# Parmenides

The Seminars of Alain Badiou

The Seminars of Alain Badiou

*Kenneth Reinhard, General Editor*

Alain Badiou is widely considered to be one of the most important Continental philosophers of our time. Badiou has developed much of his thinking in his annual seminars, which he delivered in Paris from the late 1970s to 2017. These seminars include discussions that inform his major books, including *Being and Event*, *Logics of Worlds*, and *The Immanence of Truths*, as well as presentations of many ideas and topics that are not part of his published work. Some volumes of the seminar investigate individual thinkers and writers such as Parmenides, Plato, Nietzsche, Heidegger, Beckett, and Mallarmé. Others examine concepts such as infinity, truth, the subject, the present, evil, love, and the nature of change. These seminars constitute an essential part of Badiou's thinking, one that remains largely unknown to the non-Francophone world. Their translation is a major event for philosophers and other scholars and students in the humanities and social sciences and for the artists, writers, political theorists, and engaged intellectuals for whom Badiou's work has rapidly become a generative and inspiring resource.

*For a complete list of seminars, see page 217.*

# Parmenides

## Ontological Figure, Being 1

## Alain Badiou

*Translated by*
*Susan Spitzer and Kenneth Reinhard*

Introduction by Kenneth Reinhard

Columbia University Press
*New York*

Columbia University Press
*Publishers Since 1893*
New York   Chichester, West Sussex

First published in French as *Le Séminaire—Parménide—L'être I—Figure ontologique (1985–1986)*
© 2014 Librairie Arthème Fayard

English translation copyright © 2025 Columbia University Press
All rights reserved

Library of Congress Cataloging-in-Publication Data
Names: Badiou, Alain, author. | Spitzer, Susan (Susan Jane), 1946– translator. | Reinhard, Kenneth, 1957— translator.
Title: Parmenides : ontological figure, being 1 / Alain Badiou ; translated by Susan Spitzer and Kenneth Reinhard ; introduction by Kenneth Reinhard.
Other titles: Parménide. English
Description: 1. | New York : Columbia University Press, 2025. | Series: The seminars of Alain Badiou | Includes index.
Identifiers: LCCN 2024043273 | ISBN 9780231180948 (hardback) | ISBN 9780231543378 (ebook)
Subjects: LCSH: Parmenides.
Classification: LCC B235.P24 B2313 2025 | DDC 182/.3—dc23/eng/20250103

Cover design: Julia Kushnirsky
Cover image: Shutterstock

GPSR Authorized Representative: Easy Access System Europe,
Mustamäe tee 50, 10621 Tallinn, Estonia, gpsr.requests@easproject.com

Columbia University Press gratefully acknowledges the generous contribution to this book provided by the Florence Gould Foundation Endowment Fund for French Translation.

# Contents

*Editors' Introduction to the English Edition of the Seminars of Alain Badiou*   ix
*Author's General Preface to the English Edition of the Seminars of Alain Badiou*   xiii
*Parmenides's Subtractive Ontology: Introduction to Alain Badiou's Parmenides: Ontological Figure, Being 1 (Kenneth Reinhard)*   xxiii
*About the 1985–1986 Seminar on Parmenides*   xlvii

Session 1   1

Session 2   19

Session 3   41

Session 4   61

Session 5   77

Session 6   93

Session 7   117

Session 8   135

Session 9   151

Session 10   175

Session 11   185

*Notes*   199

*Index*   211

# Editors' Introduction to the English Edition of the Seminars of Alain Badiou

KENNETH REINHARD, SUSAN SPITZER, AND JASON E. SMITH

With the publication in English of Alain Badiou's seminars, we believe that a new phase of his reception in the Anglophone world will open up, one that bridges the often formidable gap between the two main forms in which his published work has so far appeared. On the one hand, there is the tetralogy of his difficult and lengthy major works of systematic philosophy, beginning with a sort of prelude, *Theory of the Subject*, and continuing with the three parts of *Being and Event*, *Logics of Worlds*, and *The Immanence of Truths*. On the other hand, there are his numerous shorter and occasional pieces on topics such as ethics, contemporary politics, film, literature, and art. Badiou's "big books" are often built on rather daunting mathematical ideas and formulations: *Being and Event* relies primarily on set theory and the innovations introduced by Paul Cohen; *Logics of Worlds* adds category, topos, and sheaf theory; and *The Immanence of Truths* expands into the mathematics of large cardinals. Each of these great works is written in its own distinctive, and often rather dense, style: *Theory of the Subject* echoes the dramatic tone and form of a Lacanian seminar; *Being and Event* presents a fundamental ontology in the form of a series of Cartesian "meditations"; *Logics of Worlds* is organized in formal theories and "Greater Logics," and expressed in richly developed concrete examples, phenomenological descriptions, and scholia; and for reading *The Immanence of Truths*, Badiou suggests two distinct paths: one short and "absolutely necessary," the other long and "more elaborate or illustrative, more free-ranging." Because of the difficulty of these longer books, and their highly compact formulations, Badiou's shorter writings—such as the books on ethics and Saint Paul—often serve as a reader's first point of entry into his ideas. But this less steep path of induction brings its own problems, insofar as these more topical and occasional works often take for granted their relationship to the fundamental architecture of Badiou's thinking and thus may appear to have a greater (or smaller) role in it than they actually do. Hence the publication of Badiou's seminars from 1983 through (at least) 2012 makes available a middle path, one in which the major lines of Badiou's thinking—as well as its many extraordinary detours—are displayed with the remarkable clarity and the generous explications and exemplifications that always characterize his oral presentations. It is extraordinarily exciting to see the genesis of Badiou's ideas in the experimental and performative context of his seminars, and there is a great deal in the seminars that doesn't appear at all in his existing published writings.

The first volume of the seminars to be published in English, on Lacan, constitutes part of a four-year sequence on "anti-philosophy" which also includes volumes on Nietzsche, Wittgenstein, and Saint Paul. The second volume, on Malebranche, is part of a similar cluster on being, which also involves years dedicated to Parmenides and Heidegger. And the later volumes, beginning in 1996, gather material from multiple years of the seminars, as in the case of *Axiomatic Theory of the Subject* (which is based on the sessions from the years 1996–97 and 1997–98), and *Images of the Present Time* (which was delivered in sessions over three years, from 2001 to 2004).

Isabelle Vodoz and Véronique Pineau are establishing the French text of the seminar on the basis of audio recordings and notes, with the intention of remaining as close as possible to Badiou's delivery while eliminating unnecessary repetitions and other minor artifacts. In reviewing and approving the texts of the seminars (sometimes as long as thirty years after having delivered them), Badiou decided not to revise or reformulate them, but to let them speak for themselves, without the benefit of self-critical hindsight. Given this decision, it is remarkable to see how consistent his thinking has been over the years. Moreover, each volume of the seminars includes a preface by Badiou that offers an extremely valuable account of the political and intellectual context of the seminars, as well as a sort of retrospective reflection on the process of his thought's emergence. In our translations of the seminars into English, we have tried to preserve the oral quality of the French edition in order to give the reader the impression of listening to the original recordings. We hope that the publication of Badiou's seminars will allow more readers to encounter the full scope of his ideas, and will allow those readers who are already familiar with his work to discover a new sense of its depths, its range, and its implications—perhaps almost as if reading Badiou for the first time.

# The Seminars of Alain Badiou (1983–2016): General Preface

ALAIN BADIOU

## The Seminars in English

It is a great pleasure for me to write this preface to the English-language edition of the entire collection of thirty years of my seminars. The information below is intended simply to shed some light on what these thirty years of public speaking have meant, to me and my various audiences, and why there may be some interest, or even pleasure, to be found in reading the seminars.

## I. A Few Historical Reference Points

The word "seminar" should, in principle, refer to collective work around a particular problem. Instead, where these seminars are concerned, it refers to my own individual, albeit public, work on many different problems, all of which were nonetheless united by a philosophical apparatus explicitly claiming to be systematic.

Admittedly, the word "seminar" was already used in the latter sense with reference to Lacan's famous seminar, which, for me and many other people, has raised the bar very high when it comes to this sort of thing.

That a large part of my teaching took the form of such a seminar—whose ongoing publication in French, and now in English and Spanish, will show that it remained virtually free from any institutional authority—was originally due to pure chance.

At the beginning of the academic year 1966–67, while I was the senior class teacher at the boys' high school in Reims, I was appointed lecturer in an establishment that had just been created and that testified to the rapid expansion of higher education in the supremely Gaullist France of those years: the Collège universitaire de Reims, affiliated with the University of Nancy. Initially, only so-called propaedeutic [i.e., college preparatory] teaching was to be provided there (at the time, there was a first year of studies with that name, validated by a final exam that, if successfully passed, allowed students to begin their first year of university). So I was asked to teach the philosophy option in this preparatory year. But all of a sudden, thanks to one of those nasty betrayals so typical of academic life, the University of Nancy announced that, for the time being, it couldn't relinquish its philosophical powers to Reims and that there wouldn't be any philosophy option for the preparatory program to which my position was attached.

So there I was, a teacher of a nonexistent discipline. Given these circumstances, what else was there to do but hold an open seminar? And that's what I did for two years (1966–67 and 1967–68), before—I have to brag a bit here—an increasingly large audience and, what was even more flattering to me, one that was there out of pure interest since there was no final exam to reward their faithful attendance.

If I'd had the energy to look for my notes from that time long ago (when no one had either the idea or the means to bring in one of those big, clunky tape recorders to record my improvisations) and to revise those notes and turn them into a written text, I could have proudly begun this edition of the seminars with the one from

1966–67—fifty years of free speech!—, the year devoted to Schopenhauer, and then continued with the 1967–68 seminar, when my syllabus was focused on Mallarmé, Rimbaud, and Lautréamont, in that order. The *Chants de Maldoror*, however, which I had intended to begin dealing with in early May, was sacrificed on the altar of the mass movement.

And then, as a result of that May upheaval, which was to drastically change my life and my thinking about many issues other than academic appointments, I was appointed (since those appointments continued to be made nonetheless) Assistant Professor at the Experimental University of Vincennes, which soon became Paris 8.

The context in which I began teaching courses there was so feverish and politically so intense, the actions afoot there so radical, that the government decided that the philosophy degrees granted by Paris 8 would have no national accreditation! So there I was again, forced to give an open seminar since there was no state validation of our teaching efforts, despite the fact that they were highly innovative, to say the least.

This marginalization lasted for years. So—if, once again, the documentation really allowed for it—I could give an account of the free and open seminars of the 1970s, which, when all the exciting, frenetic collective action going on at the time allowed them to take place, were devoted in particular to the Hegelian dialectic, to Mallarmé again, to my beloved Plato, and to Lacan, always before audiences that were there out of pure interest alone, since there was no exam and therefore no academic credit to validate their attendance.

Actually, a synthetic account of that period does exist: my book *Theory of the Subject*, published by Seuil in 1982 under the editorship of François Wahl (English translation published by Continuum, 2009). It provides an admittedly very freely rewritten account of the seminars that were held between January 1975 and June 1979.

Beginning in those years, as a result of the so-called political normalization, things calmed down in the universities, even in the one in Vincennes, which had incidentally been moved to Saint-Denis. In the early 1980s, the government authorities decided that we of the glorious Department of Philosophy—where you could hear lectures by Michel Foucault, Michel Serres, François Châtelet, Gilles Deleuze, Jean-François Lyotard, and Jacques Rancière—deserved to have the national accreditation we'd lost gradually restored. It was from that time on, too, that the seminars began to be systematically recorded by several different attendees. Little wonder, then, that I decided to publish all of the seminars between 1983 and the present: for these thirty-odd years, abundant, continuous documentation exists.

Not that the locations, the institutions, and the frequency didn't change. Indeed, starting in 1987 the seminar moved to the Collège international de philosophie, which owed its creation in large part to the determined efforts of everyone in "living [i.e. non-traditional] philosophy" who felt put down and badmouthed by the University, Lyotard and Derrida being the two most emblematic names at the time. In that setting, I rediscovered the innocence of teaching without exams or validation: the seminar was now officially open and free of charge to everyone (for the reasons I mentioned above, it had actually always been so). It was held in the locales that the Collège secured or bargained hard to secure for its activities: the old École polytechnique on the rue Descartes, the École normale supérieure on the boulevard Jourdan, an industrial institution on the rue de Varenne, the Institut catholique on the rue d'Assas, and the main auditorium of the University of Paris 7 at Jussieu.

In 1998, when my seminar had been held under the auspices of the Collège international de philosophie for ten years, a crisis of sorts erupted: one faction of the Collège's administration viewed with suspicion both the form and the content of what I was doing. As far as the form was concerned, my status in the Collège was an exceptional one since, although I'd initially been properly inducted into it under Philippe Lacoue-Labarthe's presidency, I had never been officially re-elected as a member of the Collège. The content was viewed with suspicion because in those times dominated by the antitotalitarian ideology of human rights, rumors were going around that my teaching was "fascist." As I was unwilling to put up with such an atmosphere, I broke off my seminar midyear, thereby causing a lot of confusion.

I set it up the following fall at the École normale supérieure, where I'd been appointed professor. It remained there for fifteen years, which is pretty good, after all.

But this seminar was fated to always end up antagonizing institutions. I had to use the largest lecture halls at the ENS due to the sizeable audiences the seminar attracted, but at the start of the 2014 school year there was a dark plot afoot to deny me all access to those rooms and recommend that I accommodate around 250 people in a room that held only 80! After driving Lacan out, the prestigious ENS drove me out too! But, after all, I told myself, to suffer the same fate as Lacan was in its own way a glorious destiny. What happened to me next, however, can literally be called a "coup de théâtre," a dramatic turn of events. My friend Marie-José Malis, the outstanding theater artist and great renovator of the art of directing, was appointed artistic director of the Théâtre de la Commune in the Paris suburb of Aubervilliers. She offered to let me hold my seminar there, and I enthusiastically accepted. For two and a half years, in the heart of a working-class suburb, I stood on the stage before a full house and interspersed my final seminars, which were connected with the writing of my last "big" book, *L'Immanence des vérités*, with actual theatrical presentations. I was generously assisted in this by Didier Galas, who created the role of Ahmed in my four-play cycle, written in the 1980s and 1990s for the artistic and stage director Christian Schiaretti: *Ahmed the Subtle, Ahmed Gets Angry, Ahmed the*

*Philosopher*, and *The Pumpkins*. On January 16, 2017, my Final Seminar took place in the Théâtre de la Commune in Aubervilliers, where pure philosophy, congratulatory messages, anecdotes, and theatrical productions all combined to celebrate the seminar's long history for one last time.

---

I'd always wanted the seminar to be for people who worked. That's why, for a very long time, it took place between 8 and 10 PM, on Tuesdays for a few years, on Wednesdays for probably twenty years, if not more, and on Mondays between 2014 and the time it ended in 2017, because theaters are dark on Mondays . . .

In these various places, there was a first period—five years, from 1987 to 1992—when the seminar had a feeling of spontaneity to it as it ran through philosophy's "conditions," as they're called in my doctrine: poetry, the history of philosophy (the first seminar on Plato's *Republic* dates back to 1989–90), politics, and love. It was over the course of those years, especially during the sessions on the rue de Varenne, that the size of the audience increased dramatically.

From 1992 on, I began putting together large conceptual or historical ensembles, which I treated over several consecutive years: anti-philosophy, between 1992 and 1996; the Subject, between 1996 and 1998; the twentieth century, between 1998 and 2001; images of the present time, between 2001 and 2004; the question of subjective orientation, in thought and in life, from 2004 to 2007. I dealt with Plato, from 2007 to 2010; then with the phrase "changing the world," from 2010 to 2012. The final seminar, which was held, as I mentioned above, in a theater, was entitled "The Immanence of Truths."

I should point out that, although it was a more or less weekly seminar at the beginning, it was a monthly one for all of the final years of its existence.

## II. The Seminar's Form

As I mentioned at the outset, my seminar ultimately took the form of an ex cathedra lesson, the venerable old form known as the "formal lecture" [*cours magistral*]. But this was the outcome of a long evolution. Between 1969 and, let's say, the late 1980s, there were questions from the audience. It was obviously a lot easier to entertain questions in a room with 40 people at Vincennes than in a theater with 300. But it was also a matter of the time period. Initially at Vincennes, every "class" was a sort of steeplechase in which the hedges, which had to be jumped over elegantly and efficiently, were the constant hail of questions. It was there, as well as in the tumultuous political meetings I attended, that I learned how to stay unfailingly focused on my own thinking while agreeing with perfect equanimity to answer any question calmly, even if it was clearly a side issue. Like Claudel's God, I took crooked paths to reach my goal.

I must admit that, little by little, with the "normalization," I was able to rely on the audience's increasing unwillingness to listen to overly subjective rambling, rants with no connection to the subject under discussion, biased ideological assaults, complaints about not understanding or boasts about already knowing it all. Ultimately, it was the dictatorship of the masses that silenced the frenzied dialectic of interruptions without my having to change, on my own, my relationship with the audience. In the Jules Ferry auditorium at the ENS or in the Théâtre de la Commune, nobody interrupted anymore, or even, I believe, considered doing so, not out of fear of a stern refusal on my part but because the ambient opinion was no longer in favor of it.

I never ruled out having someone else come and speak, and thus, over time, I extended invitations to a number of people: François Regnault, to speak on theater; Jean-Claude Milner, to speak on Lacan; Monique Canto, to speak on Plato; Slavoj Žižek, to speak on orientation in life, etc. These examples give you a sense of my eclecticism.

But in the final analysis, the seminar's form, solidly in place for about twenty-five years, remained by and large that of a one-man show. Session by session, I began with careful preparation, resulting in a set of lecture notes—I never really wrote out a seminar—that provided the basic outline, a few summary sentences, and the quotations or references used. Often, I gave out a handout containing the texts that I would read and comment on. I did this because my material was nothing like philosophical references in the traditional sense of the term. In particular, I had frequent recourse to the intellectual concentration that poetry allows for. Naturally, I also engaged in logico-mathematical formalism. However, it's very difficult to make extensive use of that resource before large audiences. I usually reserved it for another seminar, one that could be called arcane, which I held for a long time on Saturday afternoons and which contributed directly to my densest—and philosophically most important—books: *Being and Event* and *Logics of Worlds*. But for the time being there are no plans to publish these "other" seminars.

### III. What Purpose Did the Seminar Serve?

It's hard for me to say in what respect my seminar was useful for people other than myself. What I noticed, however, was that its transmission of sometimes very complex subjects was of a different sort from that of my writings on these same subjects. Should it be said that the seminar was easier? That's not exactly the point. Clearly, philosophy has always combined oral activity and writing and has often privileged the oral over the written, as did its legendary founder, namely, Socrates. Even those—like Derrida—who promoted the primacy of writing were very careful never to overlook physical presence and the opportunities oral presentation provides for transference love, which Plato already theorized in his *Symposium*.

But I think that the oral presentation, as far as I myself and no doubt many attendees were concerned, conveyed the movement of thought, the trajectory of the investigation, the surprise of discovery, without having to subject them to the pre-established discipline of exposition, which is largely necessary whenever you write. It had the musical power of improvisation, since my seminar was not in fact written out. I met many seminar attendees who hadn't read my books. I could hardly commend them for it, obviously. But I understood that the thinking-on-the-spot effect of the oral presentation had become the most important thing to them. Because if the seminar "worked" as it should—which was naturally not guaranteed—the audience felt almost as if they themselves had thought up what I was talking to them about. It was as though all I'd done, in Platonic parlance, was trigger a recollection in them, whereas philosophical writing per se demanded sustained and sometimes unrewarding effort. In this respect, the seminar was certainly easy, but such easiness also left traces, often unconscious ones, of which attendees who thought they'd understood everything would have been wise to be wary.

For me, there's no question that the seminar served as a laboratory. I tested out ideas in it, either already established ones or even ones that emerged during my public improvisations, by presenting them from a variety of perspectives and seeing what happened when they came in contact with texts, other ideas, or even examples from contemporary situations in politics, art and public opinion. One of the great advantages of oral presentation is to be able to repeat without really boring your audience—which would be very difficult to do in writing—because intonation, movements, gestures, slight accentuations, and changes in tone give repetition enough charm to make it not just acceptable but even retroactively necessary. So the seminar went hand in hand with the inner construction of my thought, something Deleuze would have called the moment of invention of the concept, and it was like a partly anarchic process whose energy could later be captured by prose in order to discipline it and incorporate it into the philosophical system I've created, whose final, and I daresay eternal, form, is nonetheless the written form.

Thus, some of the seminars directly became books, sometimes almost immediately, sometimes later. For example, *Saint Paul: The Foundation of Universalism* (the 1995–96 seminar, published by Presses Universitaires de France in 1997; English translation published by Stanford University Press in 2006); *Wittgenstein's Antiphilosophy* (the 1993–94 seminar, published by Nous in 2009; English translation published by Verso in 2011); *The Century* (the 1998–2001 seminar, published by Seuil in 2005; English translation published by Polity in 2007). In all three of these cases, the content of the books is too similar to that of the seminars for there to be any need for the latter to be published for the foreseeable future.

But all the seminars are in a dialectic with books, sometimes because they exploit their effects, sometimes because they anticipate their writing. I often told my seminar attendees that I was without a doubt throwing myself on the mercy of their attention span (a two-hour seminar before such an audience is truly a performance), but that their presence, their degree of concentration, the need to really address my remarks to them, their immediate reaction to my improvisations—all of that was profoundly useful to my system-building efforts.

The complete set of volumes of the seminar may, in the long term, be the true heart of my work, in a dialectical relationship between the oral and the written. Only the readers of that complete set will be able to say. It's up to you now, dear reader, to whom every philosopher addresses himself or herself, to decide and pronounce your verdict.

# Parmenides's Subtractive Ontology: Introduction to Alain Badiou's *Parmenides: Ontological Figure, Being 1*

KENNETH REINHARD

In 1985, following his seminars on "The One" and "The Infinite," Alain Badiou began a three-year sequence of seminars on the topic of "being." The first year of the series, which is presented in this volume, was on Parmenides, the second on the seventeenth-century French theologian Nicolas Malebranche, and the third on Heidegger.[1] Parmenides and his "poem," as well as the Parmenides of Plato's dialogues, will continue to figure prominently in many of Badiou's seminars, essays, and major philosophical writings, including *Being and Event* (1988) and *The Immanence of Truths* (2018). Although there were significant earlier Greek speculative thinkers, such as Thales and Anaximander, Parmenides of Elea (6th–5th c. BCE) is often regarded as the most important of the pre-Socratics and the first Greek philosopher; in the *Sophist* Plato refers to him as "father Parmenides" and in his *Lectures on the History of Philosophy* Hegel comments that by advancing "into the region of the ideal . . . Parmenides began Philosophy proper."[2] Parmenides is often considered the first thinker to utilize deductive reasoning to make his arguments, and for Badiou this is key to his originality.[3] Unlike other pre-Socratics, Parmenides did not conceptualize the fundamental nature of things in terms of a primal element, such as fire or water, but through a nearly undetermined concept of *being*.[4] According to

Parmenides, being in itself is "ungenerated and imperishable," without difference, without a beyond: it is "a whole of one kind," "unperturbed," and "complete" (Fragment 8, p. 217). Parmenides's account of being as unified, indivisible, unmoving, and unchanging, neither coming into existence nor fading away, is so radical that it often strikes readers as ludicrous. Aristotle, for one, alternates between praising Parmenides as the exceptional thinker of his age and almost mocking him for views that seem incredible.

As Badiou remarks:

> On the one hand, he's the tremendous Parmenides, the great Parmenides, and, on the other, to think that "being is One," strictly motionless, without difference, without multiplicity, without change, and so on, actually gives nothing to be thought. What a symptom it is, this close proximity, this conjunction, between the recognition of the founder's greatness and the denunciation of the theory's absurdity! (Session 7)

Unlike his contemporary, Heraclitus, whose understanding of the world as a constant flux of becoming may seem more attuned to our lived experience, Parmenides's account of being—no doubt meant in part as a refutation of Heraclitus's—can feel counterintuitive, static and strange. In the *Science of Logic*, Hegel argues that Parmenides's concept of being is not only absolutely abstract, but also completely indistinguishable from nothingness, with which it endlessly oscillates. For Hegel, the relationship of being and nothing must be dialecticized, which, he argues, is the function of Heraclitus's notion of becoming.[5]

But what is Parmenides really talking about when he refers to "it-is" [εἶναι, eínai]? Being for him is certainly not something we experience with our senses, a substance, or what Aristotle means by nature [ɸύσις, phusis]. For Heidegger, Parmenides is the great Greek thinker of "how it is" [ὅπως ἔστιν, hopōs éstin]—which he glosses as, "How matters stand with the 'is,'" the nature of Being as such in distinction from beings, or existent things.[6] Heidegger sees Parmenides as the heir to the early Greek poets' primordial experience of Being, and the last efflorescence of real thinking prior to the forgetting of Being that begins with Plato.

For Badiou, however, the thought of being is not what defines philosophy; indeed, he argues that ontology does not fall under the purview of philosophy at all, but is the work of mathematics, which is itself one of the conditions of philosophy. According to Badiou, the philosophical discussion of being should more properly be called *meta*-ontology, since it talks about ontology rather than practicing it. And in any case, as Badiou will point out, the thought of being and its radical opposition to nonbeing is hardly original to Parmenides: concepts of being and nonbeing arise at various earlier moments and in places other than Greece (e.g., India and Egypt), just as examples of counting and arithmetic can be found in cultures all over the world, well before Pythagoras and Euclid. Yet, Badiou argues, in both these regards Parmenides marks the emergence of something truly new—both a new mode of *discourse* and a new way of *thinking*, which together will constitute the conditions of possibility for what Badiou calls "the singular and strange entanglement of mathematics and philosophy" (Session 1). Badiou argues that Parmenides initiates a new mode of knowledge and its transmission that breaks with the previously dominant ones of poetic narrative and mythical thinking. Of course, both poetry and myth continue after Parmenides, but they no longer have exclusive claims on thinking and discourse, and thereafter must share the stage of human creativity with mathematical logic and philosophical reason.

## 1. Parmenides's Threefold Ways

Parmenides's "poem" straddles this conceptual and discursive break: before entering into its properly ontological discussion, the text opens with a poetic account of a youth's mythic journey of initiation escorted by "the maiden daughters of the Sun," passing through "the gates of the paths of Night and Day," and into the abode of the goddess of Truth. There he receives her instruction concerning the three "ways of inquiry for thinking." In a first part, titled "Truth," the goddess begins by distinguishing two possible paths:

> It is right for you to learn all things,
> both the unshaken heart of persuasive Truth,
> and the opinions of mortals, in which there is no true reliance.
> (Fragment 1, p. 213)

The youth must seek the truth [ἀλήθεια, alétheia], but he should also become familiar with the unreliable opinions [δόξα, doxa] and beliefs [πίστις, pistis] held by many people, presumably in order to better evaluate them and, if necessary, argue against them.[7] For Heidegger, this path of "opinions" is defined by the failure to approach Being as such, and thus to be caught in the "frenzy" produced by the endless stream of individual beings and the inability to discriminate among them. Those who follow it "merely slurp up impressions and believe they are philosophizing . . . they remain with any one thing only for a fleeting moment, and then they bounce to something else, for they lack the sight of the essence and Being of things."[8] The distinction between the paths of truth and opinion (or reality and seeming, Being and beings) will inform Plato's metaphysics of the intelligible and sensible, as well as his construction of philosophy in opposition to sophistry, and becomes an organizing topos in the history of philosophy thereafter. But Parmenides immediately indicates another path to be distinguished from those of the truth-of-being and opinions-on-appearance— that of "nonbeing":

> the one: that it is and that it is not possible not to be,
> is the path of Persuasion (for she attends on Truth);

> the other: that it is not and that it is right it should not be,
> this I declare to you is an utterly inscrutable track,
> for neither could you know what is not (for it cannot be
>     accomplished),
> nor could you declare it. (Fragment 2, p. 213)

To follow the path of being is to pursue what is real and thus knowable, to allow oneself to be guided by its persuasive arguments in the service of Truth, while avoiding the path of deceptive appearances and uncertain opinions that leads the hoi polloi into error. To follow the path of nonbeing or nothingness, however, is futile, since it produces neither knowledge nor opinion, and resists all significant nomination. Indeed, as Heidegger points out, "there can be *no persuasion toward nothingness*" (89); unlike opinions formed on the basis of deceptive appearances, nonbeing cannot even mislead us. Furthermore, in addition to simply asserting that "never shall this prevail, that things that are not are," Parmenides also feels it necessary to forbid us from investigating nonbeing: "withhold your thought from this way of inquiry, nor let habit born of long experience force you along this way" (Fragment 7, p. 215). But although we must decide between being and nonbeing, our choice is at the same time forced: "the decision is made, as is necessary, to leave the one way [of nonbeing] unthought, unnamed—for it is not a true way—the other [of being] to be and to be true." The path of nonbeing is an "utterly inscrutable track," a road to nowhere—yet it must be counted as a path, as Badiou will insist, the one attempted, for example, by the sophist Gorgias of Leontini in his treatise "On What-Is-Not."[9] Despite the double negation of nonbeing as both impossible and forbidden, it remains in the text as the path not taken, and will return in crucial ways for both Plato and Badiou. For Parmenides, however, only being is: we can follow it as it truly is or as it only appears to be, but we cannot follow—and, at the same time, we must *choose* not to follow—nonbeing.

Having established the three paths of being, nonbeing, and appearing, Parmenides introduces the question of *thinking* and its relationship to being in one of his most famous statements: "... for the same thing is there for thinking and for being" [... τὸ γὰρ αὐτὸ νοεῖν ἐστίν τε καὶ εἶναι] (Fragment 3, p. 213).[10] Whereas nonbeing not only is-not but also cannot be thought, being and thinking are fundamentally linked or "the same"—although the precise meaning in this context of *αὐτὸ* (*auto*), the word translated as "the same," is not entirely clear.[11] Badiou follows Heidegger in pointing out that translations of *αὐτὸ* as "the same thing," such as the recent one by Daniel Graham or Kathleen Freeman's 1948 translation, hypostatize the sameness of being and thinking as a "thing," which, Badiou points out, is obviously "tautological and nonsensical" (Session 3). Heidegger translates *αὐτὸ* in this statement as *Zusammengehörigkeit*, "intrinsically belong together," a rendering of which Badiou conditionally approves. Badiou glosses Heidegger's reading as "What thinking is in its being is destinally prescribed by being itself"; rather than a reflection or representation of beings, thinking emerges only in proximity to the Being of beings. Heidegger translates *νοεῖν* as *Vernehmen*, "apprehending," rather than the more common *denken*, "thinking," in order to suggest that it involves "a process of letting things come to oneself in which one does not simply take things in, but rather takes up a position to receive what shows itself."[12] That is, to "apprehend" is to face the Being of beings, to remain open to Being, prior to conceptualizing what in particular they may be. And although Heidegger's translation might seem to involve a passive posture, he means it to imply the act of deciding about being, seeming, and nothing: "apprehending is a passage through the crossing of the threefold way. Apprehending can become this passage only if it is fundamentally a *de-cision for* Being *against* Nothing, and thus a confrontation *with* seeming" (187).[13] The mode of thinking that Heidegger calls apprehending can only "belong together" with being insofar as it makes a "de-cision" [*Ent-scheidung*], a cut, between being and nonbeing, and forces a reckoning between truth and opinion. The decision to exclude nonbeing is the condition of possibility for both the belonging-together of being and thinking and for the difference between the truth of that belonging-together and the various opinions about it. For Badiou, Heidegger's insight is key: the primary significance of Parmenides's text is not its thesis about being and thinking, but its presentation of the relationship of thinking, being, and nonbeing as requiring a *decision*.

## 2. Plato, Aristotle, and the Risk of Nonbeing

Already for Plato and Aristotle, making a decision about Parmenides's decision about being, thinking, and nonbeing was a pressing and complicated question. As Badiou points out, for Aristotle, the Eleatic philosophers (usually understood to include Melissus, Zeno, Xenophanes, and Parmenides himself) are an exception to the tendency of ancient philosophers to propose the existence of a primary element (e.g., fire, water, earth), but then to fail to explain the infinite differences that emerge from a single material cause. The Eleatics are exceptional because they accept the implications of their mono-causality and argue that reality (or being) is in fact One, static and undifferentiated—which for Aristotle is absurd, but at least rigorous and consistent. Badiou shows that Aristotle sees Parmenides as an *exception* to that Eleatic exception, insofar as he proposes not only the primary causality of being, but also a second type of causality in the decision that must be made concerning being and nonbeing, and in this he comes closer than the other pre-Socratic philosophers to Aristotle's fourfold account of causality. Nevertheless, Parmenides remains a problem for Aristotle: he is simultaneously ridiculous (as an Eleatic) and useless for the investigation of nature, but also a singular, original, and exceptional proto-philosopher. Aristotle's ambivalence, Badiou argues, is the result of his failure to understand that Parmenides's insight is not simply that being is and nonbeing isn't, but that *"there is no thinking of being except at the risk of nonbeing"* (Session 4), the "risk," that is, of including nonbeing as the excluded condition of possibility for the relationship of being and thinking. The truthful relationship of thinking to being thus is guaranteed both by the declaration of the impossibility of nonbeing, and by the prohibition of nonbeing—a prohibition that for Plato opens the additional question of *transgression*.

Parmenides is a strong presence in two of Plato's dialogues: the *Parmenides*, where an elderly Parmenides and his disciple Zeno converse with a young Socrates; and the *Sophist*, which involves a "Stranger from Elea" in conversation with the young mathematician Theaetetus and an unusually taciturn Socrates.[14] In the service of his critique of sophistry in the *Sophist*, Plato (whose perspective is usually understood as being voiced by the Eleatic Stranger) finesses his disagreement with Parmenides's prohibition of the path of nonbeing, worrying whether in doing so he might appear to be committing an act of "patricide" against "father Parmenides" (241d). The Stranger from Elea (hence himself presumably a Parmenidean), questions young Theaetetus about the nature of a "copy" or "likeness"—is it merely unreal, without being ("that which is not"), or does it have a certain reality, a being of its own, *as* a copy? The "many-headed sophist," the Stranger warns, will use this ambiguity "to force us to agree unwillingly that that which is not in a way is." In order to avoid getting caught in the snares of the sophist, "an expert at cheating and falsehood-making," however, the Stranger will have to risk agreeing with him: "we're going to have to subject father Parmenides' saying to further examination, and insist by brute force both that *that which is not* somehow is, and then again that *that which is* somehow is not" (241d). If Parmenides is the Father of philosophy, it is because of what Badiou calls his "founding gesture" of establishing the paternal law (πατρικὸς λόγοoς, patrikos logos) against nonbeing as the excluded condition of the relationship of being and thinking. And insofar as the "force" that the philosopher uses to counter the sophist's "force" involves the son's transgression of that prohibition, the Eleatic Stranger risks seeming to have turned against the Father. For Plato there is something paradoxical, indeed impossible, in such an act of "patricide"; as Badiou points out, it is "beyond the son's capacity, because it is only by virtue of this declaration that he is established as the son." Hence, Badiou continues, "Even though [the *Sophist*] appears to be a refutation [of Parmenides] it's not actually one; it's really an invention, namely that of the shift from one regime of the possible to another, or a splitting of the law. That's why it makes perfect sense to say that the refutation is impossible, that the very idea of it is crazy, and yet to carry it out." So, Plato's apparent violation of Parmenides's injunction against the path of nonbeing is not the Oedipal struggle of a son against the father, but perhaps closer to a careful act of filial piety that adjusts the relationship of being, thinking, and nonbeing in subtle ways—not by overturning, but by what Badiou describes as "splitting" the law, expanding the space within it for the establishment of philosophy.[15]

Plato takes the risk of being thought a patricide because of a real historical urgency: the rise of sophistry in Athens and the demagoguery that it has fostered:

> If Parmenides's prohibition "It is forbidden to follow the path of nonbeing" must be transgressed, if it must be transgressed by taking the path of nonbeing anyway, it is because the situation requires it. The core question of the *Sophist* is, as Lacan would say, that of a discourse that would not be pure semblance. To get at semblance in its very being, you have to figure out what the "being" of the sophist is if you want to disparage and discredit him politically, that is to say, historically.[16] (Session 6)

For Plato, sophistry's dangerous allure is that of a discourse based on "semblance," one that exploits language's ability to both simulate and dissimulate. For the sophists, thinking is not bound to being, since language is free to conjure nonbeing into existence, to deploy at will rhetorical chimeras for pleasure or power. In order to understand how this is possible, Badiou argues, Plato takes up nonbeing indirectly, by introducing a "surplus signifier": "otherness" or "difference" (θάτερον, heteron). The *Sophist* introduces Plato's concept of "the greatest kinds" or "greatest ideas," the most fundamental of the forms: being, movement, rest, the same, and additionally, the "other"—which will be the guise in which he introduces a version of nonbeing, while avoiding the term itself. Otherness is not the opposite of sameness or being, but the multiple differences that are necessary to make sense of the self-identity of any single thing. And since otherness has no being in itself, it only serves the being of the same, it is, in a sense, nonbeing. This notion of the "other" or the "different" gives Plato a way of bringing a kind of nonbeing into philosophical discourse under another name, while avoiding its sophistic embrace, and not, strictly speaking, violating the paternal injunction against it.[17] As Badiou points out,

> This Other lifts the basic Parmenidean prohibition, which is "Do not take the path of nonbeing." If I say "the Other," I am taking that path, Plato tells us, because if I say, for example, that motion is "Other than being," then in a certain sense, as Other than being, it is not. . . . to really think being, you have to name "nonbeing" and by naming it, accord it a being. Whereas Parmenides already told us that to think being, you have to name nonbeing, explicitly, since forbidding the path of nonbeing was constitutive of the relationship between thinking and being. . . . What is conceived of as a prohibition by Parmenides is conceived of as a permission by Plato. (Session 6)

Badiou will follow Plato in taking the risk of the being of nonbeing (and the nonbeing of being). For, even though it is not fully articulated in this seminar, this ontological undecidability is precisely what will define Badiou's concept of an *event*. An event is a rupture in the accepted order by which any particular situation or world is constituted and appears; in this sense, an event is, so to speak, a singular multiple, not strictly speaking part of being. As Badiou writes in *Being and Event*, "In this matter ontology remains faithful to the imperative initially formulated by Parmenides: one must turn back from any route that would authorize the pronunciation of a being of nonbeing. But from the inexistence of a mathematical concept of the event one cannot infer that mathematical events do not exist either. In fact, it is the contrary which seems to be the case" (240). In sections of *Being and Event* titled "The Absolute Non-Being of the Event" and "The Event Belongs to That-Which-Is-Not-Being-Qua-Being," Badiou shows how the mathematician John von Neumann established the ontological conditions of set theory in what he called the "axiom of foundation," which excludes sets that belong to themselves. As Badiou writes, "In ontology *per se*, the non-being of the event is a decision. To foreclose the existence of sets which belong to themselves ... a special axiom is necessary, the axiom of foundation" (304). Von Neumann's axiomatic elimination of self-belonging multiples from the ontological worlds described by set theory allows Badiou to define the event precisely as such a paradoxical multiple that belongs to itself, and thus is ontologically undecidable, indeterminately part of being or nonbeing. Within the universe of sets that are "constructible," that is, that can be established on the basis of preexisting sets or knowledge, the event, as a self-belonging multiple, simply does not exist. But if events do, on occasion, occur, they do so as ontological anomalies that point to truly new possibilities of being that are nonconstructable on the basis of the existing situation.

## 3. The Borromean knot of being, thinking, and nonbeing

Near the end of his yearlong seminar, Badiou succinctly recapitulates his two most important arguments: "Parmenides's founding gesture was a double gesture. He proposed a Borromean knotting of the three components, 'being,' 'non-being,' and 'thinking.' And he also proposed a type of discourse that was on the horizon of the matheme in that *reductio ad absurdum* (or indirect or apagogic) reasoning played a key role in it" (Session 10). For Badiou, these are the dual modes of Parmenides's "strange entanglement of mathematics and philosophy": first, the novel way in which he conceptualizes the relationship among being, nonbeing, and thinking that Badiou will characterize, following Lacan, as "Borromean"; and second, the deployment of a negative or indirect logic that breaks with the narrative structures shared by constructive reasoning and poetic discourse.[18] What Badiou calls "the matheme" in this passage, using another Lacanian term (on the model of terms in linguistics such as the "phoneme"), is a unit of mathematical thought that can be transmitted intact from one context to another, the crystalization of an idea in an irreducible material form at the zero degree of being and thinking. Parmenides's innovations are "on the horizon of the matheme" insofar as they propose and convey new ways of thinking, new modes of logic and argumentation, and new methods for the transmission of ideas.

Borromean knots (or more technically, "rings"[19]) are three closed curves linked in such a way that cutting any one of the rings will unlink the other two. That is, no two rings are connected by themselves, but only through the mediation of a third ring; there is no determined "two" in a Borromean linkage, only the consistency of a "one" made up of all three elements. The rings were the emblem of the Borromeo family in Milan during the Renaissance and have been used in a variety of contexts, including as an emblem of the

Parmenides's Subtractive Ontology: Introduction to Alain Badiou's *Parmenides* xxxv

Christian Trinity. The Borromean rings are a simple example of what topologists call Brunnian links, which involve any number of linked rings that fall apart into unlinked rings when any one ring is broken. In his 1971–72 seminar . . . *or Worse*, Lacan first used the Borromean rings to illustrate the interdependence of three verbal acts that structure transference around the *objet a* in the analytic situation: "I ask you to refuse me my offering, because this isn't it."[20] The Borromean knot became increasingly important in Lacan's seminars over the next several years, and in his seminar of 1974–75, *R.S.I.*, it served as an emblem of the relationship of the three orders of subjective organization: the real, the symbolic, and the imaginary. In his seminar of 1975–76, *Le sinthome*, Lacan presented the "sinthome"—which in French sounds similar to "symptom"—as a fourth element that fastens two or more of the Borromean rings into a rigid pathological structure which it is the work of analysis to undo.

Badiou first discusses the Borromean knot in *Theory of the Subject* (1982; based on seminars delivered in the second half of the 1970s) as Lacan's model of the "consistency" initiated by the topology of the symbolic, imaginary, and real in distinction from his earlier account of the "connection" constituted through the signifying chain.[21] Thus for Badiou the Borromean knot marks Lacan's shift in emphasis from algebraic models and the logic of the chain to topological ones and the figure of the knot. For Badiou at this point, these two conceptual apparatuses together describe the subject of politics as the linkage of State (the symbolic), classes (the imaginary), and the masses (the real). The "algebraic talent of the revolutionary" (as exemplified by Lenin at the moment of the October revolution) is to "seize the moment" of the signifier of what Badiou will theorize as the "event" and to trace the linear chain in which it unfolds from that vanishing cause. On the other hand, "the topological genius of the communist" (and here Badiou is thinking of Mao and the Chinese Communist Party) is to establish the "consistency" of the three orders as a Borromean relationship, in which no two terms are sutured to each other; hence the link between State and classes only persists through the mediation of the masses.[22] The Paris Commune of 1871 embodies both of these logics: the Communards locate the point of the impossible in Marx's theory of the state and trace out its unfolding consequences, which Marx too comes to accept retroactively; whereas—even in its brief duration—the Commune embodies the prolongation of a consistency for subsequent communist projects, including that of Lenin (who, according to legend, danced in the snow when the new Bolshevik government lasted a day longer than the Paris Commune) and the Shanghai Commune. As Badiou writes, "We thus pass from the algebraic punctuality, by which a materialist domain opens itself up to knowledge, to the topological adherence, which saturates the recurrence of conflict with memory and neighbourhoods."[23] In *Being and Event*, Badiou will develop and formalize these concepts: the revolutionary's "algebraic punctuality" will be reconceptualized as the event, and the "topological adherence" elaborated in expanding neighborhoods of consistency by the communist will be elaborated as the faithful work required of the subject of a truth procedure.

Let us return to Badiou's seminar and his discussion there of the Borromean knot. Badiou emphasizes that Parmenides's knotting of being, nonbeing, and thinking is not a theory, but a "decision-making operation." Parmenides "initiates" a linkage between being and thinking, hence the possibility of truth, through the act of prohibiting nonbeing. Moreover, this initiation is not the assertion of an "ontological" condition that nonbeing does not exist, which hardly needs stating, but the condition for *thinking* the relationship of being and thinking. And as an act of conceptual exclusion, it will be possible for Plato and Aristotle, et al. to take up and reconceptualize or "recode" the knot and locate it in philosophy in a new guise.

But in what sense is Parmenides's arrangement of being, thinking, and nonbeing "Borromean"? First of all, there is no direct fastening of any two of the three terms; each pair of terms has only a disjunctive relationship. Clearly, there can be no immediate link between being and nonbeing, since only being is, and "nonbeing" is merely a signifier without a signified. Nor can there be a real relationship between being and thinking, since they are "the same" or indistinguishable according to Parmenides, and there can be no relationship between terms without difference. Finally, there is no direct relationship between nonbeing and thinking, insofar as Parmenides asserts that nonbeing cannot be thought and prohibits any attempt to do so. As Badiou summarizes it, "Ultimately, we have impossibility, indistinguishability, and heterogeneity as relationships. Pure heterogeneity: being and nonbeing; indistinguishability: being and thinking; impossibility: thinking and nonbeing" (Session 8). Secondly, none of the three terms is self-identical or self-sufficient; each by itself only functions as a link between the other two. Since thinking and being are the same, neither can be regarded as a unique "one." Nor can nonbeing be considered self-identical because, as Hegel points out in the *Science of Logic*, pure being and pure nothingness are indistinguishable: being in itself has no predicates whatsoever, and that is also, of course, the case for nonbeing. Parmenides presents all of being's attributes in negative terms: it is unchanging, without beginning or end, or movement of any kind. And nonbeing's only predicate is similarly negative, that it is *not* being. So, strictly speaking, there is no "two" in Parmenides's constellation of being, nonbeing, and thinking—no independent connection of any two elements—and the only "one" is the knot made up of all three terms.

As we have seen, Plato recodes Parmenides's knot by reconceiving of nonbeing as otherness, and reincluding it as the internal principle of difference that allows for the truthful convergence of thinking and being. In his seminar *Vérité et sujet*, delivered a few years after the one on Parmenides (1987–88), Badiou presents Plato's substitution of the term "the other" for "nonbeing" as his way of conceiving of a "two" that is not the product of two "ones," and that is the condition of possibility for linguistic signification.[24] Badiou argues that Aristotle, on the other hand, "only saw in Parmenides an incomplete beginning, fraught with absurdities, which he, Aristotle, would complete and clarify." While Aristotle "gives [Parmenides] credit for having dared to have two principles . . . for Aristotle, thinking is linked to being *and* to nonbeing"—a suture that would seem to preclude a truly Borromean logic. Finally, Badiou argues, "neither Plato nor Aristotle will untie the knot; they'll just describe it differently. The knot remains, but the name of the knot, its process, changes" (Session 6).

Since nonbeing is not, we might ask, what does it mean for Parmenides to exclude it? Indeed, if it doesn't exist, what exactly is being excluded? As we have seen, Badiou argues that it is as a *name* that Parmenides excludes "nonbeing," and with it all the names of things that are only thinkable if nonbeing is thought—the world of sensation and becoming, of "coming to be and perishing, being and not being, changing place and exchanging bright colors" (8.219). Finally, "nonbeing is just the name in which experience is recapitulated." So, it is *experience itself*, Badiou argues, that Parmenides is rejecting from incipient mathematics and philosophy, experience as no more than a system of names, all of which are versions of nonbeing:

> Therefore, to avoid the path of nonbeing essentially means to reject experience so as to establish thinking as something separate from the

field of names where experience is manifested. It could not be any clearer. And what's foundational is that it brings forth the order of thought in its heterogeneity with respect to experience. Philosophy begins when we break with experience. . . . There is no more profound idea in Parmenides's conception than this: thinking begins by restricting language, not by opening it up, forcing it, or expanding its limits. (Session 7)

Thinking can be the thinking of being—that is, can be *truth*—only if nonbeing is prohibited, and we now understand "nonbeing" as the source of the endlessly shifting shapes and colors of sensory and bodily experience (the realm that Lacan will call the imaginary). As efflorescences of nonbeing, the world of experience and the language that represents it are the sources of the "opinions of mortals, in which there is no true reliance." For Parmenides, real thinking is not a reflection of or on experience, but requires that we *break* with the unreliable evidence of our senses.

The originary Borromean knot that Parmenides constructs, in which being and thinking are linked by the prohibition of nonbeing, functions as a matheme that will be passed on to and reinflected by later philosophers, including Plato, Aristotle, Descartes, and Hegel:

> Parmenides *initiated* philosophy, under conditions that are still being investigated, not by deciding between being and nonbeing but by declaring, in his own terminology, a *matheme*, the absolutely first matheme in philosophy, which Plato, Plato's refutation, reiterates. (Session 6)

Badiou argues that Parmenides's matheme enacts a break with Greek poetic and mythological narrative traditions in two ways: both as a repudiation of an intrinsically ambiguous kind of knowledge, one easily manipulated for sophistical purposes; and as the rejection of an unreliable system of cultural transmission, one that lends itself to distortion and degradation over time and space: "[Parmenides's] most primordial gesture . . . was to transmit the abandonment of the figure of narrative as the organic figure of mythological, legendary, religious transmission and, in so doing, to found philosophy" (Session 8). The matheme of the Borromean knot transmits itself unambiguously, without loss or residue, and what it transmits is a mode for the transmission of a knowledge that will decouple truth from empiricism, as well as from mythopoetic narration. Parmenides, of course, is a transitional figure; his discourse is not self-authorized, but given to him by a goddess; but the Borromean structure he encodes in his "poem" will open the way to new possibilities of truth in the next generations, under the aegis of what will be called Philosophy.

### 4. *Reductio ad absurdum*

But Badiou's reading of Parmenides does not stop there:

> Let's go one step further. If, ultimately, Parmenides must transmit the break with narrative, he must do so—and he can only do so—in a recognizable figure of that break. Now, what frees the statements from any enunciation, and is the matheme, is reasoning as such, the demonstration, the proof. . . . The heart of the Parmenidean foundation lies in transmitting the transmission by matheme, as a break with narrative, in the form of *reductio ad absurdum* reasoning.[25] (Session 8)

In the mode of classical logic referred to as "direct" proof, the implications of a set of assumptions (axioms, definitions, theorems) are developed in a linear sequence of inferences that lead to a conclusion.[26] In direct proof, we begin with a hypothesis that we believe is true, and then work, following rules of inference, with the intention of proving that hypothesis. Each statement is a link in a chain in which the truth of the conclusion is a direct consequence of the truth of the assumptions and the logical consistency of the intermediary steps. Badiou argues that the linear nature of direct reasoning implies a structure of explanation that in certain ways resembles that of a coherent narrative, not unlike that of a detective novel, but without the explicit assumption of fictionality.

*Reductio ad absurdum* (or "indirect") reasoning, on the other hand, attempts to reach a true conclusion by assuming the exact opposite of what it believes to be true, and demonstrating that this assumption leads to a contradiction, and thus must be impossible. If we want to prove the truth of "A" by means of *reductio ad absurdum*, we proceed by exploring the consequences of "not-A," following them wherever they may lead us, with the hope of encountering a contradiction along the way that shows that "not-A" simply cannot be true. And if we discover that "not-A" cannot be true, we have demonstrated that "not-not-A" cannot be false, which implies, according to the principle of double negation elimination, that A *is* true.[27] Badiou here follows the historian of mathematics, Árpád Szabó, who argued that mathematics in ancient Greece transformed from an empirical technology for enumeration and calculation to the radically anti-empirical and non-intuitive science that it becomes in Euclid by way of the development of *reductio ad absurdum* reasoning in the Eleatic school, and especially in Parmenides's argument for the non-genesis of being. For Badiou, Szabó's insight anticipates the profound connection between mathematics and ontology that will become central to his philosophy in *Being and Event*.[28] In Badiou's paraphrase of Szabó, Parmenides argues that being cannot be created along the following lines: if being is not originary, it must come from either being or nonbeing. If it comes from nonbeing, this would imply that there is a connection between them—but this violates Parmenides's axiom that there is absolutely no relationship between being and nonbeing. If, on the other hand, we propose that being is created from being, we would be assuming that there are two types of being, one anterior to the other—and this would violate Parmenides's axiom that there can be no difference within being.[29] So, either way of following the consequences of arguing that being arises from something leads to a contradiction, and must be rejected for the opposite thesis, that being is eternally being, without beginning or end. As perhaps the earliest known instance of *reductio ad absurdum* reasoning, and the condition of possibility for modern mathematics, Badiou adds, Parmenides's text "bears witness to an event of thought" (Session 11).

Badiou points out that indirect reasoning has often been regarded as inferior to direct reasoning, and the modern school of Intuitionistic logic rejects it entirely. But Badiou argues that insofar as *reductio ad absurdum* reasoning involves a decisive and manifest break with narrative thinking, it is "the exemplary vehicle for the emergence of demonstrative discourse," that is, of traditional logic as formalized by Aristotle (Session 9). Badiou emphasizes four ways in which Parmenides's use of indirect reasoning functions as a matheme that transmits the discursive break with narrative into the history of philosophy. First, there is what he calls its "effect of unbelief": indirect proof begins by assuming a proposition that we don't think is true. Rather than telling a story that shows how something we believe implies and leads us to other plausible things that we will come to believe, indirect reasoning begins faithlessly, with an assertion it hopes to disprove. Second is what Badiou calls its "effect of the real": it demonstrates the consistency and lawfulness of a proposition by coming up against an impossibility within the opposite proposition, and such an encounter with the impossible is precisely how Lacan defines "the real." Direct reasoning, on the other hand, produces an effect of "reality" (in distinction from the real) within the realm of the possible. Third, *reductio ad absurdum* reasoning does not persuade us to accept its conclusions by clarifying and developing the implications of its assumptions; rather, it *forces* our consent to its propositions by showing us the unacceptable implications of following the opposite proposition. And finally, to proceed down the path of *reductio ad absurdum*, Badiou argues, is to take a risk: we don't know if we will actually find a contradiction, we might wander endlessly, fruitlessly. We cannot anticipate a clear path towards our desired end; all we can hope is that we will hit upon it eventually. In these four ways, Parmenides's innovative, perhaps originary, use of indirect reasoning establishes a new possibility of discursive reasoning that does not depend on narrative or "semblance," and thus instantiates a break with the great mythopoetic tradition of persuasion. As Badiou indicates, *reductio ad absurdum* reaches a conclusion

> not because it's credible, or possible, or plausible, or narrated, or can be experienced, or because it can be shown, but . . . on the basis of the point of impossibility, because the other way is forbidden. This is a radically new mode of transmission because the fiction shows the necessary other side, as it were, of the element in which truth takes root, namely, the combination of impossibility, law, force, and the real. Philosophy springs from that, with its own, invariant knot—being, nonbeing, and thinking—but it comes to be because it is under the condition of the matheme in that precise sense. (Session 9)

For Heidegger, Parmenides's text is originary insofar as it bears witness to truth as the coming into presence of Being, an experience that is forgotten, covered over, or otherwise denied by Plato and the subsequent history of philosophy. For Badiou, on the other hand, Parmenides's text transmits "a decision about the impossible" in which truth is not present, but revealed indirectly, negatively through the assumption of a fiction. This conjunction of *reductio ad absurdum* reasoning and the logic of the Borromean knot in Parmenides transmits into philosophy a matheme that will be indissociable from its project. And as Badiou argues, "Precisely because it bears witness to an event of thought, Parmenides's text can only be understood, as regards its originary function, in terms of the intricate relationship between the emergence of the philosophical proposition and the advent of mathematical discourse" (Session 11).

## 5. Parmenides's Revenge: *The Immanence of Truths*

Badiou will continue to discuss Parmenides in his later seminars, essays, and books, primarily in terms of the implications of the Borromean knot of being, nonbeing, and thinking and the negative logic of *reductio ad absurdum*. We have seen that Badiou follows Plato in resisting Parmenides's radical foreclosure of nonbeing, and that nonbeing returns in Plato under the name of "the other" and for Badiou as the condition of possibility of an event. In the opening Meditation of *Being and Event*, Badiou frames his project as the interruption of the impasse in which ontology has languished "since its Parmenidean organization," caught in oscillating claims for the unity and the multiplicity of being: "We find ourselves on the brink of a decision, a decision to break with the arcana of the one and the multiple in which philosophy is born and buried, phoenix of its own sophistic consumption. This decision can take no other form than the following: the one *is not*" (*BE* 23). But this decision against the primacy of the one by no means leads Badiou to reject Parmenides; already in the present seminar Badiou describes the ontology of the multiple in the early atomism of Democritus as "a sort of exploded Eleaticism, in which the Parmenidean *One-being* changed into an infinity of ones, even though all of them, in their intrinsic multiplicity, have the exact same features as Parmenides's being qua being" (Session 1). In *Being and Event* Badiou will continue to praise Parmenides as, above all, the originary thinker of the matheme, and its epochal interruption of poetic and mythic thinking.[30]

In *The Immanence of Truths*, the third volume of the *Being and Event* series, Badiou argues that contemporary mathematics vindicates what is perhaps Parmenides's most counterintuitive claim: the absolute *immobility* of being. One of Georg Cantor's most important discoveries in his formulation of set theory was the existence of types of infinity that are "bigger" than that of our everyday notion of infinity (for example, the endless natural numbers). Cantor speculated that these higher infinities culminate in one that is larger than and inclusive of all the others, an *absolute* infinity, which he understood as God. Later set theorists continued to discover many "large cardinals" or higher infinities between the first infinity and Cantor's absolute, which is now known as the von Neumann universe, denoted "V," and understood as the class of all sets. V is a *class*, rather than a set, since, according to Russell's paradox, there is no such thing as the set of all sets. Badiou describes V, or the "absolute place," as "beyond any distinction between being and thinking since it is the place where there is a thinking of being. We could also say, as Parmenides did, that in this place 'the Same is to think and to be.' "[31]

Badiou's project in *The Immanence of Truths* is to show that what he calls "works" of truth—the finite material products of the four infinite truth procedures (art, science, politics, and love)—always express some attributes of this absolute. Hence just as he had earlier argued for the universality and eternity of truths, Badiou now insists that finite truths cannot be understood as relative to a particular ontological or historical situation, but must be seen as the product of a dialectic of higher infinities, and ultimately, as participating in some aspects of the absolute itself. This absolute place, Badiou writes, "is immobile in the sense that, while it makes the thinking of change possible, as any rational thought must do, it is itself foreign to that category" (39). In 1971, the mathematician Kenneth Kunen demonstrated what is known as his "Inconsistency Theorem," one of whose implications is that there is no non-trivial elementary embedding of $V$ into itself, which means that no model can be produced in $V$ that has a one-to-one correspondence with every element of $V$ and is "non-trivial," that is, different from $V$ itself.[32] As Badiou writes, "Kunen's very remarkable theorem . . . tells us that the absolute is rigid, immobile. . . . In other words, a relation from the absolute to itself that preserves the validity of the statements can only be strict identity. We will say that there exists in this case a Parmenidean dimension of the absolute" (394).

For Badiou, Kunen's landmark proof also serves, in the title of one of the final sections of *The Immanence of Truths*, as "Parmenides' Revenge"—his revenge against those, like Aristotle, who thought his theory of being as unchanging and motionless, "unperturbed," was ridiculous and *prima facie* false. After Kunen, as Badiou writes, it seems clear that the absolute horizon of the universe of sets is "invariably rigid, Parmenidean" (395). Moreover, there is in fact no real contradiction between Parmenides's thinking of the One and Badiou's of the multiple—it's simply a question of *place*:

> As tortuous as it has been, the road from Parmenides to Cantor-Kunen by way of Plato serves as a basis for two simple statements. First, being is not one but multiple. Second, the place where multiple-being is theoretically *thought* is neither multiple nor mobile; it is one and rigid. (432)

Being is intrinsically multiple, not one; yet in every situation in which multiples are included and in every world in which they appear they are limited, closed, or in Badiou's expression, "counted as one." In order to think multiple being and the works of truth that are occasionally built from them, we must pierce the finitudes in which they are wrapped, their true infinity concealed, for the sake of rediscovering the place where we find the possibility of eternal, universal, and absolute truths.

## About the 1985–1986 Seminar on Parmenides

ALAIN BADIOU

From at least 1983 on, we had to protect ourselves from any contamination by the toxic atmosphere that would come to characterize the 1980s. Activists' hopes for new forms of political emancipation receded all over the world, under pressure from a material and intellectual counterrevolution. The buzzword "democracy" masked the newfound arrogance of an oligarchy of servants of capital who, with the word "communism" finally discredited, criminalized, and (so they thought) gone forever, saw a golden opportunity for global hegemony, aided and abetted by some hardly new "philosophers."

I almost immediately named the system that sought to control bodies and minds in this way "capitalo-parliamentarianism." This configuration of the situation, the economy included, has since dubbed itself "the West," celebrating, under the democratic name of "humanitarian interventions," the "Western" powers' deeds of worldwide plunder, without much caring that in the past—and here's where the shameful secret of this whole setup is revealed—it was only fascist groups that took the name "West" for themselves. That's just the way counterrevolutionary periods are.

Even though I never stopped participating in all the local experiments that kept the thought-practice of a transformed political life alive, I began to build a philosophical shell within which it would be impossible to succumb to resignation, much less to be complicit with capitalo-parliamentarianism. It will come as no surprise that the key concept of this undertaking was that of truth. Who can believe, even for a second, that the combination of Capital's despotic and imperial brutality on the one hand, and the electoral fetish on the other, could have anything to do with the Idea of truth? If I could succeed in the project of proposing a new dialectical concept of truth, I would be forever immune to neoliberal propaganda and would be able to offer the same protection to anyone who felt the need to become indifferent to the sirens of "Western" Goods. So, in 1983, I humbly began the journey that would lead, five years later, to the publication of *L'être et l'événement* [Being and Event] with a fresh examination of the large-scale history of philosophy. The intellectual mediocrity of the prevailing democratism was so pervasive that I was sure I'd find something in this large-scale history that I could use to take down this modern conspiracy. And so I offered a series of courses at Paris 8: first, in 1983–84, under the heading of "The One," on Descartes, Plato, and Kant; then, in 1984–85, under the heading of "The Infinite," on Aristotle, Spinoza, and Hegel; and finally, from Fall 1985 to Fall 1987, under the heading of "Being," on Parmenides, Malebranche, and Heidegger.

The seminar on Malebranche, which deals with the theological figure of the question of Being, has already been published in the editorial series [*Ouvertures*] in which the present book appears—a series that will include all my seminars since 1983, in fact, for which I would like to thank Éditions Fayard once again for taking the risk.[1] The seminar on Parmenides, scheduled for publication this year, concerns the founding figure of the same question.[2] The seminar on Heidegger, who advances the thesis of a withdrawal of being in the contemporary world, is expected to be published in 2015, thus completing this ontological trilogy.[3]

As I was reading over Véronique Pineau's excellent editorial preparation of the text, I was surprised by the tone, at once erudite and intense, of my undertaking of 30 years ago. It can be explained by my need to compete, not only with Heidegger but also, in a way, with Plato and Aristotle, regarding the idea of a "foundation" of philosophy as such by this mysterious Parmenides. I am retrospectively proud, I must confess, of both the scrupulous thoroughness of my investigation and the propositions with which it concludes. The three main propositions can be presented as simply as possible in the following way:

- Proposition 1: Parmenides founded philosophy by proposing a whole new knot between three concepts: being, thinking, and nonbeing.
- Proposition 2: This knot is Borromean, meaning that each of the three components is linked to another one only by the third one. Essentially, the fact that the knot is Borromean means that, for Parmenides, being is linked to thinking by an identity relation (being is "the same" as thinking) only if the third component, nonbeing, takes the form of an act: the act of *forbidding* the thinking of it.
- Proposition 3: If all this is philosophy and not myth (in which it is often a question, in Egypt and India, of being and nonbeing), it is because Parmenides's text—albeit presented in the form of a poem and containing elements of sacred narrative—is, for the first time, based, in terms of its principal propositions, on a matheme: *reductio ad absurdum* reasoning.

Thus, this seminar's approach is clearly to attempt to *demonstrate* that there are serious reasons for regarding Parmenides as the founder of a new discipline, not because he made prophetic utterances about being and nonbeing, as many mythologies did, but

## 1 About the 1985–1986 Seminar on Parmenides

because in this poetic prophesying he invoked its opposite, namely, the absolute universal rigor of mathematico-logical procedures that, at the very same time, were taking their definitive shape in Greece, in a twofold way: the topology of a knot and the logical structure of apagogic reasoning.

Part of my approach is inevitably formal insofar as it involves unpacking the consequences of the Borromean nature of the knot between being, thinking, and nonbeing. To that end, I invent a dialectic between the *knotting*, which guarantees the "making-three" of the knot itself, and the *coding*, which specifies each of the components within the knot, as when, knotting three strings together in Borromean fashion, you avoid the indistinction between them (since each one knots the other two together) by giving a different color to each one, each One. From this dialectic of the Three (the knot), the Two (the knotting together of two components by the third), and the One (the coding of each component) amazing consequences can be drawn.

But my approach is also based on history in that it carefully scrutinizes the reasons why Plato, Aristotle, and Heidegger also regarded Parmenides as a founder, as—this is Plato's term—the "father" of philosophy. The formalism of the knotting helps explain why, even though they acknowledged this inaugural position, they were unable, for their own reasons, to fully understand how a primitive poem, an initiation narrative, could have shaped the future of a rational enterprise largely inspired by the birth of demonstrative mathematics.

There's an enjoyable aspect of suspense, of a police investigation, of a reasoned challenging of the testimony of a few important witnesses, such as Plato and Heidegger, in this seminar. Its complexity shouldn't obscure the sort of cheerful erudition behind it. What's more, the seminar took place back at a time when the audience would participate, ask questions—often very pertinent ones, or sometimes strange or even insolent ones—and I would answer right back. A few such exchanges, if not all of them, are included in the transcription offered here.

Two final points now.

First, back when I gave this seminar, I knew next to nothing about my friend and coeditor Barbara Cassin's research on Parmenides.[4] By now I'm very familiar with it, and it's once again with admiring surprise that I realize we've been working together for 25 years now without any trouble, even though we often think in diametrically opposite ways. In this particular case, Barbara Cassin looks to Homer, to his imagery and his linguistic framing of experience rather than to nascent mathematics, for the fundamental horizon of Parmenides's thought. Are poetry and language predominant? Or the matheme and formalism? Readers are invited to decide for themselves . . .

Second, there was someone, a student from those days, a talented philosopher who, even though he worked day and night at the postal sorting office, attended, recorded, took notes and commented with a rare passion on this seminar. I'm referring to Aimé Thiault, who died of AIDS not long after. I am dedicating this edition of "my" Parmenides to the memory of Aimé Thiault.

Alain Badiou, May 2014

αὐτὰρ ἀκίνητον μεγάλων ἐν πείρασι δεσμῶν
ἔστιν ἄναρχον ἄπαυστον, ἐπεὶ γένεσις καὶ ὄλεθρος
τῆλε μάλ' ἐπλάχθησαν, ἀπῶσε δὲ πίστις ἀληθής.
ταὐτόν τ' ἐν ταὐτῷ τε μένον καθ' ἑαυτό τε κεῖται
χοὔτως ἔμπεδον αὖθι μένει κρατερὴ γὰρ Ἀνάγκη
πείρατος ἐν δεσμοῖσιν ἔχει, τό μιν ἀμφὶς ἐέργει,
οὕνεκεν οὐκ ἀτελεύτητον τὸ ἐὸν θέμις εἶναι·
ἔστι γὰρ οὐκ ἐπιδευές, μὴ ἐὸν δ' ἂν παντὸς ἐδεῖτο.

**Parmenides,** *Poem*

Further, motionless in the limits of great bonds
it is without starting and stopping, since coming to be and
    perishing
wandered very far away, and true faith banished them.
Remaining the same in the same by itself it lies
and thus it remains steadfast there; for mighty Necessity
holds it in the bonds of a limit, which confines it round about.
Wherefore it is not right for what-is to be incomplete;
for it is not needy; if it were it would lack everything.[5]

# Parmenides

# Session 1

## October 22, 1985

### On the Hardly Surprising

After ranting and railing, if only for a short time, against anything that might prevent this seminar from taking place, we should resolutely decide to go on with it, and you who are attending it will be responsible for spreading the word about it with the same firm resolve.[1]

In light of this situation, I won't get right to the heart of the matter today . . . It will just be something introductory, something fairly short.

My question is: What are the hypotheses of interpretation that enable a reassessment of the facts, sequences, or examples of the historicity of philosophy? There are two, actually. A first, negative one, which gradually and surreptitiously assumed greater importance, was as follows: The central question of philosophy cannot be the question of being. I call this negative because it is the negative of another major contemporary theory—Heidegger's—which, to my mind, is *the* only other well-argued and defended contemporary theory on the essence of philosophy. According to Heidegger, it's the question of being that originarily governs the philosophical apparatus if only in the form of its forgetting. But even when philosophy is under the sway of the forgetting of its question, it is still governed by this question about its point of origin. Heidegger's exegesis consists in large part in establishing this point: The history of philosophy is entirely driven by the concern to establish that, originarily, philosophy's question—the reason why philosophy exists—was the emergence, in its Greek form, of the question of being qua being. The historicity of philosophy is the historicity of this very question. So—and this is a very crucial, albeit extremely enigmatic, point in Heidegger—when he explains that, starting with Plato-Aristotle, the question of being enters the age of its forgetting and the metaphysical regime of philosophy is established—covering an enormous arc of its history, in which the original question, which is that of being, is forgotten—he will also say that, in fact, being has withdrawn, or that the essence and ultimate historial prescription of the forgetting of the question of being is the withdrawal of being itself. That's why I say that philosophy is governed in its essential history by the question of being, in the sense that it is under the prescription of this question.

---

The thesis I'm advancing regarding this interpretive framework—the most influential one of the modern era when it comes to the reassessment of the history of philosophy—is a negative thesis: The essence of philosophy is not the question of being.

The complete articulation of this negative hypothesis, the way it is framed, which may construct certainty over the course of its elaboration, needs to be well understood. A first way of saying that philosophy's question cannot be that of being is to claim that the question of being is a point of impossibility for human understanding. That's Kant's critical approach. The Kant of the first *Critique* states that philosophy is unable to gain access to being qua being. Thus, philosophy's question can't be that of being because it's an impossible question. But that's not the meaning of the negative hypothesis I'm proposing. When I say that philosophy's question can't be that of being, it's not in a critical sense—take "critical" here in the sense of the Kantian critique. Nor is it because the question of being would ultimately amount to a negative mystery, like that of the divine presence. It's not a statement of negative theology, a statement to the effect that philosophy cannot be the discourse on being because being, qua God, is not a matter of discourse. In my view, the question of being cannot be philosophy's question, not because it's impossible but *because it has been settled*. Not because there is something inherently impossible about this question but, on the contrary, because it's an actual question. The question of being qua being is not philosophy's question because it is mathematics' question, and it is so in a fundamental sense: mathematics is the *effectivity* of this question; that is, both the protocol for posing it and the operator for answering it. And this, in my opinion, has been the case since the dawn of Greek thought.

In response to this first, negative hypothesis, a positive hypothesis developed, as always happens: The essence of philosophy does not lie in the question of being—let me stress this—not because that question is an impasse but, on the contrary, because it is a *passage*. That is, it's a "*past*" question, in the double meaning of "pass": in the temporal sense of "of the past" and in the sense of the verb "to pass." It's a question *of the past*, because the protocol for the disposition and resolution of the question is originarily Greek. Heidegger was definitely right about this. It's just that Greek originarity isn't determined at the same time: mathematics, too, is originarily Greek. It's in this sense that the question is *of the past*: The protocol for posing and disposing of the question of being was instituted in the form of the emergence of rational mathematics, right from the Greek dawn of philosophical discourse itself. The question of being is *past* in the sense that the method of treatment thus proposed is effective, i.e., it treats the question of being *effectively*. And it treats it, in fact, as it should be treated, in terms of a vast historical process of knowledge. The question of being is *constantly* being treated by people, the mathematicians, who know nothing about it . . . who know nothing about it and yet that doesn't matter at all: indeed, the effectiveness of the procedure also depends on the fact that they know nothing about it. They do mathematics, which is a clear sign that the essence of the question isn't philosophical. Or that mathematics treats the question of being without formulating it as a question of being, precisely because its formulation is a philosophical one. In a certain sense, you could say that the question is treated where it isn't posed. That's often the case. And the chief negative consequence of this is that the most philosophy—philosophy properly speaking—can do in this regard is to state that the question is being treated. Which is something that mathematics does not state. It states the treatment, but it doesn't state that the treatment is what it, mathematics, is treating, namely, the question of being. It doesn't need to. And not only doesn't it need to but it can't. And if it could, it would be unable to treat the question. So it's of the essence of the question of being to be able to be treated only if it's not posed. This is what is shown by the philosophical name for the domain where it's treated—i.e., mathematics—where it's of the essence of this question to be treated even though it hasn't been posed. Hence the origin of the confusion: The Greek philosophers, or some of them at any rate, were well aware that something interesting was going on in mathematics; this hadn't escaped their notice, but the confusion stemmed from the fact that philosophy, being responsible for *defining* the question of being, set itself up as if being were *its* question. You imagine you're in charge of naming the empty place of a question whose answer exists somewhere else, and you think that because you're responsible for naming the void of the question, this question is *your* question. But it's not! It's not because you're in charge of naming the void of a question, in which the unfolding of its effectivity originates, that you're responsible for that effectivity. That might be the case, or it might not be. That's why the singular and strange entanglement of mathematics and philosophy that developed right from the start is oblique, or convoluted. It can be argued that it is of the essence of philosophy to pose the question—and, indeed, there's no doubt that it's only philosophy that poses it—but there's a tiny yet crucial difference between the definition of the question and the place where it is answered. And it is on this that the originary entanglement of mathematics and philosophy hinges. If you want to unravel or cut through their entanglement, you actually just need to define the question—bearing in mind, however, that this act is merely one of defining: the effectivity is not responsible for philosophy. So it is a matter of designating mathematics as ontology, i.e., the whole of what can be said about being. And what can be said about being is what is sayable at any given time about being qua being, as grasped without qualities or determinations, and ultimately as a pure multiple, contained within the historial sphere of mathematics itself. And such a statement is also philosophical, in effect. The statement "Mathematics is ontology" is a philosophical statement, not a mathematical one. Assuming that the question of being is effective in the historical development of mathematics, what are the consequences? What are the philosophical consequences of this philosophical statement?

The first major consequence is that philosophy is originarily Greek because mathematics is originarily Greek. This, in my opinion, is a fundamental point of contention with Heidegger. I'll agree with him that philosophy is originarily Greek because it had to formulate and define the question of being, but I would say that it had to formulate and define that question only because the answer already existed. Therefore, philosophy is originarily Greek because mathematics is Greek. And what was the Greeks' great invention?

It was ontology: a statement that could be completely Heideggerian except that, in his view, ontology emerged at a different time. Through a very dense dialectic, the Greeks simultaneously invented ontology both in its effectivity—that is to say, mathematics—and in the philosophical sense, i.e., the protocol for defining the question, whose effectivity was linked to the origin of its formulation.

---

In light of this, what, Heidegger will ask, is the essence of philosophy? And is there one? Once the hypothesis that the question of being determines it has been discarded, is there a destiny of philosophy? Is there a clearly recognizable figure of philosophy as such? This leads us to the second hypothesis, this one positive. If philosophy is not determined by the question of being, if its destiny is not prescribed by being qua being, then what *is* it prescribed by? And is it prescribed at all? Or is philosophy only the rhapsody of the discourse of generality? That's the positivist position: in which case, actually, it could quickly be shown that it can't be univocal and that philosophy necessarily includes a lot of very miscellaneous stuff. That's why the words "philosophy" and "philosopher" refer to lots of stuff today, most of it damaged goods. Not owing to any bad intentions on the part of good authors: we actually have excellent essayists, talented writers, rigorous polemicists, occasional politicians, modern moralists, you name it. But does "philosophy" mean anything? Or is it ultimately and only a certain level of generality of discourse? If it's not a poem, if it's not a treatise on political economy, if it's not "popular sociology," if it's not . . . whatever, wouldn't there only remain a sort of empty shell when it's philosophy—in other words, a little of everything, with a few concepts floating on the surface like dead dogs, with a sprinkling of something a little exciting on top and a few references to authors canonically accepted as philosophical? This is a very important question because, when all is said and done, it's very clear that what's at stake is whether philosophy exists or not; whether it still has a destiny, a figure; whether it's still a locus of discourse. And it must be admitted that the only conceptual apparatus, in this century, that is steadfastly regarded as a possibility for maintaining the univocity of the philosophical discourse, and therefore its existence, is—in my opinion—the Heideggerian apparatus. Think what you will about it, but if it's judged from the perspective of that particular function, it seems beyond dispute to me, because it has proposed an essence of the philosophical discourse as well as a periodized history, an origin, and a destination—an enigmatic one but a destination all the same. If we ask ourselves about the univocity of philosophy, the only thinker we can turn to today is Heidegger. All the others view the end of philosophy as an unequivocal concept.

---

So the question is whether there's an alternative framework, or an apparatus other than Heidegger's, which would preserve this univocity. I suggested that the Heideggerian apparatus is wrong. Indeed, philosophy isn't based on the intrinsic question of being, without qualities or determinations, but on something that *is* in fact determined, or qualifiable. It is in that sense that I will say that, in my positive hypothesis, philosophy has an *object*. Take that in a very vague sense, so to speak. "Object" only means that in this particular hypothesis, philosophical discourse depends, as on its cause, on a recognizable process. Let me be clear: this hypothesis would be instantly rejected by a Heideggerian as one of the avatars of metaphysics, since, in Heidegger's conceptual framework, once you abandon or forget the question of being in favor of any figure of objectivity whatsoever, even the figure of God, you're in the realm of metaphysics or of the forgetting of the question. This is a difference of opinion that admits of no arbitration. It's clear that from the moment you say that philosophy depends as a discourse on having a specifiable cause—in the nature of a process, of a vanishing cause, etc.—you're getting into the epochal configurations of metaphysics, as far as a Heideggerian is concerned. In short, this is where the critique of Heidegger comes to an end. We're in two separate conceptual apparatuses so far apart that the more we advance, the less there is any system of argumentation extending from one to the other. Each is only able to interpret the other. Heidegger will say: that's the particular epochal version of metaphysics . . .

**Someone comments sarcastically:** *He won't say anything, because he's dead!*

He'll say it from beyond the grave, so to speak. He already said as much, if only in what he implied.

---

From the beginning of these seminars on the Infinite, the One, and Being, I suggested calling the sole determination of philosophical discourse "the subject-process" or "the subject." In my assessment of the history of philosophy, I said that the *subject* is its only object. Obviously, at that stage, it doesn't mean anything. It's a name, but you always have to start with a name: "the subject-process." When Heidegger starts with *being*, he, too, is starting with a name. What could be said about it at the simple stage of the hypothesis itself? It can only be described—and described in three ways.

The first description is that of lack-of-being [*manque-à-être*], a dimension of lack. Simply because it is not exactly a question of being qua being, it includes or possesses a dimension of lack-of-being, that is, there must be an indication as to the nonbeing of the singularity of this process that prevents it from being identified with being. So there is necessarily in what is called here the "subject-process" a dimension of lack-of-being. This is something that has long been known. You can read about it in Sartre, or in Lacan as well.

There is a second description: What is called "the subject" originates—in a way that is not yet thinkable for us for the time being—in a disruption in the path of being. But this can be put differently, or more modestly: it could be said that it is undoubtedly a paradoxical being. And paradoxical with respect to what? Precisely with respect to what is sayable of being qua being. The subject-process is necessarily a paradoxical multiple, a paradoxical multiple *One*. I must stress this. I am saying "One" because it is precisely in its One that it is paradoxical. And why is it? Well, because it is always the path of being that determines what is One. So it originates in a disruption in the path of being; it is a paradoxical multiple One.

The third description that can be applied to this object—the presumed invariant of philosophy—is that it all returns to being, so to speak. That's because, despite everything, it must be. Thus, the subject consists in its effects of being, because otherwise, it would be nothingness. Yet we know full well that nothingness is just another form of being qua being. So the subject must consist in its effects of being, i.e., in the effects of the process that it is, in the effects of the paradoxical multiple One that it is. This is what it consists in, in its effects as such. To put it simply, we might even say: this object is necessarily in excess of the law of being, and therefore of number, but it only consists in the effects of being of this excess. It is *extra*, but what it is are the effects of being of *the something extra*.

---

Let's keep these three points—which will be useful for what follows—in mind: lack-of-being, disruption, and consistency of the effects. And to the extent that there is an object of philosophy, it must be given these descriptions. But be careful! This doesn't mean that it is described *as such* in philosophical discourse, because the whole problem will be that this object of philosophy is not necessarily what philosophy itself *defines*, since it's an object in the sense of being the *cause* of the discourse and not in the sense of being its referent. I'm not saying that philosophy consists of texts dealing with an object that has these characteristics. No! Philosophy—you know what it's like—deals with being qua being. It deals with God; it deals with the subject, with the subject in a different sense; it deals with self-consciousness; it deals with the *cogito*; it deals with—take your pick. With epistemology, or with the art of living. So when I say, in keeping with my hypothesis, that this is the sole object of philosophy, that doesn't mean that it's its referent. It may be its cause, which is enigmatic at first. Quite simply, the consciousness of philosophy as discourse—i.e., the consciousness philosophy has of itself as discourse, or what it puts into discourse of the consciousness that it has of itself as discourse—may be completely different from its cause. In other words, to illustrate this point, let's not mistake *the* discourse of philosophy—in the sense that we'd consider it in terms of its cause—for the *self* of this discourse. That is, the philosophical self, as the ideal self-representation. Because the way the text really works may be completely remote from its explicit intentions. I repeat: Philosophy considers itself an ontology, or a critique, or an absolute knowledge, a deconstruction of metaphysics, a general ethics, a foundation of politics, or a basis for science, and so on. What are all these things? They're the images of philosophy. It's full of its own images. It consists of its images. And when you want to discredit it, you isolate these images and say: "It's bogus! It told us it was an ontology, but it isn't one. It promised us venerable wisdom, but no one believes it. It tried to prove God's existence, but it no longer proves it. It was the servant of theology, but it is no longer in service to anything." The usual discrediting of philosophy, including by philosophy itself, involves criticizing the images it has of itself, regardless of the cause of its discourse.

That's why philosophy's real object is actually only evident in the impasses of its text. This is because everything that passes through is a servant of images. What I'm calling "the subject" here— philosophy's object—is the real of philosophy, but always more or less as the empty point of a discourse of plenitude. Does that mean that the discourse of plenitude is arbitrary? No, it's necessary. It's necessary because the relationship with the cause also requires images. And this is the essentially phantasmic structure of philosophical discourse. Discourse [le dire] does not exempt us but, on the contrary, requires us to know what its object-cause is; that's the real crux of this whole business. Even if it's captivating, hidden, or mind-blowing.

There is something that may nevertheless mislead us: the explicit presence in many philosophies of a doctrine of the subject, and even of one that includes lack-of-being, disruption, and the consistency of the effects. Yet this is not necessarily a reliable guide as to the fact that the subject is the cause of discourse. And it's not true that the philosophies presenting themselves explicitly as doctrines of the subject are necessarily clearer than the others as to their object, namely, the subject. It's even quite often the opposite: it's a further obscurity. It's a bit like pretending to pretend, the better to conceal. I tell you that my object is the subject. So what remains hidden? Well, the real object, that is to say, the subject, actually, but from a different angle, in a different sense. Indeed, this concealment of the subject within the subject itself is one of the hallmarks of post-Cartesian philosophies. It reveals this concealment, of course, but when we say that philosophy's object is the subject, let's be careful not to claim that the philosophies of the subject are selectively closer to philosophy's object than the other ones. Claiming to be a philosophy of the subject is quite misleading as to the real of such a philosophy. This is also true of an individual life: thinking you're a subject is a serious neurosis. Claiming that you've gotten rid of your self, for example... What about philosophies that state: "There's no more self, I'm a transparent subject"? Ultimately, it may be better to claim to be an ontology: that's less serious, albeit paranoid, but it's less serious! So it's easy to see how the doctrine of the subject can be a higher form of concealment, but it's because in it, the subject is something other than the subject-cause of the discourse. And actually, on closer inspection, if you look at the explicit doctrines of the subject, the subject is either an ontological term—that is, a pure point of being, as in Descartes, where it could be argued that the subject is constitutive of certainty only under the ultimate presupposition of an ontology that authorizes it—or else the subject is that which is authorized only by itself with respect to its being. Or again, the subject may be a critical operator, as in Kant. And, last but not least, it may be a form of self-presentation of the absolute, as in Hegel. In every case, the subject is unable to be the object-cause of the discourse because it is only too obviously the referent, the fetish, of this discourse.

---

I'm going to use the same conceptual apparatus that I've been using for the past two years to reassess the philosophical texts this year. The assessment won't take account of the Whole: it's not a systematic review of the doctrines, because in that case I'd only be holding a mirror up to fantasies—which would be interesting for the fun of it, though tinged with a hint of perversity. So the assessment won't take account of the Whole of the system, because in a certain way you have to *encounter* it. You have to *encounter* something in philosophical discourse, not just unpack it or re-expose or rearrange its articulations but really, literally, hit a snag. Because... what is the real? It's a snag.

But we know that to encounter it you have to work hard; you have to find something askew in the text. Otherwise, you'll never encounter anything but what it has already intended for you to encounter: its multitude of images. What recourse will you have then? The one I suggested is not the only one—many other ones can be used. But the one I suggested is to follow what could be called a "vector," to follow a concept, not necessarily a key concept in the system, not the concept in which the whole system is usually recapitulated, but a concept that has a fluid—rather fluid—relationship with the general features of the subject-process in terms of its three descriptions. Thus, to take a concept, just like that, with a rather fluid intention at first; to follow it as a vector because it has some connotation echoing the threefold description of a subject-process; and then to rely on that vector to see whether it passes through or hits an impasse. Actually, it will never be central, but rather a tiny bit "diagonal" in relation to the architectonic structure of philosophical discourse.

---

These are the vectors that have guided my seminar series of the past three years. The first year, I used the One. Why the One? Because it's related to the first characteristic, the lack-of-being. Basically, the subject-process assumes that something has not been counted as being, or that something has been subtracted from being counted as one. In other words, the mode of appearing of the lack-of-being is always subtraction from a count. So if you want to follow this lead—seeing where, in a philosophical discourse, the question of the lack-of-being emerges unconsciously and not in the images—it's useful to pursue the question of the One, i.e., the question of what is counted as one, in the hopes of seeing where it breaks down and thus of determining whether something has actually not been counted and will appear in the text or in thought, in philosophical discourse, as unstable because it is unfixed by the One. So you'll have to try to find out where the count-as-one fails. And how does this count-as-one fail? Always in the same way: You always hit a point where a paradoxical being, a paradoxical multiple, is such that whether it is counted as one or not is undecidable. Naturally, you never come across anything that, explicitly and decisively, hasn't been counted, because if you could recognize and identify something that wasn't counted, you can be sure that the astute philosopher would have long since recognized and counted it. So there won't be any gross miscalculation, so to speak. That's out of the question! A good philosopher doesn't make that kind of big, stupid mistake: letting the uncounted get clean away. But what you *will* find is undecidability as to the count. Undecidability in the sense that the text hasn't decided whether something was counted or not. It's not that it didn't count it, no! It's just that it's encountered as undecidable. Neither we—nor the author, in a certain way—know whether it has been counted or not. We share his uncertainty, and that's what we encounter with this vector of the One: a relationship between the One and the undecidable. And it's here that one of the symptoms of the subject-process can be traced: whenever the question of the One ends up being ruled by undecidability, that is to say, by something that is neither One nor not-One. This is an approach I've already used: tracing the subject's symptom to the relationship between the One and the undecidable, in connection with Plato, the first year, in the *Sophist* and the *Parmenides*; then in connection with Descartes, concerning the cogito and the proofs of God's existence; and finally in connection with Kant, concerning the sequence of the three *Critiques*, because my real aim was less each individual *Critique* than the question of their sequence and asking what happened in the period between the *Critiques*.

---

Last year, I used the infinite as a vector. The infinite, as related to the second description: that of the disruption of the law of being, because the disruption of a law of being immediately exceeds representation and thus it un-fixes the order in which being is presented. In philosophy—in classical philosophy—the infinite is the name of this excess, or one of the names of this excess. Indeed, it is always the name of what is presented at the point where the linear law is disrupted. I dealt with the infinite in connection with Aristotle, whose advantage is that he explicitly denies it any being; then in connection with Spinoza, who, in diametrical opposition to Aristotle, posits the fundamental originality of this concept; and finally, in connection with Hegel, who revealed its very fascinating dialectical ruses. What had struck me then is that, insofar as it was linked to a hypothesis of disruption, of excess, the infinite was immediately related to the void and to the point; to the punctual and the void. To the void, in Spinoza, of which I gave a complete demonstration; and to the point, in Hegel, whose doctrine of the infinite is a pure punctual capacity of the finite. The symptomal site of the subject, in the case of the infinite, i.e., where the vector leads us, is ultimately its relationship with the void and the point—whence the hypothesis of an empty point, a hypothesis that is strangely necessary for any rational construction of the concept of the infinite.

This year, it's the concept of being that I'll be using as a vector—that concept through which philosophy is able to be grasped as ontology, a concept of being that is less organic or central than it is a vector. So it's the regime of its transformations, its relationships, and its impasses that will be the basis for the interpretation. This time, I'll be chronological—that wasn't the case in the previous years because chronology had nothing to do with the approach adopted—but I'll be chronological now in order to inhabit the Heideggerian construction. I'll trace its structure in several steps. I'll begin with the Greek origin of the question, basing myself, as I already told you I would, on fragments, snippets of Parmenides's poem, which are absolutely primordial, absolutely originary, in the Greek formulation of the question of being, and also, at the same time, that fragmented and materialist form introduced by the atomists of antiquity. Because historians of philosophy have long noted that the philosophy of Democritus, the founder of the school of Abdera, the founder of the atomist school, was a sort of exploded Eleaticism, in which the Parmenidian *One-being* changed into an infinity of ones, even though all of them, in their intrinsic multiplicity, have the exact same features as Parmenides's being qua being. That's why I suggested that there is an Eleaticism in bits and pieces in Democritean philosophy. Moreover, what is the source of the explosion? What is the point from which the reciprocity of being and the One in Parmenides morphs, so to speak, into an atomistic infinity? That will be the first step. Second, of course, I'll focus on the metaphysical mediation, the mediation used by onto-theology, and therefore on the era in which the question of being qua being changed into the question of the supreme being, of God, meaning that I'll be examining it at the height of its form, truly in the metaphysics of metaphysics, namely, the system of Malebranche, the Reverend Father Malebranche. Because, aside from its unparalleled philosophical oddness, his system is one of the rare systems of the great classical rationalism in which religion is an internal component of the apparatus. The onto-theological is completely—not just partially—involved in it, right down to its consequences. Descartes's "God," as Pascal pointed out, is very abstract, while the Reverend Father Malebranche's isn't. Not only is the Christian apparatus with its oddness an internal component of his philosophy, but he goes so far as to imply that the Church is a philosophical concept, not an institutional avatar. And I am moved by that audacity . . . Then, the last step will be the contemporary return of the question of being directly to Heidegger. All right, I'll stop here for today.

---

But before I leave, I'd just like to mention a few bibliographical items that will be helpful to you. Here are eight references that I have basically divided into two groups: four that are directly related to what we're going to be studying this year, and four others that are a little "diagonal." First, as regards Parmenides, there's no two ways about it: the text of reference is Jean Beaufret's *Le Poème de Parménide* [Parmenides's Poem] in his edition, with his translation and annotation. You'll find everything that survives of Parmenides in it. As for the Greek atomists, I recommend Paul Nizan's little book, *Les Matérialistes de l'Antiquité* [The Materialists of Antiquity], which, thanks to its references and arguments, will help you get an idea, through the textual fragments, of their founder Democritus in particular. From Malebranche, from Father Malebranche's enormous body of work, as enormous as the clockwork of the universe, I'll select the *Treatise on Nature and Grace*, which, in my opinion, contains the quintessence of his thought. As for Heidegger, our canonical text will be the *Introduction to Metaphysics*. So there you have it for Parmenides, the atomists, Malebranche, and Heidegger. Thus, it's with discernment and subtlety that . . . you'll begin!

---

Now, as regards the articles or short texts that I call "diagonal," they are texts that don't deal directly with the authors selected, but that I think lead to exercises of interpretation by the cut.[2] They are texts that are both closely related to, yet distinct from, the texts being studied directly. That's why they suggest the idea of a game, a play of distancing and ex-centering from the text itself. Concerning the

Greek origin of the question, I recommend you read, as a sort of dissident strategy, a text by Heidegger entitled "Anaximander's Saying," which is the last essay in the collection *Off the Beaten Track*. It's not about Parmenides but Anaximander . . . and it's incidentally a superb essay, one of Heidegger's most dense and amazing texts. Of Anaximander there survive . . . only two lines. "Anaximander's Saying": it is really what he said! Next, in connection with the Greek atomists, a text by Hegel in *The Science of Logic*. How should I give it to you? I could of course say: the Labarrière translation, volume 1, pages 134–137, or else the one in volume 1, section 1, chapter III, part B, no. 1, entitled "L'un et le vide" [The One and the Void], including and especially with the comment that follows. Next, as regards Malebranche, or rather as far as the *Treatise on Nature and Grace* is concerned, I'll suggest a text by Pascal: Écrits sur la grâce [Writings on Grace], the four writings on grace, an unfinished text, in the Pléiade edition, pages 947–1044. Finally, as regards Heidegger and the *Introduction to Metaphysics*, read one of the poet René Char's collections, *Leaves of Hypnos*, in the Pléiade edition, pages 175–233. And that about does it!

See you next Tuesday. Unless the approach of vacation is devastating. Let me know!

# Session 2

## October 29, 1985

Today's session will be fairly short: as an introduction to the study of Parmenides, it will focus on the value of using the question of being as a vector of inquiry leading to the subject as the real object of any philosophy.

So who is this Parmenides I'm going to be talking about? We're not really sure. He's someone who amounts to little more than his text. There has been no lack of scholarly studies attempting to establish the date of his birth—I'll spare you them, however—but it's all so convoluted that I don't think there's any point in celebrating Parmenides's birthday. So what *do* we know about him?

We know that he lived on the cusp of the sixth and fifth centuries BCE, so before the strictly Classical Age of Greek philosophy. That he is therefore regarded by academia as a pre-Socratic philosopher. And that he belonged to the so-called still archaic or preclassical period of Greek history. This would incidentally lead Heidegger to say about Parmenides's fragments, or rather about a passage of his that he quotes: "These few words stand there like archaic Greek statues."[1] The image of the "archaic Greek statue" is clearly like a double metaphor here, a metaphor suggesting, first, the preclassical character of Parmenides, that is to say, something originary and foundational, and, second, something whose esthetic, whose mode of presence, harbors a mystery and is not directly accessible to our understanding. We also know that Parmenides was a native of Elea, in Magna Graecia, in that remote, outlying colony of Athens. Elea was a city that we might locate today in southern Italy, just south of Naples. And because he was from Elea, the school of thought that Parmenides founded was known as "Eleatic" and his philosophy referred to as "Eleatic philosophy." But it's still an open question whether he was really its founder. It's a troubling, double question, for no sooner has one founder been identified than another one is always discovered, before him. In this case it would be Xenophanes of Colophon, and so since Parmenides was the second founder, he would be the true one. It's always the second founder who founds, because he founds what the first founder doesn't found or has left unfounded—that is, he institutes something that was not founded or able to be founded before. This was the case with Xenophanes— but we know next to nothing about him because he's even more of a mystery than Parmenides. This is a huge question that was addressed and is still being addressed by German philology... opening the way for scholars to reconstruct down to the smallest detail the philosophies of both Parmenides and Xenophanes (whose pupil Parmenides was said to have been), the connections between them, the direct influence of the one on the other, and so on. It's a work of paleontology, in a way. The pre-Socratic age of Greek philosophy is one of reconstructions: you've got a single, barely legible line of writing, and you reconstruct the doctrine, influences, origin, etc. from it. This is essentially what Heidegger managed to extract from one line by Anaximander.

    Regardless of whether he was the second founder or the first, Parmenides was really the one who provided the core of the so-called "Eleatic" doctrine, owing to the texts, the real texts that he left us. There survive from him fragments of what was once a poem. Only fragments of a whole that is half-there, to be deciphered, and half-missing, to be reconstructed. A few fairly extensive fragments, some little scraps as well . . . but enough of them to reconstruct a distinct whole and to make a coherence and a logic of the work come through despite the lacunae. There is hardly anything authentic when it comes to the pre-Socratic age: the entire constellation of texts and their interpretation come, by way of transmission throughout antiquity, from a frequently reinvented practice of writing and citations whose legitimacy remains to be proven. And so, quite often, it was the much later writers of the Christian era who cited certain of these fragments. This means that they were filtered in every case, and filtered in accordance with principles or procedures it is hard to trace. Might there have been—precisely because Parmenides was regarded very early on as a fabled and fabulous founding figure—a highly selective filtering of all his theories? . . . And that's something we can't reconstruct. Thus, the mode of expression Parmenides chose was poetic. A poem—in bits and pieces, at times veritable scraps, only a half-verse, and at other times long sequences of a unique work. It is at any rate the dominant hypothesis of current scholarship that allows us to speak of "the" poem of Parmenides. His exceptional position among the pre-Socratic philosophers, those of ancient Greece, made him a truly legendary figure, not because of him as a person or his life, as was the case with others, such as the poetic mythical figure of Empedocles, associated with the hypothesis of his suicide . . . No! There was nothing like that where Parmenides was concerned: tradition has enshrined him as a truly philosophical legend. Very early on, right from the Classical Age of philosophy, hence barely a century after his death, a conceptual legend grew up around him that placed him in an originary position, as the father of philosophy and virtually as the proper name designating the emergence, the birth, of the philosophical as such. Why? Yes, why?

The earlier pre-Socratics, who were island dwellers, like the Thales of "All is water" fame, are known as physicists, in other words, still halfway between the mythological cosmologies and the rational apparatus. So Parmenides effected a break by inaugurating a new regime of discourse, not just by developing one particular theory or another but by really inaugurating a new mode of operation of discourse—which would in fact be called "philosophy" in the Classical Age. While there is no shortage of evidence for this, the most important evidence is found in Plato, especially in the two dialogues the *Sophist* and the *Parmenides*, in which Plato's attitude toward Parmenides contrasts radically with that of all his predecessors and rivals. You know this; it's common knowledge. But let me remind you of the treatments to which the figure of Parmenides was subjected. In the *Sophist*, the metaphor of parricide appears explicitly, owing to Plato's feeling compelled to criticize certain of Parmenides's statements. To establish that there is a certain being of nonbeing is, he says, "a parricide" of "our father Parmenides," thereby ensuring that all of philosophy would have a Parmenides fixation. And note how remarkable Plato's use of the term "parricide" is! Then, in the *Parmenides*, at the beginning of the dialogue, an elaborate mise-en-scène sets up a meeting between the young Socrates and the elderly Parmenides—a meeting, if you come right down to it, between the real father and the symbolic father, because the Plato-Socrates filiation is, shall we say, a direct one, running through the whole work, whereas the other filiation, the reference to the elderly Parmenides whom Socrates supposedly met, is an explicit figure of the Name-of-the-Father, of a strictly symbolic paternity. So there's this amazing setup where Socrates, the direct predecessor, the one to whom tribute is constantly being paid, who's the main character of the dialogues, meets the person who is actually the general father, the universal father, the father qua father, that is to say, the founder of philosophy itself. This is all the more remarkable in that it is the meeting between a very young Socrates and a very old Parmenides. Socrates is so young and Parmenides so old that this meeting most certainly never took place. Plato fudged the dates. It's truly a performance, a theatrical representation. The whole reference to Parmenides, to his role as founding father, unfolds in its symbolic singularity, which shows how, in both these dialogues, as early as the time of the ancient Greeks, Parmenides's conceptual legend was already established. And by "conceptual legend" I mean the following idea here: Parmenides was the founder of a new regime of discourse on which all philosophers depend, whatever their orientation and even if they must commit a parricide, as Plato in the *Sophist* feels he has to.

This conceptual legend thereafter continued or was passed down throughout the history of philosophy—and I'll comment on it with two references, one to Hegel and the other to Heidegger.

At the very beginning of the *Logic*, when he is dealing with being, Hegel says:

> The *Eleatics* were the first to give voice to the simple thought of *pure being*—notable among them Parmenides, who declared it to be the absolute and sole truth. In his surviving fragments, he did it with the pure enthusiasm of thought which has for the first time apprehended itself in its absolute abstraction: *only being is, and nothing is not absolutely.*[2]

What do we find in this comment of Hegel's? That Parmenides enunciated the simple thought of "pure being" and the idea of "the pure enthusiasm of thought which has for the first time apprehended itself in its absolute abstraction." The idea of the "first time" is, in a way, taken up and questioned as such by Hegel.

Likewise, Heidegger, among other reverential tributes to Parmenides in his *Introduction to Metaphysics*, writes:

> Anyone today [*meaning the reader*][3] who is acquainted with the standards of such a thinking discourse [*he's referring to Parmenides's text*] must lose all desire to write books. (106)

Heidegger acknowledges not only the idea of Parmenides's absolute originarity but also that of the unsurpassed nature of Parmenidean procreation: "Anyone today who is acquainted with the standards of such a thinking discourse must lose all desire to write books." It's as though, somehow, the very existence of Parmenides in his originarity made the historical destiny of philosophy superfluous. On account of this first act of procreation, this very first time that being is enunciated in its being, Parmenides appears literally as a hero—I'm using the word in its mythological sense—a hero of philosophy, i.e., someone who accomplishes for the very first time the prodigious feat of naming being in its being and, in the process, inventing philosophical discourse as such.

That said, we'll need to reconsider, to some extent, the aura surrounding Parmenides. Not that he's a nobody, quite the contrary. But he's the kind of figure that's been turned into a statue, as it were, by history, not just in terms of its form but also in terms of what was said. Fortunately or unfortunately—because they're interwoven in a very complicated way—a counter-legend about Parmenides developed over the course of history, prompted by the desire to deconstruct him. Like every legend, that of Parmenides as symbolic father has its counter-legend. What is it? That Parmenides was certainly the first to attempt to think being but that he was to a much greater extent the founder of an abstract, rather than a concrete, approach to the question. This was of course Nietzsche's thesis—not surprisingly! It pitted Parmenides's abstract, cold, and, Nietzsche would say, mechanical immobility against what he considered to be Heraclitus's dynamic vitality. But let's leave Heraclitus aside for the moment. What's interesting is that to the great legendary figure of the founder of the thinking of being is opposed the counter-figure of the one who, instead of being the first to set thinking free, supposedly immobilized it right from the outset, that is to say, froze it right from the outset. To this counter-current Parmenides appears not as the founder of philosophy but as the founder of the danger of abstraction within philosophy itself, that is, as the founder of abstraction, or the founder of a type of philosophy that rejects life. As a result, the figure of Parmenides is saturated in that it is identified both as the founder of philosophical discourse and as the founder of the threat to that discourse.

---

What I will argue is that these two interpretations, Heidegger's and Nietzsche's (which Heidegger explicitly criticized), are both flawed. The whole problem will be to find the flaw, which is the same in both, naturally. It's the same because neither of them connects Parmenides—what Parmenides says—to the "system" of his conditions. Not, of course, in the sense of his socio-historical conditions: I'm not suggesting that when Parmenides said that immobility was the greatest thing, the rise in the price of ceramics in Sicily was hampering trade. No, of course not! It was the "system" of conditions of *enunciation* of the Parmenidean "saying" (as Heidegger would put it), of what, in fact, defined him as a founder, but not simply, or only, because it was about being that he spoke. What needs to be understood—to do justice to Parmenides, so that he's neither the Heideggerian legend nor the Nietzschean counter-legend—is the system of conceptual conditions that he complied with. There is certainly something foundational about Parmenides, or if not about Parmenides then about Xenophanes, who was, however, only a pale shadow of him. But the system of conditions of this foundation is part of the foundation itself. That's the flaw in both Heidegger's interpretation and Nietzsche's.

It must also be said that what has contributed significantly to the dramatization of Parmenides's conceptual legend is the tone he himself used. The tone of the poem is both authoritative and sacred. It's authoritative because it's in a regime of very pronounced prescriptive authority—it commands and forbids—and it's sacred because it's in the regime of inspiration, of an utterance of which Parmenides doesn't identify himself directly as the source but rather as though something had been dictated to him by an inspiration the metaphor of which is a goddess. Owing to this subtle blend of authoritative tone and sacred form, Parmenides's poem is afforded an exceptional loftiness, an utterly unique sort of imperiousness and grandeur, which has always captured the imagination.

I'm going to read you three passages from it so that you can hear the founder's tone for yourselves. Here is the beginning:

> The mares which bear me as far as my desires might reach
> were conveying me, when they led me into the many-voiced way
> of the deity, who leads the knowing mortal straight on through
> > all things.
> By this way was I borne, for by this way the well-discerning mares
> > bore me as they
> drew the chariot, and the maidens guided the way.[4]

That, you see, is the beginning! Or at any rate the one we have. It's the story of an initiation journey to a heavenly abode where the deity who is going to speak dwells, and at the same time it's the pride of the "knowing mortal."

Regarding its lofty, authoritative character, here is Fragment 2:

> Come now and I shall tell, and do you receive through hearing
> > the tale,
> which are the only ways of inquiry for thinking:
> the one: that it is and that it is not possible not to be,
> is the path of Persuasion (for she attends on Truth);
> the other: that it is not and that it is right it should not be,
> this I declare to you is an utterly inscrutable track,

for neither could you know what is not (for it cannot be
    accomplished),
nor could you declare it [or: point it out]. (213)

And, finally, Fragment 7:

Never shall this prevail, that things that are not are.
But you, withhold your thought from this way of inquiry,
nor let habit born of long experience force you along this way,
to wield an unseeing eye and echoing ear
and tongue. But judge by reasoning the very contentious
    examination
uttered by me. (215)

That is the language that Parmenides devised in order to be heard. A poetic language, a language of prophetic utterance, a language of inspiration, of authority. And the idea of a "first time"—let me stress this again—contributed to the making of his legend, the idea of the enthusiasm of the first time, as Hegel put it, but also the idea of an inspiration, knowing that what he had to say was unprecedented.

What is it basically about? What is inscribed in the opening of his poem? In *Introduction to Metaphysics*, Heidegger offers an analysis of it that is quite clear and compelling because of its proximity to the text. It is as follows: what Parmenides enunciated with the utmost clarity for the first time ever is the connection between two distinctions that do not overlap, the distinction between being and nonbeing—as you just heard: one must choose between the two ways—and the distinction between being and seeming. And this discrimination, this delimitation of these two distinctions—being and nonbeing, being and seeming—is truly constitutive of philosophy; it inaugurates philosophy. Heidegger's whole aim is to show how the delimitation of the distinctions—being/nonbeing and being/seeming—is the originary condition of philosophical discourse. Not that this discourse can be reduced to it, but it is only possible on the basis of the delimitation of these distinctions. He therefore concludes from this that poetry proposes three paths to thought—he uses Parmenides's metaphor itself here—three roads, three ways, three paths whose characterizations differ. There's the path to being, which Parmenides calls unavoidable; there's the path to nonbeing, which is inaccessible and leads to Nothing; and, finally, there's the path to seeming,—seeming-opinion; the Greek word for it is *doxa*—the path to opinion, which is on the contrary always accessible, always traveled, which is the easy way, as it were, the way of "human beings," Parmenides will say, but which can be bypassed, which we're not required to take.

Let's recap: the first path is unavoidable, the second one, inaccessible, and the third can be bypassed—it can be bypassed in the sense that, ordinarily, it's the one that's always traveled. What Heidegger shows—I believe correctly—is that Parmenides's great strength, with respect to the three paths possible for thought, lay in defining philosophy as a decision. He simply says that Parmenides's tone, the loftiness of Parmenides's tone, was that of decision, not of argumentation. So it's not quite correct to say that, in this interpretation, Parmenides was the first philosopher. Parmenides was less a philosopher than someone who *decided for* philosophy. After which there were philosophers, but there were philosophers because philosophy had already been *decided for*. And as far as philosophy is concerned, Parmenides was not *a* philosopher, not even the first. He was more than that, because he was the one who *decided for* philosophy. He did so insofar as he described its paths, and, as a result, the metaphor of the crossroads is essential for him, the metaphor of the chariot carried along by the horses to the crossroads is key, because it designates the *place* where the decision is made. We are taken to the crossroads, where it is both required and possible to decide for philosophy. But to decide for it there must of course be a representable co-presence of the paths. That's why Parmenides doesn't say: There is only one way. That, for Heidegger, will be philosophy's downfall. Philosophy will lose its way precisely when it begins to claim that there is only one way. But even more important for Parmenides: there are actually two, then three, ways—that of being, that of nonbeing, and that of seeming—and a decision for philosophy must be made *there*. Parmenides's essence, Heidegger continues, thus lies in his thinking *at the place* where ways diverge, that is, his thinking at the place where a decision is made, and especially his being the one who thinks the way of Nothing together with the way of being. Parmenides's greatness—I agree with Heidegger about this—does not lie in his having said "being is," but rather in his having decided for philosophy at the intersection of the two ways where both the being of being and the nonbeing of nonbeing are thought and to have depicted that place as the strategic crossroads of the decision for philosophy.

Heidegger sums it up this way:

> Parmenides' fragment at the same time gives us the most ancient document in philosophy that shows that, together with the path of Being, the path of Nothing must expressly be *thought* . . . (122; trans. slightly modified)

If, together with the path of Being, the path of Nothing must expressly be thought, it is because the essence of what is at stake, here, is the decision. It's not because the two must be synthesized, or thought at the same time, no! Because, if what must be decided is to decide for philosophy, then the paths of the decision must of course be thought simultaneously. Fine. This is an extremely forceful interpretation of or hypothesis about the originary character of Parmenidean thought.

What should we make of this? In that phrase "the most ancient document in philosophy that shows that, together with the path of Being, the path of Nothing must expressly be *thought*," everything hinges on *philosophy*. Everything hinges on it because of an initial problem, which is: to what extent does "deciding for philosophy" constitute a philosophical document, a document *of* philosophy? That's the first question. The second, which to my mind is much more important, is that, in reality, in that phrase, Heidegger acts as though the characterization of the two paths and the corresponding decision to be made between them—the characterization of the paths of being and nonbeing, the metaphor of the crossroads and the associated imperative of decision—described the origin of philosophy, or was the originary decision of philosophy. The whole problem is whether it is indeed true that Parmenides decided for philosophy just because he said that the paths of being and nonbeing were the place where a decision is made. Was it he who decided for philosophy or was it philosophy that he decided about because and only because he characterized what I call the "crossroads of decision," that is, the critical imperative of a decision at the place where the paths of being and nonbeing intersect? Is that really sufficient for saying that it was *philosophy as such* that was decided for there? Because it's clear that, in reality, what Heidegger will call "philosophy" is precisely what was decided for, there, under the necessity of thinking the paths of being and Nothing together. His interpretative method consists at once in saying, first, that, there, philosophy was decided for, and, second, that philosophy is what that decision established, necessarily. In other words, the interpretation conveys both meanings at once. So what is the problem? If philosophy were decided for on the basis of that issue and that issue alone—thinking the paths of being and Nothing together and establishing a regime of decision—and if that were the absolute origin of the existence of its discursive system, we would have to say, and I do say, that philosophy was decided for long before.

---

Let me begin by reading you an Egyptian text dating from three or four centuries before Parmenides, the Bremner-Rhind Papyrus. Its form, too, is metaphorical and poetic—as in Parmenides's poem, it is being, the "deity," that speaks.

The text reads:

> When I manifested myself into existence, existence existed.
> I came into existence in the form of the Existent, which came into existence in the First Time.
> Coming into existence according to the mode of existence of the Existent, I therefore existed.
> And it was thus that the Existent came into existence.[5]

That's the Egyptian text. Now, let's put ourselves in Heidegger's place. What would he say if he were dealing not with Parmenides but with this Egyptian text? And what would *we* say? We'd say: this is the originary enunciation of ontico-ontological difference. It is fully present in this text. Indeed, what is this unknown Egyptian telling us? He's telling us that there's a dialectic of "the Existent" and "existence," and it's the dialectic of "existence" [*l'étant*] and "being" [*l'être*] in the face of the uncertainty about what that word means. It means "existence;" it means "having come into;" it means "emergence;" it means "transformation," "being." It is indeed the dialectic of the Existent and existence, that of existence and being. And what the text tells us is that there is a coming-to-itself of existence and that this coming-to-itself is mediated through the Existent, as through a kind of primordiality that is self-foundational: "Coming into existence according to the mode of existence of the Existent,

I therefore existed. And it was thus that the Existent came into existence." Being that is conceived of as emergence, i.e., conceived of as originarity in self-emergence, emergence through which being comes to itself, also leaves, as a trace of itself, the Existent, which is both its principle of mediation and its effectivity. This naturally implies, already at that time, a high degree of metaphysical and ontological speculation. But will we say that the mythologizing corpus of the text, of this textual fragment, is only a myth, a story about the origin of the world, and not a decision for philosophy? That is not in itself convincing, because the beginning of Parmenides's poem also features the maidens, the goddesses, the silver-wheeled chariot, and so on and so forth: all the mythological referential ornamentation is present as the mode of utterance. So it is entirely possible to argue that if philosophy is decided for at the place where the question of being and nonbeing is presented, if philosophy is decided for as soon as the question of being and nonbeing is formulated or presented, we could then claim that it is Egyptian in origin. And we could do so all the more since what has come down to us is in a fragmentary state. Parmenides's poem, or the few surviving scraps of it, describes elements such as, on one side, "the ethereal fire of flame, being gentle, very light, everywhere the same as itself" and, on the other side, "contrarily unintelligent night, a dense body and heavy" (Fragment 8, p. 219). These are also elements of primitive descriptive cosmology. So it's not true that Parmenides's text is a text of pure ontology. It is also a text that has a cosmological purpose and ultimately aims to give a description of the procedure for classifying the elements, for distributing "the hot" and "the dry," "the wet," "the earth," "the heavens," and so on. This grouping of pure abstract or ontological dialectics into cosmological configurations is as overwhelmingly present in the Egyptian text as it is only sparsely so in Parmenides's. But why is it only sparsely so in Parmenides's text? Because *it* was filtered through the subsequent philosophical tradition. It is because the modus operandi of philosophy as such had already been established in it that what was most closely related to the material that would be retained in philosophy was gradually distilled from the founding father's text and what was clearly still mythological or cosmological was filtered out to some extent. However, philosophy *wasn't* founded in Egypt. Why not? What happened? The Egyptian text came down to us in an unsorted mass, thus consigning it to the category of cosmological, mythological, or religious texts: sacred texts, in other words. If Parmenides's text had come down to us completely unfiltered through the foundation of a specific regime of discourse—philosophical discourse—we would, I believe, have very much the same feeling about it. What can be said now is that the philosophical act cannot be decided about simply on the basis of the presence of speculations about being and nonbeing, even when they are clearly articulated in the logic of their implication.

Let's turn now to the texts that come to us from India, the hymns of the Veda. The latest ones, in this case, predate Parmenides by four centuries, the earliest ones by ten centuries. I'm going to read you one of the Vedic hymns from the more recent period, from about three or four centuries before Parmenides:

> The non-existent did not exist, nor did the existent exist at
>     that time.
>         There existed neither the airy space nor heaven beyond.
> What moved back and forth? From where and in whose protection?
>     Did
>         water exist, a deep depth?
> Death did not exist nor deathlessness then. There existed no sign
>     of night
>         nor of day.

That One breathed without wind by its independent will. There
   existed
      nothing else beyond that.
Darkness existed, hidden by darkness, in the beginning. All this was a
   signless ocean.
What existed as a thing coming into being concealed by
   emptiness—that
      One was born by the power of heat.
Then, in the beginning, from thought there evolved desire,
   which existed
      as the primal semen.
Searching in their hearts through inspired thinking, poets found the
   connection of the existent in the non-existent.[6]

That's the first text. The second, later one, is a text from the *Upanishads*, a century before Parmenides. Let me read it to you:

In the beginning, my dear, this world was just Being, one only,
   without a second.
To be sure, some people say: 'In the beginning this world was just
   Non-being, one only, without a second; from that Non-being
   Being was produced.'
But verily, my dear, whence could this be? said he.
How could Being be produced from Non-being?
On the contrary, my dear, in the beginning this world was just
   Being, one only, without a second.[7]

Some Chinese or Tibetan texts could also be found . . . What's the purpose of this detour to the East? The question is as follows: Why isn't it possible—in Heidegger's sense—to consider the Egyptian or Indian or other texts as philosophical documents? Why isn't that possible? In terms of their tone, they're absolutely similar to

Parmenides's text, and it's not poetry that differentiates them here. Heidegger himself says "The thinking of Parmenides . . . is still poetic" (161). He even adds: "and here this means philosophical, not scientific." Let's leave "philosophical, not scientific" aside for the moment and just focus on the idea that the thinking is poetic, i.e., that there's a metaphorical overlay of the discourse. There are things in Parmenides's text that might be troublesome for his commentators, such as that Being is a sphere that is "motionless in the limits of great bonds" (Fragment 8, p. 217). There's an obvious metaphorical overlay. But either you take these theses literally, and what you actually have are cosmological metaphors, or you think that they inaugurate philosophy, and they need to be deciphered and given a meaning different from their immediate metaphorical meaning. So it's not this that differentiates between them. Nor is it the immediate issue of thinking. Because in both cases the issue is not only to enunciate being but to identify the form of dialectical delimitation between being and nonbeing. And clearly these texts refer, as Parmenides does, to a whole context of polemics over the question of whether it is tenable for nonbeing to be. In the last text I read you, from the *Upanishads*, the logic of the refutation is the same as Parmenides's: if a being of nonbeing is posited, it's impossible to see in what sense being can be, what being of being is tenable if indeed there is a being of nonbeing. Or, as the first Indian text expresses it, with respect to poets, it's how the questions of being and nonbeing are connected with each other within oneself. So the issue is formally comparable, the tone is the same, it's not poetry that differentiates them, nor, as I said, is it the cosmological context.

There are two options when it comes to this situation. The first is to say: "Yes, it's not true that philosophy was unequivocally decided for in Greece by Parmenides." You accept Heidegger's thesis that it was indeed as a result of that decision that philosophy began—as regards the question of the delimitation of the distinctions and the dialectic of being and nonbeing—but you add that the assumption that it was decided for *only* in Greece is a narrow version of the thesis, and this ultimately amounts to Western-centrism. So you'd accept the discriminant kernel with respect to being and nonbeing, and you'd accept the criterion of the philosophical foundation, but you'd reject the position on the "originarily Greek" essence of philosophy.

By a strange effect of conjuncture, this hypothesis, not on the foundation but on philosophy itself, is shared by Lardreau and Jambet.[8] Jambet's *Logique des Orientaux* [The Logic of Eastern Philosophy] and Lardreau's recently published *Discours philosophique et discours spirituel* [Philosophical Discourse and Spiritual Discourse] could be mentioned in this connection. What these two works have in common is that they essentially say that the topography, so to speak, of philosophy, the established topography, is flawed: in other words, we need to abandon a Western-centered vision of philosophical discursivity, of philosophical rationality, and restructure its entire history by expressly including in it what I call "the Eastern dimension." Again, this doesn't have to do with philosophy's foundation exactly but with the general system of philosophical discourse.

Jambet thinks, for example, that the great philosophers and theologians of Islam, and especially Shiite Islam, are actually an organic part of the philosophical system, that is to say, are part of the historicity of philosophical thought, not just in the sense that they're something "extra" but in the sense that by failing to take them into account we cloud the understanding even of Western philosophers and are dealing with a historicity of philosophy that prevents us from understanding it as such. Because Jambet's thesis is that, ultimately, every philosophical system includes an Eastern dimension. The Eastern and Western dimensions will both become concepts internal to the assessment of any philosophical thought.

Therefore, the failure to appreciate the Eastern dimension of the great founders—in line with his initial material, the great speculations associated with Shiite Islam—is a pure and simple exercise in ignorance, which we must put a stop to. According to Jambet's argument, the entire history of philosophy needs to be re-established, not just supplemented but re-established.

As for Lardreau's book, in which he focused on the work of Philoxenus of Mabbug, a fifth-century Syriac monk, its subject is different: it's about the Christian space, not Islam. What Lardreau claims is that the substructure of decision can only be understood by examining a type of discourse that is different from philosophical discourse as such, as it is understood in the West. The substructure of decision can only be understood if we are open to a different kind of discourse, which he calls the "spiritual discourse," and in this way, too, the history of philosophy must be re-established. It must be re-established because we are blind to its regime of decision and fail to see that fundamental decisions about philosophy were made in a regime of discourse different from philosophical discourse—decisions that determined the future of philosophy and were, in some way, in a position of decision about the decision. Because, in reality, Lardreau's basic thesis is that the philosophical subject, the subject who decides for philosophy, can only do so in a space of pre-philosophical spirituality, whose mode of articulation is altogether different, and that the decider's system of belief requires, as operator, concept, and historical referent, the examination of the spiritual discourse, an example of which—Christian spirituality—he gives, though he doesn't claim it is the only one.

---

Both these projects, which I consider post-Heideggerian, share the current thinking that it is by incorporating and examining decisions and texts external to Western philosophy and its Greek origins that the history of philosophy, and therefore philosophical thought itself, can and must be re-established. The Eastern dimension for Jambet, the spiritual discourse for Lardreau. This exteriority, of course, in their work, was actually an unsuspected interiority. I must stress that it wasn't an addition; it was something unsuspected, something not-known in philosophical discourse itself. So their aim—because they were also Lacanians, their regime of thought was based on interpretation—their aim was to show how the not-known in philosophical and intellectual discourse, the hidden dimension of Western philosophy, is an Eastern discourse. This naturally involved drawing on specified bodies of knowledge, Shiite Islam in the one case and ancient Christian spirituality in the other, on the basis of which this demonstration was attempted. Of course, we could expand the range of hypotheses, as I did somewhat cursorily to Egypt, to India, to wherever. In each case, doing so will undermine the Heideggerian thesis of a specifically Greek foundation of philosophy. So that's the first possible approach.

The second approach to this issue is to say that the speculation, the decision about being and nonbeing, doesn't found philosophy. What, then, are the problems entailed by this?

There are plenty of them, because there are sub-hypotheses. You could go so far as to say that, at bottom, Parmenides didn't found anything at all, that in a certain way he was still an Egyptian, a refined, simplified, partly de-cosmologized Egyptian but an Egyptian all the same. How so? Inasmuch as he did not establish a new regime of discursivity: the regime of discursivity speculating on being, nonbeing, and so on existed before, elsewhere, and was perfectly consistent with religious, political, and other regimes that were quite unlike those of Greece.

But here a problem arises: if the hypothesis is pushed that far—that if there was no foundation of philosophy on the basis of the question of being and nonbeing, then Parmenides wasn't the founder—then when *was* philosophy founded? When and on what? We could simply repeat that it was founded in the Socrates-Plato system, to which Aristotle could be added—because, of course, Aristotle and Plato witnessed the birth of philosophy. But to that I would object that Plato says the opposite: he says that, in his eyes, philosophy was really and truly founded by Parmenides, that there's an indisputable Parmenidean paternity.

So the thesis that I'm going to argue is as follows—I'm going to formulate it in several propositions:

First of all, like Heidegger, I think that there is a Greek foundation of philosophy and that it is indeed a Western regime of discourse. I will thus be deliberately laying myself open to the charge of Western-centrism. A corollary of this thesis is that there are of course regimes of discourse and thought, including about being and nonbeing, that are not philosophical—nor does this detract in any way from their grandeur and dignity: they are simply something else. And this leads to my second major claim, which is that, strictly speaking, the decision for philosophy *involves more than just* deciding about being and nonbeing since there are regimes of this decision that are not considered philosophical. Whence, of course, my third claim: there has to be an additional condition. Philosophy is under condition, under condition of something other than the decision regarding the path of being and nonbeing. Ultimately, and this is my fourth claim, I will maintain that Parmenides was indeed the founder of philosophy but not for the reasons that led Heidegger to assign that role to him.

OK, we'll stop here for today. What we will be looking for in Parmenides's text and its interpretation will be the trace of this additional condition: what additional condition must a discourse meet to be historically considered as philosophical, over and above the fact that it decides about the question of being qua being and nonbeing?

And more generally speaking: where, in fact, does the idea come from that there is something originarily Greek about philosophy? And what is therefore the not-known in Heidegger's own discourse as well? In other words, why didn't Heidegger really identify what's distinct about philosophical discourse? Basically, I maintain that he was unable to prove the theory of the originarily Greek nature of philosophy: by sticking strictly to his own conceptual system he couldn't do so. He was only able to do so through some very complicated contortions, which constantly made the already-founded nature of philosophy retroact on the idea of its foundation. That's why what actually enabled him to decide that Parmenides was the founder of philosophy was really Plato and Aristotle, because it was on the basis of the loss of the foundation that they decided who the founder was. The problem is circularity: he bases himself on the founded in order to decide on the foundation, but that doesn't allow him to say that the criteria for the foundation are the ones he identified, because those criteria as such aren't discriminating. I realize that the retroactive method is being applied, but it runs up against the fact that the criteria it identifies as foundational aren't discriminating in a radical enough way. There's an additional condition . . . and it's the one we're going to attempt to find!

# Session 3

## November 5, 1985

What we need to decide on, as far as possible, this evening is what is unique about the figure of Parmenides—precisely what it is that makes him much more than just another philosopher in the long history of philosophy. What's unique about him is that he's regarded as originary. Parmenides is that philosopher who is not exactly a philosopher, because he founded philosophy.

What situation of thought have we arrived at? Let me summarize it for you: I can concur with Heidegger on almost everything. We have to agree with him that Parmenides is originary and that his poem does indeed decide for philosophy. Second of all, it is precisely because he made a decision about ontology that he decided for philosophy. I think that the foundation of philosophy requires being *in the place* where the decision is made about being and nonbeing. Third of all, I'd readily agree with Heidegger that it is the factor of decision that's the heart of the matter, not the doctrine of being. Finally, Heidegger's entire interpretation, which we'll reexamine at the end of the year in his *Introduction to Metaphysics*, can be endorsed. Except that we need to focus on the condition on which this interpretation is based: Heidegger provides a convincing descriptive protocol of the decision for philosophy; he provides a convincing description of Parmenides's decision for philosophy, but *the condition on which the decision is based is not specified*. This is crucial: if it's not specified, it's as though it were being itself that had made the decision. It's as though this decision were an epochal moment in the history of being itself, with being coming to the decision about its own being. The originarity of the decision, if it has no condition or external determinant, amounts to saying that it is itself, entirely itself, its own condition. But to say that it is itself its own condition is ultimately to say that being is the condition of the discourse on being—and this will be the whole problem of the meaning to be given to one of Parmenides's fragments, which actually bears the whole weight of Heidegger's interpretation and can be found in the Beaufret edition under "Fragment 3."

Beaufret translates it as:

*Le même, lui, est à la fois penser et être.* [The Same, indeed, is at once to think and to be.][1]

"To think" and "to be": two infinitives, right? In Heidegger's unconditioned interpretation—what I call the unconditioned interpretation is the "unspecified condition"—the fragment can be interpreted as the pure co-belonging of thinking and being, and it therefore ultimately makes being itself the self-founding condition of thinking for being, "the same" that is at once to think and to be. What thinking is in its being is destinally prescribed by being itself, and Parmenides is the *name* of this event. Parmenides is the originary *name* of the coming of being into thinking, but as pure co-belonging. Clearly, the hypothesis of an additional condition will involve a completely different interpretation of Parmenides's statement. The whole dispute will be focused on "the same." What exactly does it mean for thinking and being to be the same? This is usually translated as "They're the same thing." You'll very often find: "Thinking and being are the same thing." Here, Heidegger is to be commended for recognizing the absurdity of such an assertion, because the thingness of this "thing," having to be conceived of as the identity of being and thinking, is obviously a nonsensical reduction. It is clear that to think the thing, you need being, so to speak. So, to say that being and thinking are "the same thing" is both tautological and nonsensical. Beaufret's translation and Heidegger's can be retained, namely, "The same is to think and to be." Not "the same thing," not "the same being," but "the same." It's just that it's enigmatic, because it's not "the same this or that," it's "the same" as such. Heidegger's interpretation emphasizes the significance of the originary co-belonging, of which Parmenides is the name. If there's an additional condition, and if this condition is an extrinsic one, it won't be the same idea. Why not? Because, if there's an additional condition, it will be a condition of thinking, but not a condition of being. We'll have an additional condition coeval with the possible foundation of a regime of the thinking of being. And this condition will be a condition of thinking. Where Heidegger conceives of a co-belonging, an element of asymmetry must necessarily be introduced, conceiving of "the same" as also and at the same time "the not-same." And this will then cause problems for *us*.

You see, what's at stake in this debate on the originarity of philosophy are ultimately two issues that are completely interrelated. What are they?

First, is there or isn't there a condition? In other words, is philosophy under condition, and if so, under which one? Or does it have no condition other than Being itself? Does it have a singular condition that founds the possibility of its destiny, or does it have no condition other than Being itself, which, in a manner of speaking, un-conditions it? Second, what type of relationship is there between thinking and being? What does "the same" mean in Parmenides's poem, then? In his text he himself offers two versions of the statement I just cited.

The first version, which I've already read you, is the one from Fragment 3:

The Same, indeed, is at once to think and to be.

The second version is at the heart of Fragment 8, at line 34, page 87 of Beaufret's translation, and he translates it as:

*Or, c'est le même, penser et ce à dessein de quoi il y a pensée.* [For the same is to think and that for the sake of which there is thought.]²

"For the sake of which" is οὕνεκεν [*houneken*], which is commonly translated as "that because of which." "Because of" . . . : the history of cause is very complicated. Let's just say that Heidegger maintains the identity between these two formulations. He says as much, moreover: he maintains the consonance between the two. The first is: "The same, indeed, is at once to think and to be"; and the second is: "The same is to think and that for the sake of which there is thought." I, for my part, will suggest that these two statements are different from one another, not wildly contradictory, not conflicting, but fundamentally different from one another. And even that the thinking of the difference between them is a key point of the interpretation of Parmenides. It is—to sum it up sticking as closely as possible to the text—the second issue at stake in this debate about Parmenides, along with what remains the canonical reference today whenever it's discussed: Heidegger's interpretation.

---

Now let's focus on defining what the "additional condition" is: what "additional condition" must the statement about being and nonbeing meet in order to decide for philosophy? Since by itself, in a way, it doesn't decide for it. And let's work our way back to this condition starting from what is indisputably philosophical, that is to say, from what was established under this condition, after Parmenides. Indeed, we need to start from the point of the unquestionable establishment that Plato and Aristotle—post-foundational philosophers—represent and see whether, from that point, we can begin the analysis of the condition. So what will we take retrospectively from each of them? Well, quite simply, the way *they* conceive of Parmenides's originality, of course. How do *they* conceive of what is philosophically originary about Parmenides?

Let's begin this regressive approach with Aristotle. As you know, he was the first philosopher to systematically use the historical account of a problem, hence the advantage he offers us: he always began by saying what the Great Predecessors thought about a given problem. But what's important to understand is that he didn't do so in a spirit of eclecticism, just for the sake of seeing the succession of systems. No! Aristotle wasn't a chronicler of philosophy, or, shall we say, an academic historian of philosophy. He would relate a history under condition, a history under hypothesis. Regardless of whether it was the question of being, the question of motion, the question of politics, or ethics, or art, Aristotle would formulate a hypothesis which was either a definition of the relevant concept or a typology, i.e., the declaration of a plurality of meanings, in which case he would list the different meanings of a given concept. And the whole problem for him would be whether the list was exhaustive or not, whether it was a definitive list or not.

Take, for example, the beginning of the *Metaphysics*, Book Alpha. The basic framework of this first book addresses the doctrine of the four meanings of the word "cause." The plurality of meanings is a central idea in Aristotle's work: it is truly a founding idea of his way of thinking and his system.

In two respects Aristotle was essentially, if I can put it this way, a sort of Maoist! In two respects! When it came to conclusions, it was another matter, but when it came to the method, he was a Maoist in two respects.

The first was that he obeyed Chairman Mao's famous directive: "If you want to solve a problem, investigate its past history!"[3] When you come right down to it, he was one of the very rare philosophers, with the exemplary exception of Hegel, to apply that directive to himself. He didn't choose a couple of his predecessors just so he could refute them, argue with them, outshine them, attack them, or whatever. No! He explicitly set out to investigate the history of a problem without neglecting any point of view. And, to support the completeness of his enumeration of the meanings of a given concept, he investigated its complete past history, thus also obeying another of Chairman Mao's directives: "Don't overlook anything!" I don't know whether Mao actually said that or not, but he could have! It was absolutely his style: "Don't overlook anything!"

This leads us to the second respect in which he was again a true Maoist: he was convinced of the plurality of meanings and of the idea that the dogmatists—whom Mao called the "metaphysicians" but who were the "dogmatists" for Aristotle—are those who are doctrinaire, that is to say, those who don't know that there are a plurality of meanings and think they can combine them all into a single one. They're the ones who don't know that there are two class points of view, who don't know that when a problem is being considered it has several different aspects—one primary, one secondary, and still others—and aren't aware of the polysemy either of situations or of signifiers. Aristotle intertwined the two in a remarkable way: the awareness of the plurality of meanings was based on and connected to the complete history of the concept in question. It was this method that he applied in a quasi-general way.

If we return now to the question of the *Metaphysics*, the whole beginning of which I said is framed by the doctrine of the four meanings of the word "cause," we'll see—as you might expect—that Aristotle's predecessors failed to understand that there were four meanings of it and, as a result, they either selected one of them, or combined two, or, in the case of the cleverest ones, anticipated three, but none saw that there were four of them. They all saw one of them: the different meanings of the word "cause" were in fact seen, but they were never all seen together. Aristotle, though, with his genius for synthesis, put them all together: his thinking originated in the "putting together" of what, in the case of his predecessors, had remained scattered.

To better understand what follows, including what's at stake in connection with Parmenides, let's briefly review the doctrine of the four meanings of the word "cause." First, there's the formal cause: the one Aristotle calls "substance," substantiality, or "the what it was to be"—τό τι ἐν εἶναι [*to ti én einai*].[4] So what he calls the formal cause is, in short, the persistence of identity. It is, with respect to any entity, the fact that it coincides with its own enduring identity. The second meaning of the word "cause" is "matter" or "the substratum"—ὑποκείμενον [*hypokeimenon*]—the substratum, more likely, or "what lies beneath." This, on the contrary, is not the principle of identity persistence but rather the principle of undifferentiation. And for Aristotle there can naturally only be identity if there's some undifferentiated matter that this identity identifies. In other words, there must be matter, the substratum, in order for substance and the formal cause to exist, that is, to be something real. The third meaning of the word "cause" is the efficient cause, or, roughly speaking, what is encapsulated in the post-Galilean meaning of the word "cause," the modern meaning of cause. Aristotle will say that the efficient cause is the basis on which there is motion. Finally, as regards the fourth meaning of the word "cause," which is the final cause, or that for the sake of which there is motion, Aristotle also says that it is the Good, because all things move for their own good. This is how the beginning of the *Metaphysics* will be presented: it consists in seeking first principles or first causes. But be careful! "Cause" is said in four ways: formal cause, material cause, efficient cause, and final cause. It is this fundamental multiplicity of causes that is the framework of historical investigation. History, the history of philosophy prior to Aristotle, gains its consistency by being interrogated on the basis of the four meanings of the word "cause." Here's how he introduces this history:

> but yet let us call to our aid those who have attacked the investigation of being and philosophized about truth before us. For obviously they too speak of certain principles and causes . . . (983b 1–3)[5]

By enumerating these causes, might we find *an extra something*, an additional cause? In the framework of this investigation—the interrogation of history using the device of the four meanings of the word "cause"—where does Parmenides fit in and in what way is he originary, since that's still the issue we want to come to a decision about? For Aristotle, most of the ancient thinkers—that is, the philosophers who came before him—only conceived of the material cause. That's what he saw in their writings. When he considered philosophers like Thales, Anaxagoras, et al., his verdict was pitiless: they clearly saw the material cause, but that was all they saw. They only isolated the material cause, a single material cause—"water," "fire," "earth," or combinations thereof—and from this they proceeded to causal derivations. And it is here that, in a very cunning way, Parmenides was effectively an exception. Parmenides was an exception to this subsumption of the Predecessors under the oneness, the singleness, of the material cause.

I'll read you the passage. Pay attention, because, as is so often the case, Aristotle is a little slippery in it:

> To judge by all these philosophers [*so here he means the Predecessors in general*], one might think that the only cause is the so-called material cause. But as they thus advanced [*this again applies to all of them*], the very facts thereby showed them the way and joined in forcing them to investigate the subject. [*What is translated as "the very facts" (la réalité) is* αὐτὸ τὸ πρᾶγμα (auto to pragma), *which might be better translated as "the thing itself," the thing in the sense of the object of investigation, the object of investigation itself, what was at stake in their thinking.*] However true it may be that all generation and destruction proceed from some one or more elements, why does this happen, and what is the cause? For at least the substratum itself does not make itself change, e.g. [*Aristotle always gives these wonderful examples*], neither the wood nor the bronze causes the change of either of them; nor does the wood manufacture a bed and the bronze a statue, but something else is the cause of the change. And to seek this is to seek the second cause, as *we* should say: that from which comes the beginning of movement. Now those who at the very beginning set themselves to this kind of inquiry, and said the substratum was one, were not at all dissatisfied with themselves; but some at least of those who maintain it to be one—as though defeated by this search for the second cause—say the one and nature as a whole is unchangeable not only in respect of generation and destruction (for this is an ancient belief, and all agreed in it), but also of all other change; and this view is peculiar to them. Of those who said the universe was one, none succeeded in discovering a cause of this sort, except perhaps Parmenides, and he only insomuch that he supposes that there is not only one but in some sense two causes. [984a17–984b5] (1556–57; trans. modified)

That's typical Aristotelian history: viewed from a distance, the description is simple, but on closer inspection it's complicated as hell. What is Aristotle telling us in this passage? The first point is that the earlier philosophers posited only one cause—the material cause, the substratum, the ὑποκείμενον [*hypokeimenon*]: "water," "earth," the "elements," "bronze," "wood," or what have you. They said: *that's* the cause, the principle of being. But, says Aristotle—and this is his second point—they came up against the fundamental obstacle that the substratum itself does not give rise to any specific form, meaning that the substratum, obviously, since it's undifferentiation (if indeed it is undifferentiation that's the principle), can only be the principle of undifferentiation. Where does difference come from then? If you claim that there is only the material cause, then undifferentiation prevails without difference, and you can't think singularity. They were all stuck in that impasse, that is, they only drew false derivations: in reality, they conceived of a second cause without naming it. As Aristotle puts it: "to seek this [something else] is to seek the second cause." What was his actual assessment of his predecessors? He thought that, with their thesis about the unity of the cause, only one meaning of the word "cause"—the material cause—they were wrong, or else they had slipped in another cause, which they themselves remained unaware of. "They were not at all dissatisfied with themselves," he says.

But there's an exception here. It concerns those thinkers who, having claimed that there was only one cause, concluded quite simply from this that there was actually no difference, i.e., that change didn't exist. Those thinkers didn't fall into an impasse, nor did they fake their claims. They simply drew strict consequences from them: If there is one cause and that cause is undifferentiated, that means that the universe is undifferentiated; and, in particular, it is unchangeable because, quite obviously, undifferentiation doesn't allow change to be thought. Those thinkers, says Aristotle, maintain that the One and nature as a whole are unchangeable, regardless of the kind of change concerned. So they are rigorous: they are faithful, so to speak, to their dogmatism; they draw the strict consequences from their dogmatic position, which is not to see that there are several different meanings of the word "cause" and to retain only one of them. They have that advantage and conclude that nothing changes, being is reciprocal to the One, and unchangeableness is the law of things.

It is really remarkable that Aristotle says "*as though defeated by this search for the second cause*" because what he calls being "defeated by this search for the second cause" in his eyes means being rigorous to the point of absurdity, in terms of the cause adopted. It's of course the school of Parmenides that's being referred to. And, in this passage, there's quite a complicated judgment of it, which is as follows: the people of the "Eleatic" school, Parmenides's disciples, are superior to the other thinkers by virtue of their rigor, because they accepted the consequences of there being only one cause. But they are inferior to them in terms of common sense, because, for Aristotle, to say that nature is unchangeable is of course totally ridiculous. The other thinkers, by contrast, are frauds when it comes to their cause, but they had the good sense to try to come to terms with "reality." Clearly, Parmenides couldn't care less about "reality."

Except, what complicates matters is that Parmenides himself is an exception to this exception, because at the end of the passage—I'll read it to you again—here's what we find:

> Of those who said the universe was one, none succeeded in discovering a cause of this sort [*obviously they didn't, since they stuck to their belief that there was only one cause*], except perhaps Parmenides, and he only insomuch that he supposes that there is not only one but in some sense two causes.

First, Parmenides is credited with Eleatic rigor—he's a ridiculous rigorist—but, second, *he* is not completely ridiculous. Why? Because he brings out two meanings of the word "cause." So we'll say: "Yes! But . . . if he brings out two meanings of the word "cause" doesn't he then stop being rigorous by no longer being ridiculous?" Well, Aristotle doesn't say as much. He doesn't say as much because he stops there, and he ultimately credits Parmenides with being—and I'll come back to this phrase—"an exception within the exception." He's an exception to his own exception. There's already the Eleatic exception, which is "being faithful to the cause," even if leads to absurd consequences; then, within this Eleatic exception, there's the Parmenidean exception properly speaking, the exception of Parmenides himself, which is to imply that there are two causes, not one. Thus he avoids the most absurd consequences of the unity of the cause.

What can we apply this to in Parmenides's text? There's the decision, for one thing, and what is decided for, for another. The decision means being in the place where you have to decide between being and nonbeing; and there's what is decided for: the primacy of being, the unconditional primacy of being. Remember how Parmenides begins [in Badiou's paraphrase]:

> Being is, and you must withhold yourself from the way that would allow nonbeing to be.

It could be said that the decision, insofar as it takes place at a crossroads, assumes that there are two causes. Naturally, to decide, there has to be the Two. So, in the very place of the decision there are two causes, designated as "the way of being" and "the way of nonbeing." Then, at the point of what is decided for—namely, only being is, and there is only one cause—there, the consequences are strictly drawn. Hence this in-depth interpretation of Aristotle's statement: there is no inner contradiction between the rigorous aspect and the, shall we say, common sense aspect. The fact is that the rigor is in what is decided for: the rigor, even at the risk of absurdity, is in what is decided for, whereas the flexibility—the Two that makes the One more pliable—is in the decision. What's more, Aristotle ends up acknowledging that, in the final analysis, Parmenides's two causes are "being" and "nonbeing." The important thing, in actual fact, is the gesture by which Aristotle introduces a splitting of Parmenides. In the latter's thinking, which is seemingly all of a piece, Aristotle makes a distinction between what is strictly logical in it—the consequences of the unity of the cause—and what has to do with something prior to the order of logic, namely, the ontological decision itself. Parmenides has, first, a thesis and, second, an argument. Aristotle doesn't deal with these two things in the same way.

Now how does Aristotle tackle the refutation of the Eleatics? Let me read you two passages from the *Metaphysics* in which we once again find that strange kind of twist when it comes to Parmenides. Aristotle begins by announcing what I called "the exceptional position" of Parmenides and his school:

> The discussion of them [*the task is now to turn to the refutation, the discussion*] is in no way appropriate to our present investigation of causes, for they do not, like some of the natural philosophers, assume being to be one and yet generate it out of the one as out of matter, but they speak in another way; those others add change, since they generate the universe, but these thinkers say the universe is unchangeable. [986b 13–18] (1560; trans. slightly modified)

So what is Aristotle telling us here? That if history is responsible for verifying the completeness of the hypotheses, something about the Parmenidean texts is unusable, is historically superfluous. "The discussion of them is in no way appropriate to our present investigation of causes." If history is the test of the hypotheses, the Parmenideans are useless: they don't verify nor do they falsify. And why do they neither verify nor falsify? Because they claim that the universe is unchangeable, and that, therefore, *there is no cause of the universe*. Parmenides is utterly unique in being a historical exception, in showing that the criteria of history aren't applicable to him. Note, incidentally, how Aristotle isn't bothered when he comes up against something that's an exception to his historical framework: he doesn't change his framework; he simply does away with the obstacle. If Parmenides isn't appropriate to the investigative framework for the theory of the four causes, Aristotle will simply declare that he's historically aberrant, that is to say, historically superfluous. History is thus quite rational, provided that it is in a situation of exhaustion of meanings. If there's something aberrant, you just have to get rid of it.

Let's get back to the argument. First, Parmenides is considered as a pure and simple exception to the hypothesis of investigation. He's a nonsense effect. Then, a little later, Aristotle says: "Now these thinkers, as we said, must be [absolutely] neglected for the purposes of our present inquiry" [986b 25–26] (1560). They are therefore absolutized in their absence from Aristotelian historicity. However, here's how Aristotle continues: "but Parmenides seems to speak with somewhat more insight."

Let me read you the passage:

> For, claiming that, besides being, non-being is not, he thinks that being is of necessity one and that nothing else exists . . . but being forced to follow the phenomena, and supposing that what is is one in formula, but many according to perception, he now posits two causes and two principles, calling them hot and cold—i.e., fire and earth; and of these he ranges the hot with being, and the other with non-being [986b 28–987a 2] (1560; trans. modified).

So, once again, in the refutation step, Parmenides's status is very precisely an exception to the exception. While the Parmenideans are historically superfluous, Parmenides himself is not entirely so. And he is not entirely so because his thinking of the One is in reality a thinking of the Two. Aristotle connects this to the fact that Parmenides, unlike the lesser Parmenideans, so to speak, did not attempt to materialize the One—he didn't say "The One is matter," a thesis that Aristotle attributes to Melissus, another Parmenidean.

**Someone asks:** But who were the Parmenideans?

The Parmenideans were a group consisting, as I told you last time, of Xenophanes,[6] a person we don't know a whole lot about, nor, for that matter, did Aristotle; of Parmenides himself; of one of his disciples, Melissus; and later, of Zeno of Elea, plus a few others, some followers. But if you take a close look at Aristotle's text, the Parmenideans were actually just Parmenides himself. To say that Parmenides was more insightful is to say that Parmenides was more insightful than Parmenides, or to point out that in the very essence of Parmenides's thinking there was an excess over his own thinking. At bottom, Aristotle's thesis was quite simple: to develop a way to think the One rigorously—to be a rigorist of the One, a *real* rigorist of the One, not a phony[7]—Parmenides in fact had to posit the Two. That was Aristotle's thesis. And as Parmenides posited the Two, it became "causes" (in the plural). Because, so long as it was the One, nothing allowed him to say that the One was a cause: why would it be a material cause any more than a formal cause, and so on? If you simply say "The One is," you're outside the historical framework, you're superfluous. But if you want to say it rigorously, as Parmenides did, you're forced to posit the Two. And if you posit the Two, then there are two causes, and the difference between them is a difference of principle. Thus, Parmenides comes back into the historical framework from which he was originally excluded. So, in relation to Aristotle's historicity, in relation to the historical investigation—that of the doctrine of the four causes—Parmenides's position was to be at once superfluous and internal to it. He was historically aberrant, but, in another sense, he was, on the contrary, the founder, because he had seen that there were at least two causes—pretty good, considering that his contemporaries, the nature philosophers, had only seen one! He was better than they were: "On the right track!" said Aristotle, thus conferring on him the utterly extraordinary status of being the founder. On the one hand, the founder was completely aberrant and unable to be thought; but, on the other, he was paradigmatic. He was proof that the historical method was the right one. That's what Parmenides was! Parmenides was someone who proved that historical logic was worthless, since he was completely excluded from it, but he was also the first to prove that it was right, since he had seen that there were two causes, whereas his nature philosopher contemporaries, with their "water," their "earth," their this, that, and the other, only saw one, a material cause. Parmenides was the exception to the exception, the exception to the exception that he himself was! That is to say, he was exceptional in terms of historicity, but he was also the historical exception to that exception to history. And that's what the status of the founder was, as Aristotle presented it in the *Metaphysics*.

But Parmenides is also in the *Physics*. It is Aristotle's trademark to spread out his questions and come back to them in a different way in each of his works. Parmenides is a question in the *Metaphysics* but is also one in the *Physics*. And it isn't the same one because Parmenides is spoken about in several ways. Cause, being, and Parmenides are spoken about in several ways. There's the Parmenides of the *Metaphysics*, and there's the Parmenides of the *Physics*. In the *Metaphysics*, the issue was whether there was only one or several different meanings of the word "cause," and in the *Physics* the issue was "nature," as the word "physics" implies. It wasn't about whether there's *One* being, *One* single cause, but about whether they could be directly identified, because, according to Aristotle, if being and the One are identified, "nature" is rendered unthinkable—and the concept of "nature" is eliminated. But "nature's" existence is his basic postulate. The "There is nature" is the absolutely primordial statement, and it absolutely co-belongs with "There is motion." And by saying that there is no motion, the Parmenideans, in Aristotle's eyes, are the thinkers who do away with "nature." And so there will be the exact same dialectic again—formally, the logic of the exception to the exception. First, Aristotle says: it's pointless to speak about the Parmenideans and Parmenides! Because there's no nature as far as they're concerned.

This is how he puts it in the *Physics* (Book I, 185a):

> Now to investigate whether Being is one and motionless [*i.e., Parmenides's thesis: being is One and being is motionless, which is something explicitly stated in his poem*] is not a contribution to the science of Nature. For just as the geometer has nothing more to say to one who denies the principles of his science—this being a question for a different science or for one common to all—so a man investigating *principles* cannot argue with one who denies their existence. For if Being is just one, and one in the way mentioned, there is a principle no longer, since a principle must be the principle of some thing or things.[8]

That's the first step: when it comes to the historical framework—the concept of "nature"—Parmenides compels silence. Just as the geometer has nothing more to say if his axioms are denied, so, too, the philosopher physician has nothing more to say to Parmenides. He can say nothing more because there is no nature. Parmenides thus compels silence, and here again we find his status as an exception to the historicity of the question. If you take the different conceptions of "nature" as a historical framework, you make Parmenides superfluous. Why? Because *his* conception is that there's no nature at all. It is moreover this silence that gives rise, immediately thereafter, to the statement of Aristotle's basic postulate: he will seek in Parmenides what reduces him, Aristotle, to silence, and, against the background of that silence, he will speak; that is, he will formulate his own statement, his fundamental hypothetical statement, which is as follows:

> We, on the other hand, must take for granted that the things that exist by nature are, either all or some of them, in motion . . . [185a 13–14] (316)

Here again is the radical exception of Parmenides. But then, as in the *Metaphysics*, Aristotle reconsiders Parmenides's thesis by way of a very detailed process of refutation, even though there would seemingly be no reason to refute, since the subject is missing. Aristotle states: "What I'm speaking about, Parmenides precludes. So there's nothing left to say." But as a matter of fact there is! Later on, there will be five very dense pages of refutation of Parmenides's theses. And again, a paradox: how can you refute Parmenides on nature after you've just said that there's no nature in his theses? Simply by making the refutation bear not on Parmenides's *thesis*—what I'm speaking about doesn't exist—but on his reasoning, on his *argument*. An argument about which Aristotle, who's often scathing, will say: "The premises are false and the conclusions don't follow." It's clear that the status of a refutation of the type "the subject I'm dealing with is missing" can't be equated with that of the other type of refutation, i.e., "The premises are false and the conclusions don't follow."

In the *Physics*, Aristotle's problematic concerning Parmenides is as follows: If it's considered as a thesis on being, then this thinking is quite simply not part of the conceptual apparatus of physics. If, however, it's considered as an argument, then it's refutable. Not being part of the conceptual apparatus isn't the same thing as being refutable within that apparatus. Let's put it this way: as a thesis, Parmenides isn't encountered in the *Physics*, and nowhere are you dealing with him. As a thesis of thought, you won't encounter him. However, you can deal with him in terms of his argument. Let's bear this point in mind, since, as we'll see, it has far-reaching implications for the interpretation I'm proposing: the philosophy of Parmenides is split in two again here. It's split, on the one hand, into an *utterance* (what I called the "thesis"), into an utterance that silences because it eliminates the subject in question (nature); and, on the other hand, into an *argument* that, on the contrary, is of the order of rational debate. Parmenides is thus split into an utterance that silences and an argument that's of the order of rational debate.

It's on account of this twofold issue that Parmenides will once again prove to be an exception to the exception. There's a loftiness about him, which is that of poetic speech and which essentially implies the reception of a revelation. If you're not willing to accept such a thing, as Aristotle isn't, then you're reduced to silence. That's one aspect, poetic speech. The other is strict adherence to consequences. And *that* implies a thinking informed by what a proof is. While poetic speech is intended for receptivity to a revelation, strict adherence to the consequences is intended for something else. It is a thinking informed by what a consequence in fact is, what a proof is. Parmenidean thinking is intended for both. It is intended for those who will receive the revealed speech, for those who are open to it—"Listen to what I will reveal to you," we read in his poem—and for those who accept the argument, those who examine, accept, and assess the argument. And Aristotle treats these two kinds of messages differently: first, he makes a distinction between them, and then he treats them differently. So there is nothing paradoxical about the fact that he can say both that that there is nothing to be said about Parmenides—the first statement—and then that Parmenides merits a detailed refutation—the second statement. This double approach taken by Aristotle corresponds to the twin messages of the Parmenidean texts.

Next time, we'll see how the meaning of these twin messages once again reinscribes Parmenides in the history of physics just as it reinscribed him in the history of the doctrine of the four causes. In other words, how, by virtue of these twin messages, non-historicity is also thinkable as founding historicity. We'll see this in the fascinating and illuminating details of Aristotle's refutation of Parmenides's theses. This will take us right up to the question of the "condition" and from there, to the framework of interpretation of Plato's texts.

# Session 4

## November 12, 1985

What struck me about the way Aristotle discusses Parmenides was a contradiction. On the one hand, Parmenides is outside the framework of historical investigation. And Aristotle will repeatedly say as much: "I can't fit the Parmenideans into my vision of history! They're not part of it." He even calls them "mentally defective" in Book 7 of the *Physics*. So, on the one hand, Parmenides can't be included in history; he's superfluous to it—that's the first side of the contradiction. And on the other hand, he, Parmenides, if not the Parmenideans, is reinscribed into history. He can therefore be discussed. That's the contradiction: an undiscussable Parmenides and a discussable one.

That is why it's important to analyze the discussion, the refutation. In Book 1 of the *Physics* Aristotle attacks Parmenides about what establishes the reciprocity between being and the One, in the form of "being is One," therefore about what precludes multiplicity. That's the angle he attacks him from, which is understandable because nature is the locus of motion and multiplicity for Aristotle. He attempts to refute this thesis—the absolute unity of being—by approaching it first from the standpoint of being, then from the standpoint of the One, showing that it's incompatible with both a "proper concept" of being and a "proper concept" of the One. What is a "proper concept" of being or the One? It's a concept that gives all the meanings of it. It's a complete concept with respect to the meanings because being is said in several ways: πολλακώς λέγεται [*pollakos legetai*], "it is said variously, multiply." So he will examine three of its meanings; namely, being is said of substance, quality, and quantity. In other words, what is, is the existing substance; it's a qualitative determination of the existing substance, and it's also its quantity, its number. These are the three relevant conceptual categories for the word "being." In all three cases, Aristotle will say, regardless of whether it's considered according to quality or according to quantity, it is absolutely impossible to say that "being is One." Quality and quantity assume the need for the third meaning, substance, because they are only in a position of attribution. Take the example of the color white, which is always the one Aristotle chooses: in what sense can it be said that white *is*? Naturally not as the "idea" of whiteness, as is the case with Plato: for Aristotle, that's pure fantasy. But does this mean that white *is not*? No, it *is*: this table is white, which means that the table *is*, and also that white *is*. But you can only say that white *is* provided that something white exists. The quality only exists to the extent that it has an underlying something, a ὑποκείμενον [*hypokeimenon*]. So there's the Two: the quality and the ὑποκείμενον. Therefore, being is not One. And this is intrinsically the case. Thus, you can never claim that being is pure quality since the quality is related to the underlying something, and to think the being of white you have to think the Two of the quality and the underlying something and consequently reject Parmenides's One. The same goes for quantity: I won't go into the details, but there can only be quantity of a substance, of what can be quantitatively demonstrated. There is the Two: once again, Parmenides can't claim that his famous "One-being" is quality, nor can he claim that it's quantity. It is pure substance; that's the only conclusion. It's a pure underlying something, that is, it's a being that is unqualifiable and unquantifiable, but unquantifiable in a privative sense, or without number. If Parmenidean being—because it is One—can be neither quality nor quantity, it's because it's pure substantiality, i.e., unquantifiable and unqualifiable.

There's something very odd in the text of the *Physics*: we'd expect Aristotle to refute the possibility that such a substance exists, but that's not what happens. So how will he proceed? He'll start with the qualities that Parmenides attributes to this substance and point out the weakness of his approach. If there is a substance, if it's pure substance, Aristotle argues, it must be unqualifiable and unquantifiable, or else being is not One as such. So it cannot be finite, as Parmenides claims, because if it's finite, it is quantitatively determined. Not necessarily implying number but rather quantity grasped conceptually, to say it is "finite" is to reinscribe it under the law of quantitative assessment. Should we think of it as infinite, then? No, we can't think that either, because the infinite is a privative concept, which is only comprehensible on the basis of the finite. So thinking of it as infinite doesn't resolve the problem: to think of it as infinite you have to think the finite, you have to think that the finite is, and therefore that there's the Two. Finiteness leads to the Two.

What's of interest to *us*, here, is the issue that causes problems for Aristotle. And what is that issue? It's that there's no direct refutation of pure substantiality, as the One-being of being. He can only reach a conclusion via another of Parmenides's theses, namely, the One-being is finite. Whereas before, with the previous refutations, he had confined himself to the refuted thesis, being is One, this time around he doesn't do so: he proceeds by way of this other thesis, being is finite. These two theses are not the same, however. The best proof of this is that the infinitist Parmenideans, such as Melissus, had claimed that being was One, that there was nothing but being qua being, that nonbeing must not be thought . . . but, on top of that, that being was infinite. Why couldn't the One-being be said to be finite or infinite, or neither one nor the other? Why should Aristotle care? It's not an obstacle! Since there's a quantitative determination (being is finite), there's the Two, because you have to think the being of quantity and not just being qua being. But what interests *us* is why that other thesis of Parmenides's had to be involved, because, after all, a radical Parmenideanism could be imagined that would hold that being qua being is One and that it escapes the opposition between the finite and the infinite. In which case Aristotle's refutation wouldn't work. "Unqualifiable" could then be understood in the following sense: the One-being cannot be said to be either finite or infinite. And that's what would seem logical.

---

Why isn't this what Parmenides said? What was he thinking when he decided definitively for the finiteness of being? Why, in addition to the thesis of the radical unity of being, is there the thesis of its finiteness? As far as this is concerned, we need to go back to Parmenides's text itself, because it's far more complicated than Aristotle lets on. In the middle of Fragment 8, Parmenides begins by saying that being is not divisible. This is the assertion of the One: "Nor is it divisible, since it is all alike":[1]

> nor is there any more here, which would keep it from holding
> together,
> nor any less, but it is all full of what-is.
> Thus it is all continuous, for what-is cleaves to what-is.

Here we have a number of metaphors that restrict the radical unity: being allows neither any more nor any less. It doesn't allow divisibility, of course, "since it is all alike."

Then he says:

> Further, motionless in the limits of great bonds
> it is without starting and stopping, since coming to be and perishing
> wandered very far away, and true faith banished them.

So there is neither coming to be nor perishing, neither generation nor destruction, neither beginning nor end. Therefore, temporally, with the temporal metaphor, there is no idea of limitation. With the cessation of all beginning and all end, there is no limit to being. We haven't yet reached the assertion of finiteness. When we read: it is motionless, without starting and stopping, we, post-Galilean Westerners, have the impression of a temporal infinity.

This is how he continues:

> Remaining the same in the same by itself it lies
> and thus it remains steadfast there; for mighty Necessity
> holds it in the bonds of a limit, which confines it round about.
> Wherefore it is not right for what-is to be without end;
> for it is not lacking; if it were it would lack everything.
>     (217, trans. slightly modified)

Let me read this very obscure passage to you again: "for mighty Necessity holds it in the bonds of a limit, which confines it round about. Wherefore it is not right for what-is to be without end; for it is not lacking; if it were it would lack everything." The assertion of finiteness with respect to being is based entirely on this passage. And the two terms that refer to it aren't the same: you've got the word "limit"—πέρας [peras]—and the word "end"—τέλος [telos]. The thesis of finiteness is introduced by the poetic metaphor, in which being is said to be held "in the bonds of a limit." However, "limit," in the Greek sense, isn't a boundary that must be gone beyond or crossed, in the Hegelian sense, but rather the affirmative emergence of being itself. The limit is what being unfolds as its natural interiority, not as something that comes to it from outside and that it would have to go beyond. And by regarding this concept of the limit, which he understands perfectly well, as a concept of quantity, Aristotle trivializes it a little. The thesis of finiteness here is a general Greek thesis about the fact that a being is that which unfolds its own limit.[2] This is what Parmenides describes with respect to One-being, to being qua being: it should be thought of as an emergence that contains its interiority, not as a limited quantity. The meaning of πέρας [*peras*] needs to be clearly understood.

So that was the first formulation: there is a limit. The second is as follows: "Wherefore it is not right for what-is to be without end."[3] But the "without end"—ἀτελεύτητον [*ateleuteton*]—refers to another, completely different Greek word, the word τέλος [*telos*]. This word *telos* in fact means "the end" but also in the sense of an ultimate purpose, as in the word "teleology," as that which fulfills by itself the destiny of being. So *telos* is not exactly the "limit" either, in the sense of something that could be crossed over by an extension of quantity. And, finally, the connection between *peras* and *telos* is that the latter—the *telos* of every being—is to unfold its *peras*. The aim of every being is to set out its limit. And the word is often even translated as "end" [*fin*], but with the double meaning, the ambiguous sense, that the word "end" has in French [and in English]. The end is what is completed but also what one strives toward. But strictly speaking, whether in this passage or in the other one, Parmenides doesn't say that "being is finite" in the sense in which we intuitively understand the word "finite." What he does say is that being is in a position of having to set out its limit, and that what-is cannot be without a *telos*, or without an "end" . . . until the key is revealed in the final sentence: "for it is not lacking; if it were, it would lack everything." It is not lacking, and Parmenides gives this absence of a lack as an explanation for what precedes: "indeed, it is not lacking." The existence of the limit—*peras*—and of the end—*telos*—is related to this one point, that being must be thought of as "not lacking." He doesn't say that being is finite but that being does not lack. To us, this can seem like the opposite: you can argue that "what is finite" is that which is lacking what it could go beyond. So when Parmenides claims that the basis of being's limited nature is that it is not lacking, we can also understand this to mean that he is asserting the radical completeness of being. Aristotle's refutation founders right when it interprets as finiteness what is instead the lack of the lack. Basically, what is involved here in the explanatory figure of the lack of the lack—which is the absoluteness of being—is the absolute transitivity of the law of *telos* to being. This could be criticized, of course, but not the way Aristotle criticizes it, by interpreting "finite" in the form of a going-beyond or of quantity.

**A question from the audience:** *How should it be interpreted then?*

As the fact that being is transparent to the law and therefore nothing is lacking in it; that being is, qua being, that in which nothing can be identified as causality lacking with respect to the law, or as the subtraction of a point of the real, or as a scrap, or as a lost object. That's what Parmenides tells us: being qua being is that which has lost nothing. But the fact that it has lost nothing, if only at the cost of some extreme torsion, is interpreted as finiteness by Aristotle. Aristotle sidesteps pure substantiality, in the sense that it is lacking nothing, by interpreting it as quantitative or qualitative finiteness. Of course, if he'd had knowledge of the unconscious, he might have suggested that this figure of being is a psychotic one, because that's what psychosis is, Lacan tells us: the lack of the lack, absolute fullness. But that's not what Aristotle says. He could have attacked the lack of the lack directly instead of misrepresenting it as finiteness, but that's not what he did—he instead avoided it. There's something evasive about his text: the refutation could have been carried out in a different way. But if he didn't do so it's because he didn't want to know anything about this figure of pure substantiality in which nothing is lacking. And rather than have to know about it, he ultimately preferred to reinscribe Parmenides into history in a form that was recognizable but had lost its radicality. Something of Parmenides's radicality, even if it was a psychotic radicality, as I put it metaphorically, was avoided by Aristotle.

This is how he concludes:

> If on the other hand it is asserted that all things are quality or quantity, then, whether substance exists or not, an absurdity results, if the impossible can properly be called absurd. (185a 29–31)[4]

That's the kind of symptomal sentence I love! Because it's superfluous to say that it's absurd and then that it's impossible. It *could* be claimed that this being that lacks nothing is a point of impossibility of thought—Aristotle could say so, but he won't. He'll say it's absurd. But to say it's absurd, to refute it as such, he'll first have to extract it from its real, that is, realize it.[5] Finiteness, in the sense Aristotle means it, is the "realization" of a real, or of a point of impossibility. It is its placement into circulation in "reality"—which requires a different *name*. And what is that name? It is "quantity," which really has nothing to do with Parmenides's text. And under that name, the impossible becomes absurd.

---

Now let's approach the argument from the standpoint of the One, from the standpoint of the "proper definition of the One," by going back to the refutation of the absolute unity of being because of its incompatibility, this time, with a proper definition of the One. Like being, Aristotle tells us, the One has three senses, or is said in three ways. A thing can be said to be "One," or a being can be said to be "One," either because it is continuous, or because it is indivisible, or because its apparent multiplicity boils down to a single definition. And Aristotle refutes Parmenides by showing that he can't take "One" in any of the three senses.

Let's review what they are.

It cannot be said that "being is One" in the sense that it is "continuous," because the definition of the continuous is precisely that it is divisible or that it has parts—parts arranged in continuous fashion. So there is multiplicity: the concept of the One in the sense of "the continuous" amounts to multiplicity. It is not true that a given painting can be said to be "One" because it is a continuous surface. To say or to think as much is to acknowledge its inner multiplicity, that is, its differentiality.

Nor can it be said that it is "One" in the sense of "indivisible" because, Aristotle comments ironically, it would then be impossible to say it is "finite." This is the same trap as a moment ago. The finite is precisely what has divisibility. Finiteness includes divisibility. If I say I'm indivisible, I can't say I'm finite. But, as we have seen, Aristotle claims that Parmenides asserts the finiteness of being.

What is new comes from the third sense: the unity of definition. If "being is One," in the sense of the unity of definition, says Aristotle, then "all that is" ultimately has the same definition. If being qua being is One in the sense of the unity of definition, then there is a unity of definition of all that is, insofar as it is. So, he continues (this is a very subtle point), there is no reason to say that it is being rather than nothingness. This passage purely and simply anticipates the beginning of Hegel's *Science of Logic*.

Let me read it to you:

> Hence being qua being cannot exist in anything else. For this thing cannot be a *being*, unless 'being' means several things, in such a way that each *is* something. But *ex hypothesi* 'being' means only one thing. (186b 1–3, p. 318, trans. modified)

The first step of the argument is: being is One because it means only one thing: the word "being" does not have several different senses; it has only one, it means only one thing. So being qua being can't exist in anything else, since this other thing would have to have "being," but in fact it would then be impossible for it to be anything else, since "being" has only one meaning. Note, by the way, that it's not a problem for Aristotle for being to exist in "something else." It simply proves that the way this other thing "is" corresponds to a different meaning of the word "is" from the first one that was used. This is how it is for him: such polysemy is fundamental. You can argue that this thing "is," insofar as it is in something else; it's just that you know that you haven't used the same sense of the word "is" in both cases. If you claim, as he assumes Parmenides did, that there's only one meaning, then that option is naturally not open to you.

Aristotle then goes on to say:

> If, then, being qua being is not attributed to anything, but other things are attributed to it, how does being qua being mean being rather than non-being? For suppose that being qua being is also 'white,' and that being white is not being qua being (for being cannot even be attributed to white, since nothing is which is not being qua being), it follows that what is white is not—not in the sense of not being something or other, but in the sense that it is not at all. Hence being qua being is non-being; for it is true to say that it is white, and we found this to mean non-being. So 'white' must also

mean 'true being'; and then 'being' has more than one meaning. (186b 4–12, p. 318; trans. modified)

This is a little tricky. The crux of Aristotle's argument basically concerns *naming*. That's why he can use the example of "white" or any other term. If you say that being is being or that what is, is, hence if you have *named* being qua being, if only by using the word "being" (Aristotle uses the word "white" to make his point, but what he has in mind is actually the word "being," which already *names*), then since what that word refers to has only one meaning, the act of naming doesn't distinguish anything. And how *could* it distinguish anything, since being is "being" in the sense of having one and only one absolutely indivisible meaning? You can't expect to find a distinguishable name. You can just as easily say that it is nonbeing since, under the assumption of a single meaning, you won't be able to distinguish being from nonbeing. So, to say "being is" is no more meaningful than to say "nonbeing is." In both cases, since there's a single meaning, the predication adds nothing to what is predicated. To say, then, as Parmenides does, that we should think that only being is, is the same as to say that we should think that nonbeing is. To say "being is" is no more conclusive than to say that "nonbeing is." There would be no difference between the two statements.

**A comment from the back of the room:** That's not true, nonbeing is not . . .

Except how is that an objection? It's easy to understand how Aristotle can connect this figure of the thinking of being to that of nonbeing. But in what way is that an objection? That's the whole point. To my mind, it's not an objection, and not only isn't it one but it happens to be exactly what Parmenides says. What Aristotle's argument founders on is the fact that Parmenides, in thinking the One of being, was immediately faced with the impossibility of thinking nonbeing. It is as one single thought that being is thought, in terms of its name, as well as nonbeing. So the objection is only valid if it's impossible to think nonbeing. That's its stumbling block: to think the One of being all the way through you necessarily have to confront the impossible thinking of nonbeing. Yet that's the very essence of Parmenides's thesis: the way of being inherently brushes up against the impossibility of the way of nonbeing. Parmenides repeatedly shows that the prohibition of the way of nonbeing is an integral part of the decision of thought itself and that it's at the intersection of these two ways that thinking is decided for. Saying that "being is One" immediately confronts you with nonbeing, with the problem of nonbeing. There is a principle here that Aristotle failed to grasp: Parmenides's fundamental problem is not the existence of being and the nonexistence of nonbeing but far more the question "What does it mean to think?" And when it comes to this issue, not only does Aristotle's argument not refute anything but all it does is emphasize the crux of the problem: *There is no thinking of being except at the risk of nonbeing.* Aristotle's refutation does indicate that, but, once again, in a way in which the impossible real is, for no reason, regarded as absurd.

---

Two statements will elucidate the interpretation of Parmenides for us. One of them is in Fragment 3: "The Same, indeed, is at once to think and to be," and the other is in Fragment 8: "For the same is to think and that for the sake of which there is thought." The impossibility of nonbeing—the inaccessibility of the way of nonbeing— arises from the point where being is the same as thinking, right where it is thinking that's at issue with respect to being. It's because "the Same, indeed, is at once to think and to be" that the way of nonbeing is inaccessible. It's the knot between thinking and being that is decided for in the impossibility of the way of nonbeing. Parmenides cannot be understood without reference to the knot between the three components—being, nonbeing, and thinking—and without taking into account that the impossibility, here, the impossibility of nonbeing, is in fact the impossibility—unless there's a decisive rejection of nonbeing—for thinking to be the thinking of being, therefore thinking *tout court*. The way of nonbeing must be rejected in order for thinking to become established as the thinking of being. In short, nonbeing is in a Borromean position in relation to thinking and being . . .

**Someone interrupts:** *What's the meaning of the word "Borromean"?*

. . . Well, it means that unless the way of nonbeing is inaccessible, thinking and being cannot combine . . .

**The same person interrupts again:** *"Borromean" doesn't mean anything!*

OK, but you've just got to learn, man! You can learn the meaning of the word "Borromean." I could tell you what it means, but I don't want to right now.

**The questioner becomes more insistent:** *All right, but that's not democratic!*

Oh, here we go, democracy! . . . Anyway, as I was saying . . . being, thinking, and nonbeing are in a Borromean position, meaning that each of them links the other two. There you go! The most important point in interpreting Parmenides is why his text takes the form of an imperative.

Take Fragment 6, for example. Let me read it to you:

It is right to say and to think that what-is is, for being is [or: it is
   for being], and nothing
is not. These things I bid you consider.
From this first way of inquiry <I withhold> you,
but then from this one, which mortals knowing nothing
wander, two-headed. For helplessness in their
breasts directs a wandering mind; and they are borne
both deaf and blind, dazed, undiscerning tribes,
by whom to be and not to be are thought to be the same
and not the same, and the path of all is backward-turning. (215)

"These things I bid you consider." What is it that he bids be considered here? The impossibility of nonbeing, the impossibility of nonbeing as the creation of the possibility of the thinking of being. Thinking can only be thought—i.e., "truth"—under a prohibition: there has to be a prohibition for there to be thinking as the thinking of being. But the prohibition is not of the order of refutation or of the empirical: it constitutes thinking itself. For thinking and being to be "the same," there has to have been a prohibition.

Why? Who are these people with wandering minds, who are deaf and blind? They are those, says Parmenides, "by whom to be and not to be are thought to be the same and not the same." Therefore, those who do not think, or who are blind, are the ones to whom nonbeing has not been prohibited, and for whom everything is mixed together: "to be and not to be are thought to be the same and not the same." They're blind in that they don't know where the impossible is. They're not blind because they don't see but because they see "too much." Parmenides intervenes to utter the prohibition and indicate, in this very way, that there is a place of impossibility, as a result of which, he says, he founds thinking as thinking, thinking as the thinking [*penser*] and the thought [*pensée*] of being. But to say that it's the thinking of being is a tautology, since "the same is at once to think and to be." So what he founds, we might say, is thinking *tout court*, which is obviously the thinking of being. That's why there is an imperative structure. Aristotle's error lies in failing to understand that what's involved is the relationship between thinking and prohibition, and not just a thesis about being. Where Aristotle seeks to make the impossible absurd, Parmenides, by contrast, constitutively, identifies the real of the impossible by a prohibition—which is a completely different operation.

It's extraordinary that Plato, before Aristotle, went straight to the structure of prohibition. With the metaphor of the parricide, he embarked on the path that Parmenides had forbidden. These are two completely different approaches. There's that of Aristotle, who gave everything that could be given in what I'd call a "regulated relationship" with Parmenides's decision. On the one hand, he recognized that Parmenides was an exception to the exception. But, on the other, he only saw in Parmenides an incomplete beginning, fraught with absurdities, which he, Aristotle, would complete and clarify. By contrast, in Plato's approach, with Parmenides there was a founding *gesture*. Not a beginning, which would later be developed, expanded, and consolidated, but a true founding gesture. And that gesture was essentially in the form of a prohibition. While for Aristotle the problem was completeness, for Plato it was transgression. It would be a refounding, because for Aristotle philosophical maturity had been reached, while for Plato, it would be a refounding because a point of resistance to the prohibition was necessary. These are very different visions of the gap and the foundation.[6]

This is what we'll see next time, with regard to Plato, when we begin with the Parmenidean structure of prohibition as a structure of intelligibility of his foundation of thinking.

# Session 5

## November 19, 1985

Nothing is more beneficial to us, or more important, in a life based on the Idea, than Plato's founding gesture, than that moment of rebellion, of transgression of Parmenides's prohibition tied to the thinking of being. It is on this gesture known as "Plato" that the current disposition of my philosophy is based: to reaffirm, through filiation, the possibility of the articulation—transformed, of course, but still recognizable—of the being-subject-truth triad.

Last time, however, we weren't dealing with Plato yet. A conclusion had been reached about Aristotle, about Aristotle's relationship with Parmenides, from which there emerged—surrounded, hunted down, but not stated—the idea that thinking can only be tied to being if the way of nonbeing is forbidden. This statement, despite appearances, is not obvious. Sure, you might say, thinking can only be tied to being if it is not tied to nonbeing. But that's not right! I say: the act of prohibiting the way of nonbeing is *how* thinking is tied to being. So there is a founding prohibition, discernible in what I called Aristotle's *splitting* of Parmenides. He was in fact, for Aristotle, in a wavering position between his historical impossibility—of not fitting into any analytic category for the history of thought—and his historical primacy. He was both historically impossible and first. And it's this ambiguous position that is the foundation.

---

Now what about Plato—Plato, who will be the second act of the backward move, of the regressive method? He mentions Parmenides a number of times, but we'll focus on two of his dialogues: the *Parmenides* and the *Sophist*.

In the dialogue that bears his name, Parmenides—our hero—is in fact a character, a theatrical character, who mounts the Platonic stage, which is truly remarkable. So he's no longer just a text; he's a person, a personality. As Captain Ahab in Melville's *Moby-Dick* says of himself, "A personality stands here": Parmenides. He's the only pre-Socratic philosopher who is present, in flesh and blood, in Plato's dialogues. By contrast, in the *Theaetetus* dialogue, Heraclitus, not being a character, is methodically refuted. The staging of this drama in the *Parmenides* is highly instructive. In a supposed meeting between the character Parmenides and Socrates, Plato dramatizes his double filiation. It's almost like a scene between the two fathers: the remote conceptual father, Parmenides, the founding father or the father of the line, the ancestor, on the one hand; and the immediate historical master, Socrates, on the other. In this scene, a scene of the double origin, the origin apprehends itself as double insofar as it is a very elderly Parmenides who is in discussion with a very young Socrates. The meeting very likely never took place, but it's all the "truer" for that. Truth here is in its fictional form: something of an essential truth is revealed to us here by this meeting, which is like an event of thought. Furthermore, this chance meeting between the ancestor and the immediate father is itself placed at a remove, distanced by a very elaborate narrative technique. At the beginning of the dialogue, a certain Cephalus—the first vanishing element of the frame story given that he quickly fulfills his role—arrives in Athens from

Clazomenae and meets one of his friends, a certain Adeimantus. This Adeimantus has a brother, Antiphon, who knows one of Zeno's disciples, and *his* name is Pythodorus. Bear in mind that the latter, who comes to see Cephalus, is a Parmenidean, a third-generation Eleatic, because he's a disciple of Zeno, not a direct disciple of Parmenides.[1] So it all begins with the fact that someone knows someone who knows someone else who knows a third-generation Eleatic. That's it! Plato defines the time frame: back when Pythodorus associated with the Eleatics and Zeno, he says, and back when the discussion supposedly took place, Parmenides was sixty-five and Zeno forty—which is exactly the timespan of one generation, twenty-five years. It was then that the meeting between Socrates, Parmenides, and Zeno took place. That's the first time frame. Pythodorus witnessed that discussion and was so blown away by it that he remembers it by heart. Considering what that discussion was like, he deserved a lot of credit! So Pythodorus, the third-generation Eleatic, gave a faithful account of it to Antiphon, who is so overwhelmed by what he hears that he, too, memorizes it and will tell it to Cephalus, who has come to Athens for just that purpose. And he, too, will probably memorize it. Between Antiphon and Cephalus, there's Adeimantus who completely fulfills this role of intermediary.

Just think what a string of extraordinary events this meeting—which is not just remote in time but is also the deliberate staging of a "precariousness" of transmission—depends on. It's an enigma that is fascinating in and of itself. Why did Plato feel the need to dramatize something so implausible? Nothing prevented him from saying: "One day, Socrates, Zeno, and Parmenides met, and here's what they said to each other." A lot of dialogues begin that way, so there's no inherent problem. Naturally, there's a meaning to it: Plato was absolutely determined that this transmission should be highly implausible. Here, Parmenides's foundational dimension is metaphorized, so to speak: first, by pure and simple distance, temporal distance, geographical distance, the distance of the transmission that's staged at a temporal remove—that's the first time frame of the founder; and second, the foundational dimension is also dramatized by the precariousness of what is transmitted of it. This transmission does not have the guarantees of an orthodoxy. We'll see how important this is in what follows.

Let's return to the dialogue. What happens at the beginning? Once the narrative device is in place, the account of the meeting between Parmenides, Socrates, and Zeno gets right underway. Zeno, a second-generation Parmenidean, or supposedly one, sets out his arguments—apparently reads his book—against motion and multiplicity, arguments that would remain extremely famous throughout all of Antiquity and well beyond. Zeno's arguments are aimed at the refutation of Parmenides's critics. These arguments are not represented as the Parmenidean "body" of doctrine but as refutations of refutations: silencing the critics is the goal that Zeno, as a zealous disciple, sets for himself. Yet Socrates tears Zeno's arguments to shreds. Zeno is forty, and Socrates is presented as very young, really very young: for him to have met Parmenides he would have had to be almost a kid. And this kid completely demolishes Zeno's arguments, in a very sarcastic way, actually, in the way of someone saying: "What a joke this all is!" And to that end he uses the doctrine of the Ideas and participation, that is, Platonism already. So this young sixteen- or seventeen-year-old adolescent is ahead of the game. Armed with the weapons of mature Platonism, he destroys Zeno's arguments and treats them with a certain arrogance, typically adolescent perhaps but itself a very important sign, something I'll come back to later. Parmenides is there: he'd gone out but had come back in and witnesses the scene. What happens then? Well, he's overjoyed! Parmenides is overjoyed that his disciple was torn to shreds. "That's great! Well done! You're really letting him have it, that's terrific!" Not only does he not defend his disciple but he congratulates Socrates, at first. Later, though, he attacks Socrates's refutation head-on. He, in turn, will destroy the arguments with which Socrates had torn Zeno to shreds. However, he does so in a different way from Socrates. With the firm hand of a master, he leads the impetuous young man into a philosophical impasse. It's crucial for Parmenides to be portrayed as the Master in this particular episode and to occupy this position of mastery vis-à-vis Socrates, who had earlier set *himself* up as Zeno's rival. The sons had had a fight . . . Parmenides had gone out; then, when he came back in, he saw that one of the youngsters was bashing the other, so he bashed the basher. All right! So here he establishes himself as the master again, and that's what he'll remain thereafter throughout the dialogue.

---

This mastery is artfully depicted in three respects, which could be called its three instances. Parmenides is presented in three different guises.

First, he is the only master because he rejects, or has the capacity to reject, spontaneous judgments, or, shall we say, average opinion—something Socrates still has trouble doing. With regard to the Ideas and the Forms, he says to Socrates: "You spoke about the Beautiful, the Good, and the True, sure, but is there an Idea of mud, for example? Is there an Idea of hair? Your Ideas are wonderful, but if you really want to give a comprehensive account of the sensible world, you also have to admit an Idea of mud and an Idea of hair." And Socrates replies: "Oh, man, I've often thought about doing that, but if I were to admit an Idea of mud or of hair I'd sound ridiculous!" "Then you're not a master yet," Parmenides retorts, "because you're someone susceptible to spontaneous opinions; you're still sensitive to ridicule. You lack the radicality of mastery; you're too young." That's what he tells him in so many words. Socrates is not yet able to express discursively the singularity of his theory, which he confuses with average opinion through that fundamental mediation, the fear of ridicule. Mastery requires holding fast to *the singularity* of one's theory when confronted with the tyranny of opinions.

In the second place, Parmenides is the master because, in his assessment of Socrates's line of argument, it is less the argument that he examines than its sticking point. He cuts straight to its point of the real. Parmenides's refutation isn't exactly the same as the one Socrates used against Zeno: it is, rather, a radicalizing of Socrates's position to its point of impasse. This time, mastery is presented as "the place of the pass," that is, the point where the place that *must* be passed through, and which the other person fails to pass through, is identified. And this is very different from refuting an argument.

Finally, in the third place, Parmenides is the master because he can provide training exercises: he can devise the appropriate training for *the pass*. He'll say so explicitly—here's what he says in the passage—when Socrates is in a complete impasse: "Which way will you turn if you have no answer for the questions I'm asking you? You need to radicalize your position. I'm asking you a number of questions and you fall into an impasse . . ."

And Socrates replies:

For the moment at least, I am not really sure I see.[2]

Parmenides continues:

No, because you undertake to mark off something beautiful and just and good, and each one of the forms too soon, before being properly trained. I realized that yesterday [which proves that the Master had been observing this promising young man for quite a while], when I heard you discussing here with Aristoteles [not Aristotle!]. Believe me, your impulse toward argument is noble and indeed divine. But train yourself more thoroughly while you are still young; drag yourself through what is generally regarded as useless, and condemned by the multitude as idle talk. Otherwise, the truth will escape you.

Socrates worriedly asks:

What is the manner of training, Parmenides?

And Parmenides, smiling, explicitly suggests a thought exercise to him, a dialectical exercise on the One. It is in this respect that he, philosophy's founder, is also the founder when it comes to the three instances of mastery: the decision for singularity, the pass, and training.

Here a very surprising question comes up: what exactly is Zeno's role in Plato's setup, since the instances of Parmenides's mastery vis-à-vis Socrates derive from the refutation of Zeno? What exactly is his role, and what is therefore the status, in Plato's eyes, of the second-generation Eleatics? Because the question of the founder is clearly related to that of the second generation: who are the direct disciples? Who comes right after the founder? And, first of all, is Zeno really an Eleatic? Is he really a Parmenidean? Oddly enough, in Plato's *Parmenides*, Zeno is in a certain way not considered as one by either Parmenides or Socrates. That's really something! The philosopher with the greatest fame in history where Parmenidean argumentation is concerned is not regarded as a serious Parmenidean by either the old master or the young man in Plato's dialogue. Parmenides's point of view is very clear. He witnessed the scene between Zeno and Socrates but won't say anything about it directly. He does, however, imply that Zeno wants to defend his master—of course he does!—but that he never gets beyond sensory anecdotes. So Parmenides patronizes him as a nice guy, who obviously defends him but never rises above a very modest level of argument. As for Socrates, with all the youthful respect he feels for Parmenides, he considers Zeno a "nobody" throughout the whole dialogue and refutes him in no time flat. It's as though the character of Zeno, the direct disciple—people often say "Parmenides and Zeno" when they talk about the Eleatics—was the figure of the dogmatic second generation in Plato's dialogue: the generation that, being in a defensive position in relation to the founding theses, led them into the opponents' territory, into what Parmenides called "the sensible world."

The objection to Parmenides, as you know, had to do with his doctrine of the One, which precluded motion and multiplicity, but especially precluded motion, i.e., denied Nature. What Zeno was focused on, it would seem, was turning the tables by protesting against the possibility of motion: your motion, he shot back at his master Parmenides's critics, is ultimately no more tenable than our non-motion! An argument that was still inferior, however, and that, like every negation of negation, carried the risk of a dogmatic closing-off of discourse.

In a recent, highly amusing article entitled "La technique littéraire des paradoxes de Zénon" [The Literary Technique of Zeno's Paradoxes], excerpted from his latest book, *Détections fictives* [Fictional Detections], Jean-Claude Milner proposes implicitly (because this wasn't his immediate objective) to address the question "Who exactly is Zeno?"[3] This is the question we're asking here, which Plato's dialogue effectively prompts us to ask. Milner claims that Zeno uses a literary technique, that of showing that his now-lost book is one whose structure borrows from literary methods and references, which are not exactly speculative. In particular, his technique borrows from Homer's, but from a Homer revised, so to speak, by popular wisdom. A Homer contaminated or rewritten by Aesop's fable "The Tortoise and the Hare." A prime example is the ever-so-famous argument of Achilles and the tortoise, according to which Achilles will never catch up to the tortoise because, to do so, he would first have to get to where the tortoise was when it started, but by the time he gets there the tortoise would have moved ahead, and so on. Achilles will never catch up to the tortoise because he always has to cover the distance, however minuscule, that he covered between the tortoise's previous starting point and the end point. This argument had an extraordinary success. Milner proposes the hypothesis, which he supports with an extremely erudite linguistic and literary demonstration, that it's first of all a reference to the famous episode in the *Iliad* where Achilles chases Hector around the walls of Troy, an episode in which, even though he's "the fastest," "the fastest man alive," he would not have been able to catch up to Hector if Athena hadn't intervened directly, or if the game hadn't been rigged. In his argument, Zeno treats as isomorphic, so to speak, Achilles's fatal pursuit of Hector and Aesop's comic, popular fable about "Slow and steady wins the race."[4] It's a technique by means of which a chiasmus occurs: Zeno combines two elements that are posited as identical, Achilles-Hector and hare-tortoise, in the form of a simplistic treatment of the epic.

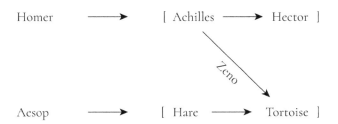

That was Milner's first conclusion. The second, which follows immediately, is that the real site of this technique is comedy, namely, the comical humbling of anyone considered great, in this case the reworking of the epic tragedy by the popular fable that undermines it. Hence, the chiasmus of the greatest of heroes with the humblest of animals, Achilles and the tortoise. Finally, Milner's third conclusion is that Zeno merely evened the score with those who ridiculed Parmenides's thesis and treated it as a joke. So, strictly speaking, Zeno's lost book was a humorous book, a conceptual comedy. Bravo!

Two comments should be added to this. The first is that the comic treatment of the great man, the comic arguments, must have cut Plato to the quick, because Aristophanes had turned Plato's master Socrates into a farcical character on stage. Reread *The Clouds*, of course. Next time, I may read a couple of scenes from it so you can see what it's all about. Plato often expresses, particularly in the *Apology*, the hurt caused him by Aristophanes's savage, farcical portrayal of Socrates. So Zeno is brought in, as a kind of "counter-*Clouds*," not in connection with Socrates but with Parmenides. The second comment is that a founder triggers an inevitable free-for-all below him, so to speak, a comic free-for-all in which supporters and opponents alike have lost the position of mastery and farcically pit ludicrous objections against equally ludicrous defenses. Countless examples can be given of such a spectacle! It is this comic free-for-all, caused by the loss or subtraction of the position of mastery in which the foundation originated, that Zeno exemplifies. That's Milner's thesis. Plato, though, intends to restore seriousness. This is a fundamental aspect of his relationship with Parmenides. Even if he mentions the comic aspects, Plato intends to restore the seriousness of the Parmenidean foundation, in three ways. First, through the effect of distance: it's originary, therefore, like every origin, even one that is close to us in time, it is very remote. Distance is not just a matter of remoteness; it's the likelihood of a partial loss of meaning. All of this is expressed very clearly in the *Parmenides*. Second, through the three instances of mastery—singularity, the pass, and knowledge—already expressed in the filiation, since Parmenides is the master of Socrates, who is himself portrayed as Plato's master. So he's the master's master, the ancestor and mastery being embodied here in this very touching figure of the master's master. And third of all, through the critique of Zeno, through the destruction of the comic aspect, Plato restores the foundation. In Milner's thesis, the destruction of the comic aspect is at the very least the destruction of the inferior, or dogmatic, argument. And this, in my opinion, is how the ground is cleared for the metaphor—this one tragic—of the parricide. The comic aspect had to be utterly destroyed in order for the tragic metaphor of the parricide to come into play. It's not in the *Parmenides* that it does so but in the *Sophist*.

The *mise-en-scène* of the *Sophist* . . .

**Someone in the audience interrupts:** *Excuse me, didn't Plato himself ever refute Parmenides's arguments about certain lowly Ideas—for example, hair, mud, or things like that? Wasn't that always a problem for Plato?*

I think it was, yes.

**The same person:** *It's really quite amazing that Plato sort of puts himself in a position of vulnerability vis-à-vis Parmenides and, through him, his own contemporaries.*

I agree with you that this passage is utterly extraordinary. It's extraordinary because, in a way, it goes so far as to credit Parmenides with having a type of mastery, which it is unclear whether Plato agrees with; in any case, a type of radicality concerning the question of the Ideas of hair and of mud. I'm sure that when he has the young Socrates, haunted by the fear of ridicule, speak, something of himself is being expressed. I really think so. With Plato there's always—and we'll come back to this—the feeling, related to that of a partial loss, of a Parmenidean radicality in relation to which he, Plato, is in an intermediary position and which he's unable or unwilling to agree with completely. There's that impulse, as well as the impulse to free himself from Parmenides. Clearly these Ancients were ambivalent!

---

The *mise-en-scène* of the *Sophist* is very elaborate. Once again, it's a matter of complexity effects, but with a different purpose. It's important to understand, first of all, that this dialogue directly follows that other dialogue, the *Theaetetus*, the way chapters follow one other in a novel. They are linked, one by its beginning and the other by its end. The *Theaetetus-Sophist* pair is related, in a certain sense, to the Heraclitus-Parmenides pair: the refutation of Heraclitus in the former, the parricide of Parmenides in the latter. By setting these two refutations side by side, the dialogues are joined together by a narrative transition.

How is the *Theaetetus* set up? Somebody by the name of Eucleides, not to be confused with Euclid, the mathematician, transcribed (*he didn't learn by heart; he wrote down*) the discussions between Socrates, the young Theaetetus, and a third character, Theodorus, who *was* a mathematician. Eucleides has the text of these conversations read to one of his friends, Terpsion, by a slave. But the backdrop to this scene is actually very tragic: two deaths are looming on the horizon. The occasion for this reading is the imminent death of Theaetetus: he is dying of a fatal wound he received in the war that Athens and Sparta are waging against Thebes. Then there's the death of Socrates, who was put to death, as you know, after a trial in which he was accused of impiety. The dialogue is set just before Socrates's death:[5] at the end of the *Theaetetus*, at the end of the dialogue, he goes to his death. But what's more, at the end of the text the slave reads to Terpsion, at the end of this supposed discussion between the three men—Theaetetus, Socrates, and Theodorus—Socrates, in the text, exits the stage, saying: "We won't be able to continue our discussions tomorrow because I have to go to my trial." Let me read you the passage, this tragedy's ending:

> Now, however, I have to go to the porch of the king and meet the indictment of Meletus which he's drawn up against me. But at dawn, Theodorus, let's come back here to meet.[6]

It is in fact Socrates's death, the shadow of his death, that acts as a caesura between the two dialogues, the *Theaetetus* and the *Sophist*. Bear in mind that the meeting arranged at the end of the *Theaetetus* carries over Socrates's death sentence to that other dialogue, the *Sophist*. As a result, the man who appears in the *Sophist* is in actual fact a man condemned to death—a dead man walking, over whom the shadow of tragedy already hangs—who will be the other characters' interlocutor. The text is read after Socrates's death, and, in the text, he goes to meet it.

I'm going to read you the very beginning of the *Sophist*, which follows on from the end of the *Theaetetus*. It is Theodorus the mathematician who begins:

> Here we are, Socrates, true to our agreement of yesterday, and we bring with us a stranger from Elea, who is a disciple of Parmenides and Zeno, and a true philosopher.[7]

Note how the beginning of the *Sophist* is a follow-up to the *Theaetetus*, marked by the death of Socrates, who nevertheless still features in it, so it's clear that the parricide that will be discussed in the *Sophist*—the conceptual parricide of Parmenides—is itself an echo of that other one, the death sentence that was passed by Athens on the man whom Plato regards as the City's most eminent son. This heinous act is, in his eyes, the City's murder of the man who was its finest son. Consequently, the extraordinary tragic interlocking of the ensemble formed by the *Theaetetus* and the *Sophist* is entirely marked by death. Indeed, this is what eliminates the comic aspect of the argument, as Zeno used it in support of his master Parmenides.

Moreover, you could say that Socrates is dead to speech in the *Sophist*: he's not the one who conducts the dialogue. He's still alive, but he's the figure, in the text itself, over whom the shadow of death looms, and he's not the one who will speak, whereas in the *Theaetetus* he still conducted the dialogue from beginning to end. This is truly the precise moment when Socrates disappears from Plato's text, the moment when someone else takes his place. And the person who takes his place is the Eleatic Stranger. Who? One of Parmenides's disciples. It's as though, in the very place of the second parricide—the murder of Socrates by his own City—only the founding ancestor, in the guise of his disciple, could be brought in. As though the death of the second founder required turning to the disciple of the first one. But what will this Parmenidean decree? Well, he'll decree the parricide. So it all becomes complicated again: Socrates has just been put to death; in his place comes the first founder; in the latter's shadow comes his disciple . . . But he will decree the second parricide, the fundamental parricide, that of Parmenides. And so what comes about is a complete work of death, if I can put it that way: by the end of the *Sophist*, both Socrates and Parmenides have been figuratively or literally put to death. What is engendered here? Plato is, inasmuch as *he* is now the living founder. Plato was Socrates; Plato was, in addition to Socrates, Parmenides—the conceptual filiation . . . In a certain sense, the shadow of death hangs over Socrates because of this heinous murder perpetrated on him by the City; and the one who replaces him, the Stranger, who will conduct the dialogue, is a Parmenidean. And what will this Stranger decree? This: the elimination of what remained obscure in the first foundation. And this gesture will engender Plato, in the figure of the completed murder of the father, that is, in the figure of Platonism, in the figure in which Plato is no longer a son. No longer to be a son, for a philosopher, is to be forever equal to Platonism.

So the *Sophist* is, in my opinion, the engendering of Platonism. It doesn't matter whether it is doctrinally so; it is subjectively so. The *Sophist* is the engendering of Platonism through the resolution of the question of the foundation. That is why the *Sophist*, which is an inexhaustible text, is in my view the greatest text in the history of philosophy because it is also this tragedy, because it is also—without ever biographizing, without ever deviating from pure conceptual rigor–truly the legibility of the engendering, of the engendering of Platonism, in which we can see how, even for Plato, Platonism is in excess over Plato. Over which Plato? Over the son-Plato, that is to say, over Plato as the offspring of Socrates, of Parmenides, and no doubt of much else, but let's say *symbolically* of Socrates and Parmenides. It's absolutely staggering that Plato's mind was such that it placed the parricide of Parmenides in a figure in which it is carried out by someone replacing the absent Socrates, by a Parmenidean, because only a Parmenidean could *name* the absence of Socrates. Otherwise, the realm of filiation would have been abandoned. This birth of Platonism dramatized in the *Sophist*, in the drama, in the tragedy of filiation and death, is something truly extraordinary.

We'll deal with what this tragedy tells us about Parmenides next time, in connection with the workings of nonbeing, that is, with what I suggested we call "the Borromean knot of thinking, being, and nonbeing."

# Session 6

## December 3, 1985

Believe it or not, I forgot the notes for my lecture! So it will have to be reconstructed, and if anything's missing I'll fill it in next time. What I wanted to begin with is a summary review of how what I referred to as the clarity of the transmission is articulated, i.e., how Plato depicts the way that something of Parmenides was transmitted to him, how Plato's text presents what I called the *precariousness* of the transmission.

Remember: what Plato instituted is actually a foundation—the foundation of Platonism—and it is with the *Sophist* that he designates himself as founder. So the transmission also unfolds through the distance this foundation takes from the deaths of both Parmenides and Socrates, which the *mise-en-scène* organizes in a four-step sequence. Between the first dialogue, the *Parmenides*, in which the very young Socrates's direct and respectful relationship with the undisputed founding master, Parmenides, is played out in lively exchanges, and the second dialogue, the *Theaetetus*, which is between the young Theaetetus, almost on his deathbed, and Socrates, in his guise as master, summoned before the tribunal of the city to answer the charges brought against him by Meletus, the death of Parmenides has occurred. Between the *Theaetetus* and the next dialogue, the *Sophist*, with which it forms an articulated ensemble, the death of Socrates will occur. While in the *Theaetetus* Socrates is still the initiator of the dialogue, in the *Sophist*, on the contrary, the discussion with the Stranger—which will be followed by a third dialogue, the *Statesman*, in which the characters of the Eleatic Stranger and Theaetetus are reunited—takes place in the presence of Socrates, certainly, but a Socrates who is effaced in that he's no longer the initiator or even the leader of the dialogue. He is there merely as a silent witness. The shadow of death looms over this Socrates, who has been replaced, as it were, by Parmenides's disciple, the Eleatic Stranger. Finally, in the *Statesman*, another dialogue, the *Philosopher*, is announced that may apparently have formed a trilogy with the *Sophist* and the *Statesman*, since it is said in the *Statesman*, in the voice of Socrates: "I'm greatly indebted to you for having introduced me to this admirable Eleatic Stranger." To which it is replied: "You'll admire him even more when you see how, after having dealt with the sophist and the statesman, he'll also deal with the philosopher."

Yet no such dialogue exists.

What conclusions can be drawn from all this?

First, it's clear that the double-origin hypothesis is being set up here. The double origin of what? Of Platonism. There's a double origin, whose signifiers are Parmenides and Socrates, a double origin that is revealed in the *Theaetetus* and the *Parmenides* by the position of mastery those two characters hold in them. That's the first point: the double origin.

Second, at the actual time of Plato's writing of these dialogues, both masters were dead.

Third, they were consequently replaced by a single character, the Eleatic Stranger, who leads the *Sophist* and the *Statesman* and who evidently was also supposed to lead the *Philosopher*, as the capstone and culmination of the whole. So we have to assume that "the Eleatic Stranger" is actually the name of Plato, that the significant hypothesis of the double origin supporting the textual construction is that this Stranger stands for *him*, Plato. And he then replaces the other two, Parmenides and Socrates, to whose silence he is directly connected. Socrates, condemned to death, silently witnesses the advent of "the Eleatic Stranger" as the one who "speaks."

Bear in mind that *there are two parricides* in the *Sophist*, not just one: an explicit parricide—the refutation of Parmenides's theory—and another one, no less astonishing, which is the reduction to silence of Socrates. And in a certain way, one man—the Eleatic Stranger—combines these two parricides. So there is good reason to think that he stands in the place of the double filiation, in Plato's place. This is even clearer from his name: the Eleatic Stranger, i.e., the one who, through his connection with Parmenides, is in a double relationship of co-presence—he's from Elea, his conceptual or symbolic homeland is Eleaticism—and expatriation, since he's the Stranger. Plato designates himself in two ways, beginning with the *Sophist*: first, as the one who can now speak in his own name, the one on account of whom Socrates is silent, and, second, as the one who expels Eleaticism from itself, or who exiles Parmenides from his homeland, from the doctrine of Being, from the Parmenidean doctrine of Being. Young Theaetetus will have the same position vis-à-vis the Eleatic Stranger in both the *Sophist* and the *Statesman* as the one he held vis-à-vis Socrates in the *Theaetetus*. From one dialogue to the next, from the *Theaetetus* to the *Sophist*, then to the *Statesman* and the nonexistent *Philosopher*, what transits is the disciple, as an invariant element. The master can only be replaced via the invariance of the disciple. It's not the pair of them that changes; rather, the same disciple changes masters. There must be a same in order for there to be an other, and the other master is based on the sameness of the disciple. In the *Parmenides*, Socrates himself held that position vis-à-vis Parmenides: he was his disciple in the same way that

Theaetetus was one, first of Socrates, then of the Eleatic Stranger. Hence the problematic of the "sons"—"son" being understood here in the same way as the metaphor of the father is: the one to whom something is transmitted. So there are two successive sons: the young Socrates and Theaetetus, which makes Parmenides, if you take the complex of the four dialogues as a whole, the only one who is presented only as a father figure. I said double origin, Parmenides and Socrates: yes, in relation to Plato, but in a certain sense, and in a different scheme, linearity: Socrates himself—as a youth—is presented as being ultimately dependent on Parmenides and features as his son, as his last disciple.

Consider the complex relationship that develops.

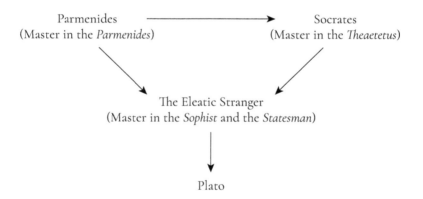

This first diagram shows that Socrates and Parmenides are historically the two masters. Of whom? Of Plato.

An additional relationship will set up the filiation mechanism: Socrates is not just in a position of mastery; he is also in the position of son in the *Parmenides*, and in the *Sophist* he's effaced, silent. The diagram becomes:

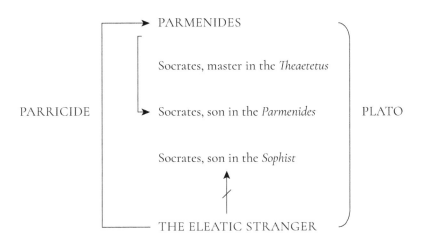

Only Parmenides appears in the guise of the founding father. But when Plato comes in, when, as the "Eleatic Stranger," he establishes his right to speak, all of them, fathers and sons, are dead. Everyone who played a role is dead: Parmenides, Socrates, and Theaetetus as well. So, with the writing of the dialogues, Plato becomes Platonism: his own speech is no longer mediated by anyone else. The previous general system of filiation, and those who embodied it, are gone. Or have been foreclosed.

What, then, is Plato's position on mastery? In a sense, it is linked to the real of the master's death; it is not simply his having been superseded. So long as the master is alive—and alive from the standpoint of the real—his symbolic killing is not a guarantee of truth. This is how Plato portrays it. Plato has real filial piety, precisely insofar as the point of the real of the master's death must be invoked so that the space of filiation can be unfolded and the autonomy of the founding declaration can emerge within it. So the parricide has to have already occurred, but without any admission of guilt: the audacity of the parricide stops short of attacking the living master.

The subjective genesis of Platonism, or of the autonomy of the declaration, depends on it: it is linked to the fictional parricide that no one is guilty of.

But why did he nonetheless require the symbolic parricide? What leads to it, to the refutation of Parmenides, is the need to describe the sophist. What's more, Plato's need to criticize sophistry and the Sophists, and therefore to give a clear concept of the sophist, reflects not only an intra-philosophical requirement as to truth but also a political requirement: indeed, it is fundamentally a political requisite, under condition of philosophy. Through the *Sophist*, what is targeted is what might be called the cynical use of democracy. Because as past master in that art, the sophist is clearly the one who trains and educates the demagogue. He's the smooth talker who can turn the legislature around. And Plato, owing to his conception of philosophy, undertakes to destroy that figure, to criticize, disparage, discredit it. It's a crucial ideological struggle. So what leads to the refutation of Parmenides is, in the final analysis, a "situation": one in which the Sophists are flourishing. In the *Sophist* it's always a situation that leads to a transgression. If Parmenides's prohibition "It is forbidden to follow the path of nonbeing" must be transgressed, if it must be transgressed by taking the path of nonbeing anyway, it is because the situation requires it.

The core question of the *Sophist* is, as Lacan would say, that of a discourse that would not be pure semblance. To get at semblance in its very being, you have to figure out what the "being" of the sophist is if you want to disparage and discredit him politically, that is to say, historically. It's clear that if Plato is led to this question of the being of semblance, it's because there is a historicity of it, which the Sophists embody. But ontologically, Plato will maintain that semblance doesn't exist—thereby remaining a son of Parmenides, the Eleatic Stranger. He will maintain that semblance is not, that the simulacrum, the false, is not. Except, even though ontologically it is not, it nevertheless has a powerful historicity. Even if it has no being qua being, it has a "situational" being whose status must absolutely be defined.

This is how the Eleatic Stranger introduces the attack (in the *Sophist*, 237a):

> Such a claim already dares to assume that what is not is; only on that assumption will a false thing said or believed turn out to be something that is. But, my boy, from the time we were boys the great Parmenides never stopped testifying against it, whether expressing himself in prose or in verse: "For never shall this prevail," so his lines go, "that the things that are not are; / Keep you your thought, as you search, back from that path." So we have his testimony . . .[1]

I'm going to highlight a few points from this paragraph, in which the problem of the relationship with Parmenides is introduced. The first point is that it's about the "great" Parmenides, he who attested and testified against the way of nonbeing. Although the criticism must be radical, it isn't meant to be polemical, as it could be in the standard Platonic refutations of the Heraclitans. It must allow the greatness of the person being refuted to be preserved, *because we are his descendants*. That's the second point. To whom did the great Parmenides testify against it? To us, "from the time we were boys." Consequently, the metaphor of the father is clearly lurking in the figure of the boy that the Stranger was back then; and the great Parmenides duly testifies to this. So there's a connection between the preservation of the greatness and the father figure that leads the criticism onto as unpolemical a path as possible, and therefore a particularly perilous one. In citing the imperative nature of Parmenides's declaration, i.e., its prohibitive form—"For never shall this prevail: that the things that are not are; /Keep you your thought, as you search, back from that path"—Plato is less concerned with criticizing a theory than with prohibitory paternity itself. It's not a specific father that is really at issue but prohibitory paternity itself. Thus, the third point: the unparalleled audacity of this undertaking. What does audacity mean? It means the transgressiveness of the undertaking. These are the things that immediately distinguish the approach to the question: paternity, prohibitory paternity, greatness that must be preserved, and audacious transgression.

Plato will compound the difficulty by giving Theaetetus all the Parmenidean or post-Parmenidean arguments that make the undertaking impossible, that make the transgression impossible. On the entire following page, the person who speaks is truly the Eleatic Stranger—someone who is an Eleatic well-versed in Parmenides's arguments—and it is he who will lead the young Theaetetus into a complete impasse. How so? He'll tell him: "Here's what's needed: having the courage to transgress the Parmenidean paternal prohibition on nonbeing! These are the reasons why it's impossible!" He then goes on to give a lot of traditional Parmenidean arguments about the impossibility of saying anything at all about nonbeing. He'll go so far as to say:

> So do you see [*he's talking to Theaetetus*] that it is impossible, correctly, to express or to say or to think what is not in and by itself; it's unthinkable, unsayable, inexpressible, and unaccountable. [238c] (131)

That's a rigid Parmenidean conclusion stringently argued by the Eleatic Stranger before a Theaetetus who had been excited by the idea of a quick transgression but who soon finds himself in an absolute impasse.

Subsequently, once the situation has been hardened with its element of prohibition and impossibility, there comes the time of the transgression, in three stages. Let me read them to you and comment on them one after the other:

Stage 1:

THE STRANGER: And there's this other thing I'd ask of you even more.
THEAETETUS: What's that?

THE STRANGER: That you don't take me to be turning into some sort of parricide, as it were.
THEAETETUS: How so?
THE STRANGER: In order to defend ourselves we're going to need to cross-examine what our Father Parmenides says and force the claim through both that what is not in a certain way *is*, and conversely that what is also in a way is not. [241d] (136)

Stage 2:

THE STRANGER: For that reason we must take our courage in our hands and go for a frontal assault on the paternal claim. It's either that or leave it totally alone, should we hesitate for some reason to do the deed. [242a] (136)

And finally, Stage 3:

THE STRANGER: Well, there's a third small thing I have still to ask of you.
THEAETETUS: You have only to ask.
THE STRANGER: When I was talking a few moments ago I think I said that I've always found mounting a challenge on these matters too much for me, and never more than now.
THEAETETUS: You did say that.
THE STRANGER: Well, that makes me afraid I'll seem mad to you for doing an immediate about-turn. In fact it's for your sake that we'll be setting about challenging Parmenides' claim, if we actually manage it.
THEAETETUS: Well, I certainly won't think you are acting in any way inappropriately if you proceed straight to this challenge of yours, and your proof, so carry on, with confidence on this score at least.
THE STRANGER: So come on, how should one begin such a hazardous discussion? [242a-b] (136–37)

A few comments now on this remarkable moment of thought.

First of all, it begins immediately with the parricide metaphor, which will thereafter run throughout the text—a metaphor I've already commented amply on in connection with Parmenides's prohibition. The transgression itself is presented with some very violent language: "In order to defend ourselves we're going to need to cross-examine [*the expression "mettre à la question"—"to put to the question"—means "to torture," so we're going to need to "torture"*] what our Father Parmenides says" and then "force the claim through . . . that what is not in a certain way *is*." Note how the transgression is a violent forcing-through, which naturally develops and supports the parricide metaphor, how it's the forcing-through of an impasse and not an ordinary dialectical refutation.

In the second stage, the time has come to go for a frontal assault on the paternal claim—πατρικὸς λόγος [*patrikos logos*]—which is "the saying [*dire*] of the father," but also, if you like, the "concept of the father," the "reason," the "thinking of the father." It is nothing less than a frontal assault on this father. It's the conceptually founding father who is attacked in his very paternity, not in one or another of his secondary attributes. In other words, in the declaration that establishes him as such, his reason in the strongest sense of the term, his *logos*.

Finally, in the third stage, the transgression is declared impossible. Why? Because it's beyond the Stranger's powers—it has always been beyond them and will still be beyond them. Something, here, is a point of impossibility with respect to the son's capacities. The attack, the refutation of the **πατρικὸς λόγος** [*patrikos logos*] or the paternal declaration, is, by its very nature, beyond the son's capacity, because it is only by virtue of this declaration that he is established as the son. And so he only has the "powers" attributed to him because of the **πατρικὸς λόγος** [*patrikos logos*] itself, the paternal declaration itself. It's a symbolic field that is being defined here. What does that mean? It means that the refutation, the transgression, is beyond the powers of the person who proclaims it. That's all. And, since it does happen, since it will nevertheless happen, carried out successfully, this means that it had to do with something other than his powers. That's all that this means. And it's easy to understand: going beyond his powers, which established him as the son or kept him beholden to the paternal declaration, causes an excess, a hole, in the symbolic system that produced him. The Eleatic Stranger will found, including for himself, what will be said here, thereby bringing forth a regime of power and capacity that was not the one he was originally under. The foundation, in this case the foundation of Platonism, is necessarily beyond the powers of the Parmenideans. Yet the Eleatic Stranger *is* a Parmenidean. So it is by *going beyond himself* that he'll become the founder. And going beyond himself in order to become the founder is one and the same gesture as defying the πατρικὸς λόγος [*patrikos logos*], the paternal declaration.

The *Sophist* makes us witnesses here of something exceptional: an invention. Even though it appears to be a refutation it's not actually one; it's really an invention, namely that of the shift from one regime of the possible to another, or a splitting of the law. That's why it makes perfect sense to say that the refutation is impossible, that the very idea of it is crazy, and yet to carry it out. Being intransitive, such an effectuation is also intransitive to its own conditions. There is no way to implement it within the space of the paternal declaration.

And the funny thing running through this whole discussion is that young Theaetetus is asked for permission. The kid is asked, three times. Take a look at the text: the first request is "Don't take me to be turning into some sort of parricide." That's an odd request, since he's just explained that he *is* a parricide, and in what sense he is one. That's the first point. The second request is: "Give me permission not to back out." He'll have to give the whole thing up should he hesitate for some reason to do the deed. This is when Theaetetus says: "Let's not let anything stop us, c'mon, let's go for it!" And then the third request is: "Don't consider me a madman" as regards this idea, which I've just explained to you in what sense it's crazy. So, what is the meaning of the permission, requested three times of Theaetetus by the Eleatic Stranger, to go ahead with the parricide? What is his role? Well, *Theaetetus is the unconscious.* He is truly the unconscious of the situation, in the sense that, grounded in dependence on the Stranger, in complete dependence on him (it's clear that the Stranger knows perfectly well that the response to his three requests will be "yes;" there's no doubt about that), he's incapable of knowing what's at stake. "So," you might say, "is the Stranger just asking an idiot for permission?" No, he's not! His non-awareness of what's at stake is a metaphor for courage in this situation. It involves an element of unconsciousness—his unconscious courage—which the Stranger will rely on, fleetingly, to bolster him in his new mastery. Theaetetus is the one to whom the new paternal declaration will be directly addressed.

(And a brief discussion about the nature of this element of courage now arises:)

**Someone asks:** *Would it be an exaggeration to say that what is intrinsic and absolutely necessary could be called love?*

Plato might possibly call it that; he'd have no objection to that. It's very clear that the Eleatic Stranger loves Theaetetus.

**The same person continues:** *This reminds me of a discussion we had a long time ago—remember, I asked you: "Why don't you demolish that idiot?" And you replied: "But Plato wants Theaetetus to be an idiot!" But I don't agree. I don't agree because Plato can't want Theaetetus to be an idiot because he's a brave man who dies at the end and is also a mathematician.*

*Plato can't make someone who stands for his ideal, the brave man of the City and the mathematician, an idiot. It's true he's idiotic, but he's idiotic for* us, *in the same way that we always find sweetly idiotic two people in love, one of whom is swooning over the other. But someone who loves us doesn't seem idiotic to us. Plato doesn't see Theaetetus as idiotic, because the Stranger loves him. We're the ones who find him idiotic, the way we find sweetly idiotic two lovers on a park bench, one of whom says to the other . . . I don't know what they might say to each other, but Plato doesn't see that and doesn't want to see it. Quite simply, the element of courage involved here is called love.*

I'm not so sure about that, first of all because there's something you're not taking fully into account: we're not dealing with the Socrates-Theaetetus relationship anymore. What you said would most likely apply to that, but the style itself and the portrayal of the character differ from those of the *Theaetetus*. I'm willing to believe that, in the way Plato dramatizes the relationship between Socrates and the young Theaetetus, of whom it's just been said that he's dying a heroic death in combat, and so on, there's the admiration typical of the love relationship with a young man. But here, it's different: nothing like that is presented as the basic hypothesis of the relationship between the Eleatic Stranger and Theaetetus. I still think that, in the *Sophist*, he's an idiot. Everyone laughed a moment ago when I read it.

**The same person:** *Well, I say it's touching. It's a kind of idiocy that in effect touches us. But I think that for Plato he's not plainly idiotic, he's no more idiotic than someone who says the things to us that people in love say . . .*

What I just wanted to say is that as regards Theaetetus, there's something new: *he changes masters*. That's undeniable: he changes masters. So is the humorous aspect a literary tactic of Plato's, or not? Indeed, maybe not, maybe he doesn't see it, maybe we see something *he* doesn't see. But does that mean it's something that's not in his dialogue? Plato may very well have decided that Theaetetus was comical, and possibly even idiotic, but with a completely different intention, namely that, in spite of everything, this young man is in the process of changing masters and he is being asked for a permission that affects him, since it is what he is going to determine or orient his thinking by. Seeing no harm in it. That's what's a little comical: he doesn't see any harm in it.

**The same person:** *I don't want to argue too much about this point, which is trivial, after all.*

Not only, not only . . .

**The same person:** *No, it's not! But actually, to return to what, in my opinion, may not be a trivial issue, it's that element of unconscious courage. Isn't there another problem in that this element of unconscious courage, which is intrinsic, has a specific source that is love? Because otherwise, if you will, an element of unconscious courage, it's . . . well, there's nothing. There's got to be a tangible, identifiable source, there's got to be . . . unless we're dealing with a total robot, this element of unconscious courage, subjectively, has got to have a source.*

Of course, of course! But why love? *I* think the metaphor may be related to the one you're suggesting, but it's the metaphor of youth, quite simply. What does the Eleatic Stranger ask of Theaetetus? He asks him to say "Go for it!" without really knowing what it's all about. Because that's what "Go for it!" means, and it will end with "Come on!" But he just needs for him to be young: right from the start of the dialogue Theaetetus is all for going through with it. It's just that he's not able to understand what's at stake, that it's a parricide, that it's a new conceptual space, a new foundation, and so on and so forth. Theaetetus is someone who deals with the problem in its particularity. And as such, he is completely internal to the situation, and as he's internal to the situation, he has the necessary courage for it. It's this courage that provides the Stranger, that is, Plato, with the support needed to take the plunge, but without the young man's having any idea of the danger involved. Sure, he'll say "Let's go!" but without any understanding as to what's at stake being prospectively possible for him. He will thus be taken point by point through the very long proof, confirming each of its steps. That's all I wanted to say.

**Someone else ventures a comment:** *Basically, the Stranger would like someone to go along with him . . .*

That's exactly right! He'd like someone to listen to him, and this listening, the fact that someone is listening, is a necessary condition for him.

**The same person adds:** *Of course, it's no ordinary dialogue. He has to listen . . .*

That's why I had no radical objection.

**The previous questioner comments again, insisting:** *OK, I don't mind your calling it youth, but in that case, you have to thematize what youth is. That's an important point, because assuming that the other person says "Well, no, I don't agree," then it's all over, right? So there has to be some complicity, some agreement. That's what I call love. You can call it something else if you like, I'm not claiming ownership of the name. But it seems to me that in your conceptual framework there's no thematization of that* point. I think it's love, but call it whatever you want. But I would have liked you to recognize it for what it is and . . .

If you say there has to be some complicity, or something of that sort, an agreement to listen, or a desire to listen, I'll agree with you. But I think love is already inscribed in Plato's work, and very emphatically so—whether in the *Phaedrus* or the *Symposium*—in a situation that's really different from that one. That's why I'm a little reluctant to introduce the analysis of love that is elaborated elsewhere by Plato. Complicity, yes, I think . . . but it seems to me that it's based on the fact that the young man he's talking to is up for any radical adventure, for considering any radical adventure. But why does he ask him for permission? Because he tells him: "Careful, your act is very radical, it's a parricide, it's horrendous, it's practically madness." He ramps up the drama as far as possible, only to be told "OK." But OK with regard to what complicity? That's what youth is: it is thematized as the courage of the situation with regard to a radicalism of the undertaking or the adventure that Theaetetus accepts, because he's young and because he's not a philosopher, and *he* has no need of a reflective mechanism. That's what I mean by "unconscious."

**Another person comments**: *The adventure, at first, isn't shared; it's the Stranger's adventure. That's why he [Theaetetus] can say: "Go for it!" He doesn't see himself as being involved in the adventure . . .*

But, as a young man, he immediately sympathizes with any adventure. This is the very thing that defines him as a possible interlocutor. To be sure, the specific adventure—the trajectory of the parricide of Parmenides—isn't his, and there's a formality about the young man: "I'm listening to the account of the imaginary adventure, I'm listening sympathetically, approvingly, and enthusiastically to the story." There's a principle of enthusiasm here that is pure and on which the Eleatic Stranger will rely.

All right! We can move on now . . . OK?

**Someone persists in commenting**: *I think that if we called that "love," Platonism would gain something thereby. That's why it's also called "foundation," which is universality, that is, the fact that there's no longer any need for the disciple to be amazed. That, in a way, goes back to you . . .*

One of the aspects of the Platonic foundation, the one that's not the Socrates-Parmenides register, is that Plato thinks that his dialectical articulation—that is, the essence of his foundation—is such that the disciple doesn't need to be amazed. I think *that's* true. The Platonic foundation is a foundation that dramatically transforms the question of the master and the disciple. We'll come back to this. It's the very heart of the question of Parmenides and leads, in a way, not exactly to the disciple's disposition, but to a status . . .

**Someone interrupts**: *An academic status?*

At any rate to a completely different status.

**The questioner from earlier comments, grumbling**: *Precisely, I agree with that idea. But precisely because the foundation took place, because where they went . . . I mean, I'm not talking about Plato's disciples but about the character of Theaetetus vis-à-vis Parmenides. In my opinion, it's not just vis-à-vis what you described. I'm not going to go on about it, but I think that in this case what we agreed to call "complicity" would merit further discussion . . .*

All right. What will happen next in the dialogue will be the tortuous process of the refutation. Let me emphatically remind you again here that, in essence, this refutation is actually a declaration. This explains why Theaetetus has to be what he is: someone who listens to a declaration, not someone who follows an argument. He of course *appears* to be following it, but essentially he's someone who listens to a declaration. So he has to be able to testify to it and not just to have followed it.

---

I will naturally not go back over Plato's method of refutation. I already dealt with it two years ago and I'm not going to revisit it.[2] I'll get right to the concluding point: using Parmenides's arguments, Plato, or the Eleatic Stranger, pushing Theaetetus into an impasse, concludes (may I remind you) that nonbeing is absolutely inexpressible, unsayable, unthinkable, etc. So nonbeing must occur in the form of a surplus signifier, which will not in fact be nonbeing. The invention I was talking about is that of a name that will subsume nonbeing in its being. The whole problem will then be to accord a being to nonbeing—that's what Parmenides forbids. And, to accord a being to nonbeing, calling it "nonbeing" is not a way out of the conundrum because so long as nonbeing is only called "nonbeing" Parmenides is right. So the method will be to come up with an additional name, and to say "addition" is to say "a list"—the list of what the addition is an addition to. What is it in the *Sophist*? It's the list of what Plato calls "the greatest kinds" or Ideas. There are four of them, namely: being, motion, rest, and the same.

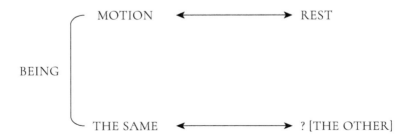

Here we naturally find the basic Parmenidean theme as the first greatest Idea: nonbeing will appear under the name "the Other." The technique—or the ingenious trick—is supplementation. There is actually no direct discussion of Parmenides's theory. What I mean by this is that there's no affirmation, *without a signifying supplement*, that nonbeing is. There is an additional signifier, "the Other," about which it can be said that, through it, a being of nonbeing can be thought, a certain being of nonbeing can be named and thought. Therefore, strictly speaking, nonbeing is, but it is "in addition." So an ambiguity will remain, an undecidable ambiguity as to whether the nonbeing Plato talks about under the additional name of "Other" is really the same as the one Parmenides talks about under the name of "nonbeing." The ambiguity about this is undeniable. What's more, when dealing with the details of Parmenides's thinking, Plato constantly says "in a way," "in some respect," or "from a certain point of view," thus letting doubt remain as to the enigma that is the parricide, because it is carried out not by means of something less but by means of something more. The parricide isn't a metaphor for that something that once was and is no more. No! We are told that this "something more" partly lifts the prohibition. That's the first aspect of the enigma. The parricide is ultimately an additional "no," a "no" to the Law of the Father, but this "no" [*non*] is actually a "name" [*nom*]. The "no" is a "name." But Plato's "no" is absolutely maintained in the strictest sense: he did indeed attack the πατρικὸς λόγος [*patrikos logos*]. As for the second aspect of the enigma, something remains or may possibly remain—we'll never know—of what Parmenides in fact called "nonbeing."

**Someone in the back of the room interrupts:** *But isn't it a "name" in the sense that it differs from memory?*

What is memory here? It's the Parmenidean filiation. So, in effect, the signifier "Other" isn't part of it. It is therefore necessarily ambiguous compared with what you call memory, which is the πατρικὸς λόγος [*patrikos logos*]. This could also be put another way: this Other is not in the paternal declaration. It lifts its basic prohibition. Plato *does* say that: this Other lifts the basic Parmenidean prohibition, which is "Do not take the path of nonbeing." If I say "the Other," I am taking that path, Plato tells us, because if I say, for example, that motion is "Other than being," then in a certain sense, as Other than being, it *is* not.

---

Ultimately, to lift the prohibition, you have to, as it were, give a nickname to the forbidden path, the path of nonbeing, or rename it another way—Other-wise, so to speak! So, in the end, how is the enigma presented? What, in actual fact, does Plato say that is different from what Parmenides says? What is this difference, so crucial in his own eyes that for him it's the entry into obsolescence of the πατρικὸς λόγος [*patrikos logos*], that is, the end of the paternal declaration? And yet, what does he tell us that's different? Essentially: to really think being, you have to name "nonbeing" and by naming it, accord it a being. Whereas Parmenides already told us that to think being, you have to name nonbeing, explicitly, since forbidding the path of nonbeing was constitutive of the relationship between thinking and being. So it can be argued (and this is what's enigmatic about this dramatized break whose meaning we're trying to uncover) that nothing happened, in the end, since the relationship in the triad—being, nonbeing, thinking—is maintained. What is conceived of as a prohibition by Parmenides is conceived of as a permission by Plato. That's it. The prohibition named by Parmenides as "Do not take the path of nonbeing" is conceived of by Plato as "I am taking the path of nonbeing; you are allowed to take the path of nonbeing." Except that, for the prohibition to change into permission, the name has to be changed, not the path.

Where it used to be called "nonbeing" it now has to be called something else. But the fact remains that something of the original name has not, strictly speaking, been done away with. What hasn't been done away with is the fact that there's a knot tying together thinking, being, and nonbeing. The only difference is there was a knot in the figure of prohibition (two paths and a crossroads) while here there's a knot in the figure of permission. But I maintain that it's the same knot. By being an enigma because it's simultaneously conceived of as a radical break, this identity shows us what the Parmenidean act of foundation really was. And because Plato has to repeat it—while in fact switching to something else—he shows us the original invariant of the Parmenidean foundation, that is to say, what founded philosophy.

---

Parmenides *initiated* philosophy, under conditions that are still being investigated, not by deciding between being and nonbeing but by declaring, in his own terminology, a *matheme*, the absolutely first matheme in philosophy, which Plato, Plato's refutation, reiterates. It's in this sense that he can be considered as the founder: this matheme states that being, nonbeing, and thinking are in a Borromean relationship. There's a Borromean knot, which is to say that each of them is bound to the other by the third one. Except, as we know, there are many ways of thinking the consistency of the Borromean relationship. What does Parmenides say? "Thinking is linked to being only insofar as it prohibits nonbeing." This is one possible formulation of the Borromean nature of the three components: thinking is linked to being only insofar as nonbeing is prohibited. Plato, on the other hand, provides a completely different formulation of it: thinking is linked to being only insofar as it is also linked to nonbeing. This now sheds light on Aristotle's critique of Parmenides, when he gives him credit for having dared to have two principles.

You remember, don't you? Assuming that being is, said Aristotle, there's nothing that can be gleaned from it. But it's not as simple as that, because Parmenides is both outside history and an exception to it. That was the matrix. Which means that, for Aristotle, thinking is linked to being *and* to nonbeing; there are two principles, and Parmenides had glimpsed this truth of the Two. So for Aristotle the formulation of the knot is as follows: thinking is tied to being and nonbeing. That's his own doctrine. These are three formulations, shall we say, three approaches to the Borromean nature of the knot. Parmenides: Being is linked to thinking provided that nonbeing is prohibited. Plato: Thinking is linked to being only to the extent that there is a being of nonbeing. Aristotle: Thinking is linked to both being and nonbeing.

Parmenides is the founder of the theory, that of the Borromean nature of the relationship between being, nonbeing, and thinking. Hence the question: why did this foundation take the form of *this* description of the knot and not another? Or why was the foundation of the recognition of the Borromean nature of the thinking/being/nonbeing relationship formulated, for the first time, originally with Parmenides, in the following form: "Thinking is linked to being only to the extent that it prohibits nonbeing"?

Our investigation is becoming clearer, then, and it is this investigation that will lead us to philosophy's conditions. Parmenides linked together and created this type of knot, and philosophy, in its development, is historically, even historically, the discontinuous process of the repetition of this knot. It's in this sense that Parmenides is the founder. On the other hand, though, he provided an unusual version of it: he proposed it only via the prohibition of nonbeing. Why is it this form that's foundational? A form within which Plato and Aristotle will thereafter operate. Because, I must stress, neither Plato nor Aristotle will untie the knot; they'll just describe it differently. The knot remains, but the name of the knot, its process, changes. So why did the Parmenidean form turn out to be foundational of philosophy?

This is the question I'll devote the next session to. Here's a clue, however, so as not to overdramatize things: it's because the schema underlying this description of the knot is *reductio ad absurdum*, and because it's the demonstrative, discursive figure of *reductio ad absurdum* that underpins not the invention of the knot as such but the possibility of its original figure. And that's how we'll turn to the latent presence of mathematics in all this.

# Session 7

## December 10, 1985

What Parmenides institutes, the way he determines his philosophy, can't be summed up in a theory. What defines Parmenides, his very essence, is not that he established that "being is being," let alone that "being is One," or that "being is unique," or that "there is nothing but being." No! No theory of that kind takes his full measure. Instead, what he institutes is a *knot*—the knot of thinking, being, and nonbeing—and this, strictly speaking, cannot be summed up in a theory, unless the knot is untied. That's the essence of Parmenides's operation: the tying of the knot of thinking, being, and nonbeing. It's important to understand all the subtlety of the Parmenidean decision—it is not a matter of saying "There is a knot," or "There is a knot of thinking, being, and nonbeing." No! *We're* the ones who say that—in our obligatory dissection of the "knot," in our retrospective description of it, in which we've been guided by Plato and Aristotle. What needs to be understood is that Parmenides *ties* the knot. But tying a knot is very different from just saying that there is one. Besides, does he really say there's one? Doesn't he even think the opposite? His decision doesn't consist in suggesting that they're tied together but rather in tying the knot: so it's a decision-making operation, not a saying. And he is acutely aware of this: Parmenides calls the sayings or the statements—such as "being is this, that, motionless, etc."—*signs*.

These, he says, are signs referring to being, to thinking, and so on. They *signify* the operation, but none of them *is* an operation. This is not even a theory but a use of the *signified* to describe what is said about being. A crucial use. Why? Because it allows us to distinguish the operation from the signs. The operation is the tying of the knot, and the signs are only particular processes that accompany the operation and yield partial, fragmentary results. Whenever we try to summarize Parmenides's thinking in one statement or another, we should remember his rule. When we attempt to *describe* the operation, we're not performing the operation itself, which alone is really foundational and alone is the Parmenidean decision. This explains the critical oscillation in history—with Hegel, with Nietzsche—between the near-unanimous recognition of Parmenides's greatness as the founder, on the one hand, and, on the other, the idea that his theory is patently absurd. On the one hand, he's the tremendous Parmenides, the great Parmenides; and, on the other, to think that "being is One," strictly motionless, without difference, without multiplicity, without change, and so on, actually gives nothing to be thought. What a symptom it is, this close proximity, this conjunction, between the recognition of the founder's greatness and the denunciation of the theory's absurdity! A theory that's usually summarized as "Only being is, and it is One." This is what eradicates any thinking of difference, motion, multiplicity, and so on. But in reality, this oscillation reflects the fact that the foundation is the tying of the knot and that, on the contrary, the theory that's supposedly absurd simply involves isolating a sign. Indeed, it is surprising that the most frequently isolated sign should be "Being is One," which hardly even appears in Parmenides's text, or at any rate in the text as it has come down to us. The misjudgment of the signs—of the explicit statements, the summary in statements—is also shown by the fact that, ultimately, the usual way Parmenides is summed up isn't even one of Parmenides's real, written signs, quite simply because isolating a sign renders the operation invisible. No wonder, then, that in the end a sign is ultimately *made up*. As a result, the operation gets lost. But let's go back, prior to the signs, to Parmenides's decision: what he instituted was the knotting together of thinking, being, and nonbeing in a unique form.

**Someone asks:** *When you say that isolating a sign conceals the operation, isn't that true for the father, the founder himself, for Parmenides himself? Isn't there a necessity, a kind of inevitability, about the fact that merely saying it conceals the essence of what is said?*

That might be overgeneralizing a bit. In line with your question, let me read the beginning of Fragment 8:

> Only one tale is left of the way:
> that it is: (215)

Just as an aside: this "that it is" is one of the great mysteries of Parmenides's text, which doesn't say "that being is" but "that it is": ὡς ἔστιν [*hōs estin*]. It's in the French translation that the pronominal "*il*" [it] was added; literally, it reads: "namely, is."[1] This goes to show that, even here, Parmenides's text cannot be summed up in the theory "Being is," which Parmenides almost always avoids in the Greek text. He writes ὡς ἔστιν [*hōs estin*], not τὸ εἶναι ἐστιν [*to einai estin*].

Parmenides goes on:

> and on this are posted
> very many signs; that what-is is ungenerated and imperishable,
> a whole of one kind, unperturbed and complete.
> Never was it, nor shall it be, since it now *is*, all together,
> one [*this is the only time that the word "one" is mentioned*], continuous.
>    (215–217)

The fact that there's always a conflict between the operation and the sayings can be considered as a contradiction, actually. But it was reflected on by Parmenides himself. He regarded all the statements about the ungenerated, the imperishable, the One, etc. as a use of signs through which the essence of his theory, or his utterance, or his saying [*dire*], was expressed, but he didn't claim that any of these signs exhausted this saying or truly restored its essential gesture. We should at least not underestimate Parmenides's awareness of the necessary distinction between the enunciative signs, through which the operation takes place, and the operation itself. Nevertheless, it's true that the knotting together of thinking, being, and nonbeing is unique, occurring in a form that I'd summarize as follows: for being to summon thought to think it, there must be a decision—the decision to prohibit the way of nonbeing. That is essentially the protocol in which Parmenides declares the knotting. The characteristics of this protocol are of two types. What are they?

The first is that nonbeing is how thinking and being are linked to each other. They're linked to each other since there is no guarantee that it is really by being that thinking is called into play other than by forbidding the path of nonbeing. Therefore, nonbeing is indeed what makes it possible to say how thinking and being are linked to each other. That's the first type.

The second is that what's involved here is a prohibition. Or an imperative, a negative imperative: "Don't do that!" Let's take a closer look at this: nonbeing is how thinking and being are linked to each other. Yes, but be careful: this doesn't mean that nonbeing becomes an object for thought. Thinking is not simultaneously linked to being and nonbeing. Parmenides doesn't say that. Rather, he says: the consistency of being of thought is only achieved by prohibiting nonbeing, prohibiting the way of nonbeing. Nonbeing is knotted together with the other two—thinking and being—but remains unthinkable: it is not a given for thought. So what is the real of nonbeing? Or what is prohibited here? It's clear that there is a paradox involved in prohibiting thought from thinking what is itself unthinkable. Why must the thinking of nonbeing be prohibited, given that there is no thinking of it? Simply because "nonbeing" is a *name*. Because it may be that nonbeing is not, but the *name* "not-being" *is*. It's absolutely impossible to get out of this dialectic without the mediation of language. So it will have to be declared that nonbeing is *a pure name* and that, strictly speaking, the prohibition is on a name. It's the path indicated not by nonbeing, which is not, but by the *name* "nonbeing," that must be avoided. What will be forbidden is a name.

Let me read you a passage from Fragment 8, around two-thirds of the way through it [36–41]:

> For nothing else <either> is nor shall be
> beside what-is, since Fate shackled it
> to be whole and unmoved. In relation to this have all things been
>     named,
> which mortals established, trusting them to be true:
> coming to be and perishing, being and not being,
> changing place and exchanging bright color.
>     (217–219)

In this passage, Parmenides says that, since nothing is "beside what-is"—therefore, that nonbeing is not—everything associated with nonbeing is just a name. Naturally, he extends this strict nominalism to all the concepts that in his opinion derive from nonbeing, such as birth, death, change, multiplicity, etc. All such things, for Parmenides, are only thinkable if nonbeing is thought. Since there is no reason to think it, the upshot is that, when you speak about those things, you're only saying names, empty names. But of course, what he's talking about here—"all things ... which mortals have established ... coming to be and perishing ... changing place, and exchanging bright color"—what is it? It's experience, immediate, sensory experience. So nonbeing is just the name in which experience is recapitulated. And its foreclosure—Parmenides's imperative—shows us that the order of thought, νοεῖν [*noein*], has nothing to do with that of experience. This is what would have been called, following Althusser, the "epistemological break," or the radical rupture with the immediacy of experience and the system of names that goes with it. The gesture here will then be to reject experience via its system of names, the cornerstone of which is nonbeing. Therefore, to avoid the path of nonbeing essentially means to reject experience so as to establish thinking as something separate from the field of names where experience is manifested. It could not be any clearer. And what's foundational is that it brings forth the order of thought in its heterogeneity with respect to experience. Philosophy begins when we break with experience.

However, there is still a very serious problem, which has to do with names: we can admit that nonbeing is just a name, but Parmenides says that the way opened up by this name, "nonbeing," the way that must be avoided, the way that must not be taken, also happens to be unnamable. Hence, *nameless*.

Thus, in Fragment 2, lines 6–7:

> neither could you know nonbeing [*it is impracticable, he says*] nor could you express it. (Badiou's translation)

Or, in Graham's translation:

> For neither could you know what is not (for it cannot be accomplished),
> nor could you declare it [or: point it out].[2] (213)

And especially this altogether crucial passage from Fragment 8, lines 16–18:

> . . . is or is not[3]. It is therefore decided as a necessity that the other way [*"is not"*[4]] is a nameless unthinkability [*One might say an anonymous unthinkability.*] Indeed, it is not the road of truth, and so only the other one proposes itself and is truth. (Badiou's translation)

Or, in Graham's translation:

> . . . it is or it is not. Thus the decision is made, as is necessary, to leave the one way unthought, unnamed—for it is not a true way—the other to be and to be true. (217)

The problem is as follows: nonbeing is just a name, whereby it eliminates, prohibits, the naming system of experience, but, on the other hand, what nonbeing, the word, the pure name, i.e., experience and its naming system, controls is actually unnamable, nameless. So, at this point in our investigation, the situation is as follows: nonbeing is just a name and it has no name; it is just a name and it is unnamable; it is just a name and it is nameless. That nonbeing is at once a pure name and something nameless needs to be explained. And to explain it, we need to think in terms of a split in naming, that is, an ambiguity as to what has a name and what doesn't have one. In Parmenides's text, being a name and being unnamable, or nameless, operates in two distinct regimes of the question of names, where both terms will find their meaning. The text is not a demonstrative one but rather a text of prophetic utterance, hence of ambiguity.

This, too, will be Parmenides's absolutely foundational gesture, the distinction between two regimes of language. Hence the dialectic: in one of them, nonbeing is a name, and in the other, it is unnamable. The first regime is language adequate to thinking—I'm using "thinking" [rather than "thought"] because it's νοεῖν [*noein*] that's used, not νοῦς [*nous*]. We, too, should use the gerund: language adequate to *thinking*—here, the only name is that of being. In this regime, there is no name except that of being, and nonbeing cannot be expressed in words, which means that if you express nonbeing in words, you're no longer thinking. You express it all the same, however, and this will involve the second regime of language, which concerns experience, what mortals imagine or dream about. So, in the naming regime of experience, there's a name of nonbeing in the sense that there is nothing *but* the name, that is to say, nonbeing is just a name. And what is just a name, like nonbeing—what therefore operates in the regime of the language of experience—*that*, from the standpoint of the regime of language related to thinking, is unnamable. In other words, when language is related to thinking, there is no name for what is just a name. Because, as such, a name gives nothing to be thought. It may give something to be experienced, but it gives nothing to be thought. And therefore, in this regime of language related to thinking, that is, to being, there is no name of the name, there is no name of the pure name. Nonbeing is indeed a pure name in the sense of the language of experience, and, as a result, it is unnamable insofar as what is just a pure name is not nameable *in truth*.

All the foregoing boils down to a famous statement of Lacan's—and of Wittgenstein's: there is no metalanguage. There is no name for names. There is one for being but not for names. By contrast, in the regime of experience, there are nothing but names. Specifically, as there are nothing but names, they can't be named, named in thought. So, if you want to think, a prohibition has to be imposed on whatever is just a name. And what is prohibited is nonbeing, since it represents everything that is just a pure name. This solves our original problem: nonbeing has indeed never been thought. It is inherently unthinkable, but there is a naming regime in which "its" pure name, this pure name, does exist. Therefore, the prohibition by which the language of thinking is purified consists in prohibiting this name.

---

Thus, Parmenides's decision fundamentally establishes a new regime of language and splits or divides something in the language. This foundation, this splitting, or this division, involves prohibiting names, and specifically the name "nonbeing," the cornerstone of the language of experience. What is thus restricted—because it is also an operation of restriction, of restriction in the order of language—results from an inner division of language that prohibits the experiential regime of the pure name. And this restriction amounts to an *opening* of thinking.

There is no more profound idea in Parmenides's conception than this: thinking begins by restricting language, not by opening it up, forcing it, or expanding its limits. The capacity for thinking, or its organic linkage with being, establishes a primitive formalization (let's call it that; I think the term is justified) prohibiting a whole regime of language, which the word "nonbeing" crystallizes, not just with respect to itself but with respect to its path. It is indeed this whole regime of language that is prohibited by a formalizing operation, in the original or primary sense of the term: not "formalizing" in the symbolic and ideographic sense but precisely in the sense of *limiting* language by prohibiting what is only a regime of the pure name. It is then in this new regime of language, complicated by limitation, that Parmenides ties his distinctive knot of being, thinking, and nonbeing, in a form that's that of the law. This is of the utmost importance: the formalization is what makes it possible to express the knot in the form of a law. Because once you've formalized, you can distinguish between two regimes of language: the one that's been divided and limited, and the one that has not. The law will state that it is not permissible to conflate the naming regime of nonbeing—which is the regime of the pure name—with the naming regime of being—which is that of thinking.

---

This is the key point of Fragment 6, which has attracted much critical commentary because it gave the impression that there were not two ways but three. Listen very carefully to this passage:

> It is right to say and to think that what-is is, for being is [or: it is
>     for being],
> and nothing is not. These things I bid you consider.
> From this first way of inquiry <I withhold> you,
> but then from this one, which mortals knowing nothing
> wander, two-headed. For helplessness in their
> breasts directs a wandering mind; and they are borne
> both deaf and blind, dazed, undiscerning tribes,
> by whom to be and not to be are thought to be the same
> and not the same, and the path of all is backward-turning.

Two prohibitions appear in this fragment: "From this first way of inquiry <I withhold> you, but then from this one [. . .]"

What is the meaning of this double prohibition? I propose to explain it on the basis of the first one, which is a formalizing prohibition: "I bid you consider that it is necessary to say and to think that what-is is"—λέγειν [*legein*] and νοεῖν [*noein*]—since saying and thinking are absolutely interrelated. It is necessary to both say and think.

**Someone asks:** *Is the prohibition an order?*

Yes! The first prohibition is an order not to express nothingness. Then comes a second imperative: not to conflate the two orders thus distinguished. The naming regime of being must be distinguished from the naming regime of nonbeing: that's the formalizing gesture. But within the space of this formalization, you shouldn't think you can have it both ways. This is in effect why there would seem to be a third way, but it isn't really one: it is simply forbidden to go back on the formalization by thinking that the original division is compatible with a simultaneous use of both these orders. First, there's the imperative of limitation—that's the formalizing gesture: the regime of the language of being that is the regime of thinking must absolutely be distinguished from the regime of pure names, from the regime of nonbeing—and, second, there's the law stipulating that the distinction be maintained: *From now on, you must stay within the limits.* You must first limit, then consider what is limited to be the entire site of thought. You must not be "two-headed," as it were. What does "two-headed" mean? People who are deaf and blind, dazed, and undiscerning are the ones "by whom to be and not to be are thought to be the same and not the same." What does Parmenides tell us? He tells us very strictly: the imperative of the formalization, of the separation between two diametrically opposed uses of names, must be obeyed, because, otherwise, we will use the pure name, that is, what is unnamable, from the standpoint of the formalized regime. The imperative must be obeyed because the formalization is *the entire site* of thought.

Ultimately, the knot of being, thinking, and nonbeing, Parmenides's Borromean knotting, is as follows: only within a restrictive formalization, in which certain words or names have been expressly excluded, is it possible to say with absolute certainty that being is really what thought thinks. Thus, what Parmenides institutes is the end of the continuum of language; it's the idea that *thinking, with regard to language, is a restricted action.*[5]

My last point will be to return to and draw some conclusions about the positions Plato and Aristotle take on the crux of the Parmenidean foundation. They propose what I call two other *codings* of the same knot. What is the coding of a knot? When is there one? There is a coding of a knot, a knot with three strands, when the One and the Two come into play, and not just the Three. In its abstract or ideal form, the Borromean knot is the pure Three, so to speak. It's the pure Three because two of its components, its strands, are knotted together only by the third one. Each of the strands, from this strict point of view, is indistinguishable from the others. What we know about each one is that it is linked to each of the other two only by the third one. You can clearly see the essential indistinguishability here: it's the pure Three. Nothing individually distinguishes one strand from the others. This is indeed the problem in Lacan's presentation of the Borromean knot between the real, the symbolic, and the imaginary: each strand, in turn, can be any one of the three orders. Nor does anything distinguish their relationship: they are linked only by the third one. There's no inherent relationship between any two of them. To have one, you have to cut the third. But what happens if you cut the third? Well, a separation happens: two are separate, precisely because there's no relationship between them. So there is only the Three in the ideally conceived Borromean knot. You can see in what sense I say this. There is no One, in the sense of the thinkable specification of each of the three components. Nor is there any Two, if what is meant by Two is the inherent connection between any two of the components. So I call such a structure "coding," a descriptive protocol into which the One and the Two are reintroduced—that is to say, the additional conditions, added to the strict three-way relationship, which make it possible to differentiate the One or the Two. This is a completely different relationship from that of being linked by the third one. For example, take a knot made up of three strands, each distinguished by a color—a blue one, a red one, and a yellow one. To say that this one's the blue one, that one's the yellow one, and the third one's the red one is to reintroduce the One. If I put two yellow ones and a red one together, I could speak of the two of the same color. That would be the Two. But to get what I call the "coding" of a knot, those two would have to be linked together by the third one; the knot would have to be Borromean.

So, is there a coding with Parmenides? Yes, very clearly! There is one: being and thinking, he says, are "the same." This term, "the same," is both thinking and being taken individually, and counted-as-two. It is therefore a coding element. But we know very well that, in actual fact, it's both a coding element and a knotting element, because Parmenides only says they're "the same" insofar as nonbeing is prohibited—so they'll remain linked together by the third term anyway. This is so obvious that he will never say: nonbeing and thinking are the same. No, he'll never say that!

So there's a knotting and a coding—or even better, every knotting is in the context of a coding, unless you do the pure mathematics of the Borromean knot, i.e., its ontology. If you do that, you'll have the "pure Three," with the three components having an inherently indistinguishable nature. Once you're no longer in that pure ontological context, there is always coding. Indeed, it's a sign of the absence of a pure ontological structure. In the singular field of the Borromean structure, you must always be attentive to the coding procedure in which the Borromean nature of that structure appears. There is always the One and the Two—it's never the pure Three, except in the mathematics of knots. So there is a Parmenidean coding, and we'll come back to the reason for *that* coding. A coding, then, that, as regards the One, clearly assigns the One to nonbeing, necessarily. It is to it, nonbeing, that the One is assigned: it has the particular One of being *a pure name*, which is not the case with thinking and being. And because it's a pure name, nonbeing is prohibited. But the fact that it's prohibited does not detract from the distinction, afforded it by the One, of being *a pure name*. As for the One, there is nonbeing, and as for the Two, there's a specific relationship between thinking and being: "the same." The Parmenidean coding of this Borromean structure consists in assigning the One to nonbeing, in the form of *the pure name*, and in thinking the Two of thinking and being.

---

What I claim, then, is that Plato and Aristotle propose different codings. They weren't interested, so to speak, in the same One, or the same Two, the underlying Three being invariable. What was Plato interested in? The distinction between thinking and being. It's this that triggers a completely different coding. The Parmenidean relationship between thinking and being is "the same." So, in a way, it's the lack of distinction between thinking and being that grounds their relationship to each other. Because, together, they are indistinguishable. But they are both distinguishable from nonbeing. Now, what Plato is interested in is not the lack of distinction between thinking and being but rather the *distinction* between them. He doesn't ask "How is it that being is what thinking thinks?" (that's Parmenides's question); Plato instead asks how it is that thinking is the thinking of being. It appears to be the same question, but it isn't, because the emphasis shifts, quite simply, from being to thinking. The sufficient guarantee isn't sought in the same place. Indeed, Plato will require that nonbeing be *renamed*. That's the solution to his problem: *renaming* nonbeing. Where should it be renamed, though? Well, in the field of language that's the field of thinking, in the other field of the two regimes of language. If I want to solve this problem, he'll say, I have to rename nonbeing in the conceptual regime, the regime of truth. So he'll maintain that there is a name of the name. To Parmenides, who claimed that anything that circulates in the regime of experiential language is unnamable, unnamable in the regime of thought, Plato will reply: no, I can rename it! He won't transfer it as is, naturally. He won't call it "nonbeing." He'll rename it and call it "the Other." Plato isn't opposed to the abandonment of nonbeing as such in the register of experience. He won't say, for example, that there's an *idea* of nonbeing but rather that there's an *idea* of the Other, "idea" being what belongs to the register of the language of thought. And the idea of the Other is a renaming in thought of nonbeing, hence a name of the pure name.

**Someone asks:** *Is there a prohibition for Plato?*

For Plato, it is still forbidden for nonbeing to be, absolutely. The word "nonbeing" will not, as such, migrate into the other language status. But the essence of Plato's move is that every prohibition presupposes a more fundamental permission. More fundamental than the prohibition. Such a permission means having to think the prohibition. The prohibition can remain, but it has to be thought. And to think it, you have to be able to formulate what is prohibited, even if it's a name, in the conceptual order of naming. Plato codes things differently: there is a different coding because he names the prohibition. But to name the prohibition, since it's the prohibition of a name, there has to be a name of this name, something that Parmenides in fact prohibited. To allow it, in Plato's eyes, is much more fundamental than to prohibit it. Thus, by naming the prohibition, by designating a name of the name, Plato will think the relationship, the Two of thinking and nonbeing. In other words, the Two of thinking is in this way truly established. It is therefore a different coding, a fundamentally different coding.

As for Aristotle, he proposes yet another one. What *he's* interested in is distinguishing between being and nonbeing, but distinguishing between them because this distinction is itself a relationship in the doctrine of the many meanings of being, which is absolutely fundamental, originary: "It is said in many ways." However, in actual fact, being and nonbeing are for Aristotle only "sayings in many ways" of being itself. Besides, he thinks nonbeing as a physicist, as a Greek, that is, someone who holds that all of being is Nature. For him, nonbeing, if it's not just a word, is matter; it's absolute undifferentiation. It's this meaning of being that is the unthinkability of being, this level of being that is indeed its unthinkability but that nonetheless does not cease to be. Therefore, Aristotelian nonbeing is pre-substantial being, i.e., indiscernible, unthinkable, and unsayable. But as indiscernible and unsayable, it is a mode of being. It is the dual relationship of being and nonbeing, the Two of being and nonbeing, in the mode of the One of being. In the mode of the One of being, that is to say, in the mode of the many meanings of the word "is." And, on the basis of this coding, he will of course criticize the earlier codings. This is what immediately places us in a context of ongoing genesis.

I should perhaps come to a provisional conclusion now.

What can be said today about Parmenides's coding? Is there a connection between the inception of the knotting and the particularity of the coding? Did the universality of the knotting have to emerge within the particularity of the coding? Using a regressive method first, we saw that, although the knotting remained the same, Plato and Aristotle proposed different codings. They each proposed a "better" coding to think the knotting. But both of them showed us that other codings are possible under the hypothesis of the knotting, coded by Parmenides. In this way, the Parmenidean coding founds philosophy as a new regime of discourse, because it is authorized by the Borromean knotting. But that doesn't get us very far, as we know. We're going to have change methods and test a different hypothesis.

Let me suggest three to you. Here they are. First, Heidegger's: the relationship between coding and knotting in Parmenides is arbitrary. There is no system of reasons necessary for this coding, which is only due to Parmenides's particular genius. The second hypothesis is Hegel's: the coding is necessary, since the knotting can express only this coding. This is Hegel's hypothesis of the beginning: the coding is deduced from the knotting. As for the third hypothesis, it's mine: this knotting is assignable to a point of exteriority, and I will argue that there's a relative heteronomy between the coding and the knotting.

# Session 8

## January 14, 1986

Last time, I said that the *knotting together* of the three components—being, nonbeing, and thinking—must be Borromean, that is, must be an instance of the pure Three: any two components are linked together by the third. And that the *coding* of this knot, i.e., what introduces the One or the Two into it (the self-identity of one of the components or the particular relationship between two components), can vary: Parmenides's, Plato's, and Aristotle's codings differ from one another. So is there a connection, or none at all, between what Parmenides proposed about the knot of being, nonbeing, and thinking—thus deciding for philosophy—and the particular coding that he chose? Now *that's* a well-formulated origin question, even if I do seem to be patting myself on the back! It's a well-formulated origin question because it's specific. It doesn't speculate on the origins of the origin! No, it identifies a proposition, a certain coding of this proposition, and asks whether the connection between the proposition and its coding is arbitrary or not. So we could vary the form of the question. We could ask, for example: couldn't Plato's coding, too, have been foundational? Or even Aristotle's? And ultimately, making our way through the Parmenidean foundation, we'd get to the question: Is there something necessarily primary about the coding of the original Borromean proposition? Does it shed light on philosophy's *conditions*? On the conditions of emergence of this singular discourse that was historicized as philosophy?

A first answer would be as follows: if we're dealing with a Borromean proposition—the idea that being, nonbeing, and thinking are linked together by the Three—what's most originary is what's most closely related to the proposition of the Three. We could say: the originary purity of the proposition, that is, what establishes it as such, is precisely that it's the proposition of the knot, of the Borromean nature of the relationship between being, nonbeing, and thinking, hence of what is least at variance with, least impacted by, the code. We could have the following conception of the history of philosophy: the proposition of the knot is followed by the history of the codings, i.e., the work on the singularizations and the dualities, and therefore the implementation, actually, of a dialectic—that of the Borromean nature of the knot and the coding. Hence the temptation to assume that, with Parmenides, we're dealing with a pure, or quasi-pure, form (since, as I said last time, the pure form is only ever the mathematical concept of the Borromean knot), a quasi-pure form of the Borromean proposition, after which the dialectical work of coding began with Plato and Aristotle, and has continued right up to our contemporaries. That's the theory that deals with the purity of the origin.

That there was originally purity, and that historicity and the dialectic tainted it by interpretative saturation, or by sedimentation of the codings, and that this then led to a call for the return to purity, by abandoning the codings, by un-sedimenting, by restoring the original proposition, by sticking to the purely Borromean—namely, Parmenides—is precisely what Heidegger claims. The best we can hope for is to finally hear Parmenides again. So let's examine the arguments in favor of this theory, using the codes of the Two.

First, let's take the relationship between being and nonbeing. If you look at Parmenides's coded relationships, the one between being and nonbeing is actually a non-relationship. It's impossible to code any lower, so to speak. It's impossible to code any lower than what Parmenides codes as the relationship between being and nonbeing, since it is exclusion or radical heterogeneity, not even—I repeat—in the form of the unity of contraries but in the form of absolute difference. The fullness of the real, on the one hand, as Parmenides thinks or attempts to think it, and the absolute transparency of an empty signifier, on the other. So it's the paradigm of non-relationship. And it has remained so ever since. We can therefore argue that, in this case, the coding is practically a non-coding, that is to say, this dual relationship is precisely the one that Borromeanism assumes, i.e., that being and nonbeing are linked together only by the third component but that, intrinsically, they aren't linked together at all. In other words, there is no genuine Two, in the sense of relationship. This is the absolutely minimal coding.

If we take being and thinking now, it's not a relationship either, strictly speaking, since they are indistinguishable from each other. For a reason similar to the one that affects the relationship between being and nonbeing, thinking and being have no relationship other than being "the same," but the same is not a relationship because no Two is thinkable in it as distinct from the other. For there to be a relationship, the Two of the relationship has to be thought. But if I say to you: "They're the same, thinking and being are the same," you aren't thinking the relationship. You're thinking an identity, you're thinking the One—the One that impacts the Borromean Three, it's true!—but, let's not forget, that's not exactly our problem. Our problem is whether there's a relationship or not. And as Leibniz emphatically pointed out, indistinguishability does not constitute a relationship because it establishes no Two. So, once again, we can say that the coding is really minimal.

Finally, if we turn to the relationship between thinking and nonbeing—our third relationship—there isn't one either. There isn't one either, because Parmenides says that nonbeing is impossible to think. That's the very content of the prohibition. Due to the effect of the prohibition, there is no relationship: thought doesn't really think nonbeing, so nonbeing is unthought, and insofar as it is unthought there is no relationship between thinking and nonbeing.

So I can easily argue, in a reasoned and cogent way, that the Parmenidean coding is strictly minimal. The relationship between being and nonbeing is the paradigm of non-relationship; the relationship between being and thinking is a relationship of indistinguishability that does not constitute a relationship; and as for the relationship between thinking and nonbeing, it is prohibited. Ultimately, we have impossibility, indistinguishability, and heterogeneity as relationships. Pure heterogeneity: being and nonbeing; indistinguishability: being and thinking; impossibility: thinking and nonbeing. Impossibility, indistinguishability, and heterogeneity are the three minimum instances of relationship.

But let's go a step further: the differential marking itself—the fact that each component is One—is nonexistent in Parmenides. As for the Two, it's minimal, as we've just seen. But what about the One? As for the One itself, this marking preserves or maintains the rotational nature of the Borromean capability. To be One is to be a component that links the other two together, that's all. Clearly, thinking and being are indistinguishable. Thinking and that for the sake of which there is thought are "the same," Parmenides will say. Therefore, distinguishing doesn't distinguish, so to speak. Even though I have the two signifiers—"thinking" and "being"—I have no rule of attribution. So it all comes down to the being/nonbeing differential. Is there, then, in this case, an operative rule of distinction that would make it possible, on the basis of the being/nonbeing signifying difference, to singularize the One? Parmenides rules that out right away where thinking and being are concerned. So is it possible where being and nonbeing are concerned? But there's a categorical Hegelian refutation of that at the beginning of his *Logic*: if the predicates of being are all negative, if being qua being is what has no particular property, then it is indistinguishable from nonbeing. Remember that page:[1] he moves from being to nonbeing when he realizes that nothing about being, pure being, can be singularized. This is because as soon as you speak about it, you are determining it. But then it becomes a *specific* kind of being, not being as such. As a result, the determinations of being are actually non-determinations. So being and nonbeing can't be distinguished. If all the predicates of being are negative, pure being will be strictly identical to pure nonbeing because, quite obviously, all the predicates of nonbeing are negative.

Now, the problem is that, for Parmenides, all the predicates of being are also negative, in what he calls the doctrine of signs. Many signs, he tells us, allow us to define being. But how? Being is successively: ungenerated, imperishable, indivisible, motionless—in the strict sense of the word: without difference, Parmenides will say, it is always the same and in the same state—strictly homogeneous, i.e., without the variable heterogeneity of non-differentiation. Therefore, ungenerated, imperishable, indivisible, motionless, without difference, and homogeneous are all predicates that cannot distinguish it from nonbeing. Yet it would seem that Parmenides's whole foundational text is about the being/nonbeing difference:

> Never shall this prevail, that things that are not are.

The whole dynamic of the text is really driven by this differential. However, what should be maintained is that it is a signifying differential, but not a coding differential. And the fact that it's only a signifying differential is clear from the negative character of the predicates. So it is entirely possible to claim that thinking and being are indistinguishable—as Parmenides says—but that being and nonbeing are, too. Indistinguishable, although distinguished, sharply distinguished, from each other. But just because they're sharply distinguished from each other doesn't make them distinguishable. We know that desire is articulated but that it is not articulable,[2] and that being and nonbeing can be distinguished from each other but not be distinguishable. The negative character of the predicates precludes thinking that they're distinguishable. This is indeed the important point: there is no singularizing operator of distinction between being and nonbeing. What's more, it's easy to understand why not: only being *is*. So how can you expect to distinguish nonbeing? It cannot be distinguished. Of course, it may be distinguished by its name, except that it *is* its name. And its name, therefore, is not what distinguishes it. If you wanted to differentially mark nonbeing, what would you have to mark? What it is. But what is it for Parmenides? Its name. So you'd need a metalanguage: a name of this name. That's what Plato will do. He'll distinguish nonbeing by giving it a different name, by saying: there is a name of its name. "The Other" is the name of nonbeing. Parmenides would have retorted: "OK, but that's the name of a name!" "The Other" is the (other) name of the name "nonbeing." The situation is not this: nonbeing is a *name*, and being is what *is*. You won't have the instance of possible distinguishing because you'd have to distinguish a name, and, as nonbeing can't be distinguished, being can't be distinguished either, because any distinguishing would imply a difference. The Parmenidean coding doesn't allow for that kind of logic. It doesn't allow distinguishing either being or nonbeing. How can this be seen? In terms of nonbeing, because, as it's a name, there is no name of this name; and, in terms of being, because there's no difference: it is ungenerated, imperishable, indivisible, motionless, without difference. All you can do is assign predicates without predication to it, i.e., predicates that predicate of it that it's *not* this or that. But not that it *is* something.

When you come right down to it, there is hardly any Parmenidean coding, whether of the Two or the One. Parmenides is the pure Three.

**Suddenly, from the back of the room, someone comments:** *Excuse me for interrupting you, but there's something I don't understand: the introduction of the minimum. If we take your propositions one by one, they're about whether there's coding or no coding. And you introduce the minimum. I can see that this is something very important.*

There's always a coding, except in pure mathematics. So I carried out an analysis of Parmenides's method by showing, on the one hand, how he coded, and, on the other hand, how you could argue that each of the components of this coding wasn't a coding. It's this coding as quasi-non-coding that I call minimal coding.

**The same person continues:** *But first we've got to agree that the fact exists. If you like, I can put the question to you in a different way. My question may seem impertinent to you, but it's fair, in the sense that one can easily be in the position of a philosopher who takes what you just said literally: objectively, being and nonbeing is a non-relationship, and so on. So at the outset there has to be some minimum agreement on the existence of the knot. Consequently, the question arises as to how we're made aware that there's a knot. Because it would be perfectly fair to say—a philosopher (or anyone else, for that matter) couldn't be blamed for doing so—that there is in effect nothing but non-relationship. To argue as you do, it has* to have been granted or assumed to have been granted to Parmenides that there's a knot.

Yes, that has to be granted.

**The person continues:** *So the question is how we're made aware that there's a knot. In my opinion, there's something crucial about that.*

**Someone else adds:** *But regarding the question of the minimum, and the knot, couldn't we say that there's a knot as opposed to there perhaps not being one, on account of the coding? There would be a knot at the point where, for example . . . You said that nonbeing has negative characteristics, just as being does. But in a way, there's something different: in one case, thinking predicates being as without difference, and so on, while in the other case—nonbeing—it doesn't do so. From that standpoint, it would appear that there's a minimum, and that there's at least one knot, and that this makes a knot, except that there's a minimum. Because you can differentiate being and nonbeing, since in one case you could say—it's not forbidden to say so—that being is effectively without difference, homogeneous, etc., while, in connection with those conditions, those prescriptions, you couldn't say that about being.*

About *nonbeing.*

*About nonbeing, sorry!*

OK.

*That's where the knot will appear. The knot will appear through . . .*

**The previous questioner adds a restriction:** *But only if there's a circulation of meaning. That is, there's either meaning or there isn't. If you're*

*Parmenides and you say there is, then there can be meaning for you. But not for me. But it's just as legitimate and defensible for there to be meaning as for there not to be.*

Only mathematics does away with meaning.

**The other person asks:** *But isn't the knot ultimately a sort of pre-coding here?*

Careful! Let's separate out the points. First, nothing in what I said calls into question the fact that there's a knot in the sense of a knot of the Three. I simply said that it could be argued that, with Parmenides, there was, strictly speaking, no knot of the Two. That said, your question is very important, but very complicated, because it's twofold, actually. First, it asks—and I rather like your formulation—how are we *made aware* that there's a knot? That's a genuine question because, in fact, we're made aware of it by the coding, not by the knot itself. Because the transmissible metaphor of the knot is the linkage, the relationship. So, in a certain sense, it's conveyed by the Two. The reason there's always coding is that it's through coding that the fact that there's a knot is transmitted to us, even if this coding isn't one of a relationship but of a non-relationship. To think non-relationship, you have to be made aware that there is relationship. That's what you pointed out to us. I think Parmenides makes us aware that there's a knot, that there's a relationship, in the mode of the Three, that is, in the mode of the fact that the establishment of meaning implies the triangular configuration of thinking, being, and nonbeing. So we're made aware of the knot by the instance of the Three.

That was the first aspect of your question. The second was: someone can categorically deny that there's a knot even though Parmenides informs him that there is one in order for there to be meaning, and therefore philosophy. Yes, but what will establish the knot denier as a philosopher? That's the whole point that matters to us, because the figure we're concerned with isn't the hypothetical denier but rather what will establish someone who claims that there's no meaning as a philosopher. I say that what will establish him as a philosopher, as a skeptical philosopher, for example—skepticism is a figure of philosophy—is the knot itself! He'll present himself as someone who cuts the knot and who, in cutting it, says that there isn't one. Which, on account of the Borromean structure of the knot, is always possible. You may claim, says the skeptic, that these components are linked, but they aren't, since, if I cut the third one, which may not exist, or may be an artificial construction, or may be an additional guarantee from who knows where, what do I get? Complete unlinking. The skeptical figure is itself a philosophical figure *only* under the assumption of the knot. This is an old refutation, but it's in my view a very strong one. Anyone who makes philosophy out of the denial of meaning is operating under the assumption of meaning.

Now, meaning can be denied non-philosophically, which is a different matter entirely. There can be active nihilism, or non-philosophical nihilism. That is, non-what? Well, which doesn't assume meaning. But if it no longer assumes meaning, then it acknowledges that it's not transmissible. Because what immediately introduces the paradox of the skeptical philosopher is that he wants to *transmit* the figure of meaninglessness. But he naturally needs that minimum of meaning attached to the operations of transmission. He never gets out of this predicament, as we all know. The fact that he never gets out of it doesn't mean that there's not an interesting, even historically fundamental, greatness about what he claims, but he claims it under the historial assumption of meaning. That's why Parmenides was the founder. Even if he was, he was also the founder of skepticism, of course, which could be shown to be an operation on the knot—an operation that, instead of being a specific coding, is a cut. But it's a possible operation.

So it could be argued that Parmenides's coding is borderline non-coding, and that, at bottom, Parmenides's presentation is as close as possible to the pure knot—which would constitute its original form—but under the fundamental condition of not thinking of the prohibition as a relationship. Everything hinges on this: on not thinking of the prohibition (on nonbeing) as a relationship. That is to say, on not thinking what links thinking to nonbeing and is the figure of the prohibition, on not thinking of it as a relationship.

It's true, there's a weakness here, which could be put this way: the non-relationship between thinking and nonbeing is an effect. It's true that there is no relationship, but it's an effect. It's an effect of that possibly fundamental relationship, the prohibition. Plato will pounce on this weak link and say "Careful! There's a prohibition, therefore there's a relationship, because to prohibit, there's something even more fundamental than the prohibition: the recognition of what's prohibited." So he'll go so far as to claim that there is an actually fundamental relationship between thinking and nonbeing. That's why I don't think, let me repeat, that Parmenides's theory, despite some very strong arguments in its favor, is correct. I don't think that the originary nature of Parmenides's coding stems from its purity. That's not its originary essence; that doesn't determine its essence. I think, in fact, that the prohibition, or the instance of the law, is the fundamental limiting power here, and that it's a relationship.

That Parmenides's coding, as purity, is originary is Heidegger's theory: Parmenides's pronouncement is originary in the sense that it is that of a lost presence that supposedly controls us, always beneath it. This is absolutely not my approach. What will mine be, then? What will the focus be on? On the prohibition, directly, since that's where the point of impurity is. And we'll ask why, originally, it's the prohibition of nonbeing that links thinking to being, why it's this prohibition, this bar placed on the signifier "nonbeing," that is the

Parmenidean coding. It won't be the theme of purity at all. What Parmenides founds, which is evident in *this* coding, is actually a structure of transmission. A structure based on the idea of the matheme, that is to say, based on the idea of an integral transmission. But be careful! Be careful of the subtlety and complexity of this idea: I'm not saying that the Parmenidean coding was required *for* an integral transmission—that would be to confirm it as pure, as if it were the only integrally transmissible coding, the only one that transmits the proposition integrally. No! I would ask you to concentrate on what I'm about to say.

When I say that we need to seek the solution in the structure of transmission, always bear in mind that I'm not saying that the Parmenidean coding was that of the right transmission, which would then be followed by other codings of an inferior transmission. That would lead us back to the paradigm of loss, of decline. We would merely have shifted it from the proposition to the transmission. What I'm saying is that Parmenides's coding transmits the transmission, i.e., transmits a new regime of transmission. And that it was required for transmitting not only the proposition but also the fact that this proposition was connected to a new regime of transmission. *That's* what was foundational! Naturally, the foundation, in terms of its content, is the proposition itself. But what was foundational about this content was that a new *idea* of transmission, focused on the matheme, was transmitted—the idea of integral transmission.

What was abandoned—and marked a break—was the narrative form of transmission. That was Parmenides's fundamental break. His most primordial gesture, which would determine the coding itself, was to transmit the abandonment of the figure of narrative as the organic figure of mythological, legendary, religious transmission and, in so doing, to found philosophy. Because philosophy is a doctrine of being, so to speak, and this means that narrative is not its form of transmission. This is what's at stake in Parmenides's poem:

the abandonment of narrative in favor of the matheme, in favor of unambiguous transmission, as opposed to the ambiguity of all fables. As a result of which philosophy supplanted mythology. What accounts for Parmenides's absolute originarity is the Borromean proposition, of course, but the Borromean proposition not subject to transmission in the figure or form of narrative, myth, or religious fable. And, in this regard, there is a break with the narrative form only on the horizon of the matheme. That's the thesis I'll argue for, where Heidegger, it seems to me, falters.

So, you might say: "But there are narrative elements in Parmenides's poem!" Sure there are! The mythological element is still present in it, but it's strictly limited to the initiation. Remember, at the beginning: "the mares will carry you, I saw the Goddess, the Goddess told me this and that," and so on. We're dealing with an initiate, and the initiation structure is presented in a poetics of narrative. It's just that the narrative element is limited to the subject of the enunciation. The statement per se is separate from it: the narrative is assigned to the subject of the philosophical enunciation, but, when it comes to the statement, it, on the contrary, escapes the figure of narrative, and it replaces it with something else. The authority of what is said—and this is the most important point—will not be the authority of the narrative, because along the way there will be a change of law. Still, in the figure of narrative, at the beginning, the *subject* Parmenides is not authorized by himself but by *the Goddess*. That's true! And, being authorized by the Goddess, he's caught in a fictional web of guarantee. However—and this is the clear sign of the break in the text—at the same time as he's deeply embedded, a change of regime and terrain will occur: the statements will no longer be authorized by the authorization given the subject by the Goddess; their authorization will have an entirely different source. An intrinsic source, so to speak, since it is demonstrative.

Thus, the investigative framework of the solution I'll propose is as follows: narrative/matheme, two regimes of the guarantee of truth. What will constitute the break? It's that truth will no longer be trapped in the structure of the narrative, trapped in the sense of what it's guaranteed by. When you move from a validation structure in narrative to a different validation structure, you necessarily uncouple truth from empirical assumption or from belief. This is where the real inaugural condition is. It is not yet located—I must stress this—in the extranarrative authorization of the subject, of the subject of philosophy—which Socrates will embody. Since Parmenides isn't self-authorized, the myth narrative has neither disappeared nor been prohibited, but the statement breaks free from it. The statement breaks free from the narrative of the enunciation. It is in this shift from the authorization of the subject to the authority of the statement that the break, and therefore the foundation, will lie. The authorization of the subject still lies in the narrative, and the authority of the statement is on the horizon of the matheme.

Let's go one step further. If, ultimately, Parmenides must transmit the break with narrative, he must do so—and he can only do so—in a recognizable figure of that break. Now, what frees the statements from any enunciation, and is the matheme, is reasoning as such, the demonstration, the proof. In this case, it will be *reductio ad absurdum* reasoning. Or indirect reasoning, or apagogic reasoning—to take the three names recorded by history: *reductio ad absurdum* reasoning, indirect reasoning, and apagogic reasoning. The heart of the Parmenidean foundation lies in transmitting the transmission by matheme, as a break with narrative, in the form of *reductio ad absurdum* reasoning.

I'll stop here for today, so as not to open a new line of inquiry. Let me just give you an idea of what the next part of the seminar and its conclusion will be like. We'll have to prove:

- first of all, that *reductio ad absurdum* reasoning contains, in its very essence, the most radical break of all with the figure of narrative; that *reductio ad absurdum* reasoning contains, in a fundamental way, and ultimately in the only tenable way, the break with the figure of narrative. Which is something that constructive or positive reasoning only does halfway;
- second of all, that the specific function of *reductio ad absurdum* reasoning in Parmenides's text brings about the shift from the authorization of the subject to the authority of the statements;
- and, finally, we'll have to propose hypotheses about philosophy's conditions. The historical and philosophical examination of this point will be undertaken with reference to the book *The Beginnings of Greek Mathematics* by the Hungarian Árpád Szabó. See you next time!

# Session 9

## January 21, 1986

Last time, I said that the use of *reductio ad absurdum* reasoning, also called indirect or apagogic reasoning, was, in my opinion, at the heart of Parmenides's founding of philosophy. Indeed, it is the discourse mode that is exemplarily capable of breaking with the mythological foundations based on fable or narrative. This point needs to be clarified, especially since, in a classical logico-epistemological tradition, *reductio ad absurdum* reasoning is very often regarded as inferior to constructive, or direct, reasoning. Among the major contemporary movements, a whole school—the intuitionist school—explicitly rejects the use of indirect proofs, which are considered to be inconclusive. However, as regards our particular objective, given that it concerns the birth of philosophy, I maintain the opposite. I do so precisely because *reductio ad absurdum* is the exemplary vehicle for the emergence of demonstrative discourse. Here, it is what effects a break in the mode of its transmission. This point needs to be substantiated, because *reductio ad absurdum* is typically regarded as an impure, or even an ersatz, type of reasoning. Whenever it can be replaced by a constructive proof it's considered progress.

We'll only give it an exemplary value, in the break with the figure of narrative, after we've distinguished it from direct or constructive reasoning. Constructive reasoning involves deriving statements from previously accepted statements, deriving them directly, in accordance with certain rules or laws of derivation and demonstration. The matrix is as follows: if I know that Statement A necessarily implies Statement B, if I've been able to prove this, and if, in addition, I know or can prove that A is true, I will immediately conclude that B is true. This is the absolute matrix of constructive derivation. As you can see, the truth of B, in this case, is derived from a fundamental connection with Statement A, namely, A implies B, and since I know A is true, I know B is true as well. There's a connection between statements, at the heart of the matter, that underlies or justifies my moving from A to B, from the truth of A to that of B: the two statements are not unconnected. This constructive reasoning operates here in a homogeneous element, so to speak. Moving in accordance with rules from one true statement to another, constructive reasoning always appears as a kind of explicitation, teasing out, or unpacking of the consequences contained in the previous statements. That's also why it is usually considered to be superior, because it seems to convey additional information: it explains, explicates, and reveals the system of effects contained in the previous statements. With constructive reasoning, I feel not only as though I'm proving something, of course, but as though I'm operating in the homogeneous element of an explanation. That's why, for those who think objects are involved, constructive reasoning is always regarded as providing information about the objects referred to in the statements, that is, as a type of reasoning that clarifies the essential nature of the objects concerned. But this type of reasoning, with its unity of plane and its explanatory value, doesn't show, in its form, the break with narrative. Careful! I'm not saying that constructive reasoning is the same as a novel. I'm saying: it doesn't show, it doesn't convey, the break with narrative because what it has in common with it is that it doesn't call attention to the fiction. Why? Because you've got "This happened" as its permanent axiom. The fiction doesn't present itself as fiction. Now, in a way, there's the same homogeneity of plane in constructive reasoning, with no inner gap or break between the different planes, which would suggest a boundary, or a border, or an articulation, or a dialectic of the fictional and the true. And if we agree with Lacan—I'll come back to this later—that truth reveals itself in a fictional structure, that it calls for fiction, then this is no more evident in constructive reasoning than it is in narrative, as I am using "narrative" here. In narrative, there's a "this happened," which produces a homogeneous effect of reality or presents itself as a vehicle for a homogeneous effect of reality; and in constructive reasoning there's a "this is the explicitation of truth," which also presents itself as a homogeneous effect of truth. We could further say that constructive reasoning at no time calls attention to its own exterior; it asserts neither the fiction nor the falsity. It makes it seem as though it were possible to navigate, autonomously and independently, through the homogeneous element of truth by a series of moves. So it can potentially—I repeat, "potentially"; I'm not saying "essentially"—but it can potentially be regarded, outwardly or formally, as a coherent narrative, as can be seen in the final deductions in classic detective novels, which use the constructive reasoning form for purposes of fiction.

**Someone asks:** *But what is the fiction?*

The fiction is simply the external, yet necessary, element for successively establishing true propositions. The fictive element implies a fictional contrivance, an assumption within which the trajectory, whether it's the narrative or demonstrative one, operates. In both cases there's an axiom requirement, of course, and so first principles don't differentiate here, because there are also first principles in narrative, if you think about it. Every narrative is secretly axiomatic, that is to say, it begins by postulating axiomatically that it's possible that what the speaker is relating actually happened. So there's an initial axiom that is the position of the subject of enunciation as a possible position. Whether in narrative or in constructive or *reductio ad absurdum* reasoning, there are first principles. But that's not the point. The point is whether the approach calls attention to an exterior. If it doesn't—and it's this exterior that for the time being I'm calling the general element of the fiction—if it doesn't call attention to its exterior, then it comes across as either a homogeneous effect of reality—the figure of narrative—or as a homogeneous effect of truth—and then it's the figure of constructive reasoning. This, I repeat, is why constructive reasoning can pass for a coherent narrative. Just as an exercise, it would be very interesting to try to imagine a detective novel in which the detective would mainly use *reductio ad absurdum* reasoning. It would be an impossible task, because the assumptions about the world that it would involve would be exorbitant. So he'd have to use constructive reasoning and convergence of evidence, deductive verification, otherwise he'd have to make exorbitant and unfounded assumptions about the world, or about its overall coherence.

Another feature of constructive reasoning, related to the invisibility of its exterior, is that the truth strategy cannot be presented as such—the strategy, or the subject effect which, at this particular point, would indicate a statement, or isolate a statement, as the statement to be proved. Of course, you can announce at the outset that you're going to prove this statement, but that's irrelevant. The strategic effect isn't essential to the proof because the proof moves from true statement to true statement, and therefore it is characterized by what I'd call the "equivalence of truth," in exactly the same way as it's characterized by its homogeneity; it's characterized by the uniformity of truth, its monotony.

**Someone in the back of the room asks:** *Could it be said that constructive reasoning is based on the rules of proof as something internal, that is, intrinsic, to it? The proof that unfolds continuously, whereas with* reductio ad absurdum *reasoning it's not related to the rules of proof, it's something that occurs retroactively* . . .

Yes! It could be said that, intrinsically, in constructive reasoning strictly speaking, there is only something that's a fragment of continuity, that is to say, something that's characterized by a presumed equivalence of all the true statements, within which a particular path is proposed. So, in a way, constructive reasoning involves examining consequences, always, but doesn't contain any indication of purpose in itself; it doesn't identify anything as its objective. When it does, it does so extrinsically; it's not internal to the proof process itself. The proof process consists in examining consequences. And among these consequences there is what will be called the "right" consequence. But it's by looking at the explicitation of the consequences that you find what will be designated, externally, as the "right" consequence—the theorem sought, etc. Thus, once again, constructive reasoning, strictly speaking, has no anticipatory function; it does not anticipate. "Explicitation" should be opposed to "anticipation" here. This type of reasoning is explicatory, not anticipatory.

To sum up, I will ascribe three essential features to direct, or constructive, reasoning, whatever the type: first, a unity of plane with no other side, or that doesn't call attention to any other side of itself; second, the fact that the fiction, if there *is* a fiction, is therefore purely latent, never manifest; and third, it is a-strategic, that is, non-anticipatory.

---

*Reductio ad absurdum* reasoning is of a completely different type. Suppose that A is a statement I want to prove by the absurd. I must then say, first of all, that it is indeed A that I want to prove. There's a regime of decision and therefore something originally strategic. It's a type of reasoning in which there must always be an anticipation of truth by certainty: I will only use it because I'm certain that A is true. But, in terms of the proof, I have no idea whether it is or not. So, in a certain sense, I'm clueless. Truth will be determined by the anticipation of certainty. And I'm forced to anticipate it since my starting point will be a negative assumption: the way I'll anticipate the truth of A will be by assuming the truth of not-A, with the strategic idea of drawing untenable consequences from it. You can clearly see that the very essence of the assumption of the "truth" of not-A is the anticipation of the truth of A through the certainty of A. So it should be noted—we'll draw the consequences of this later on—that in the element of certainty I assume the false. This false assumption may be true in the element of truth, if my strategy fails. But in the element of certainty, I assume the false: I assume that it's not-A that is true, while, because of my anticipation of certainty, it's A that is. So what can be expected from this assumption? You can see here how the subjective-strategic regime controls the whole process. What do I expect from this assumption that's the explicit denial of my certainty? I expect consequences from it, naturally! And consequences contrary to already established truths. My anticipation of certainty consists in assuming not-A, even though I'm certain that A is true, and in drawing all the possible consequences from this, in the hopes of hitting upon or encountering a statement B that's explicitly contrary to established, previously established, truths. If, at this point, I do come across it, I will consequently reject the not-A hypothesis. And in rejecting it I will conclude that A is true, which means that I'll have equated truth with certainty. This is the essentially strategic and, so to speak, highly voluntaristic aspect of *reductio ad absurdum*, voluntaristic because it attests to an indomitable will, whereas constructive reasoning attests instead to a sense of consequence.

**Someone interrupts:** *Is it a sort of challenge?*

Yes! There's something challenging about it, and also a little daring or risky.

On the basis of this broad outline, let's examine the conceptual features of *reductio ad absurdum* now. I'll suggest five:

First of all, the strategic aspect of this configuration of thought, *reductio ad absurdum* reasoning, is totally explicit. I announce what I want to prove, and I am all the more forced to announce it inasmuch as I have to assume its opposite. Quite obviously, the fact that the strategy is explicit means that there's an element of chance and risk, because if I explain the consequences, if I assume, by denying my own certainty, a statement that I think is false—not-A—I am anticipating that I'll encounter a contradiction. Of course, to do so, I'll use the rules of inference as skillfully as possible. But the whole time I'm waiting expectantly like this I'll be operating in the element of what, from the standpoint of my certainty, is false, quite simply because the consequences of falsity can't be maintained in a regime of truth. Some of them may be true and others not, but you just don't know; there's no way to tell them apart. There's no guarantee in my original assumption that I'll encounter something explicitly contradictory since that assumption is only in the regime of denied certainty. If I'm wrong, or if my certainty is unfounded, I'll go on wandering forever, I'll never encounter a contradictory statement.

**Someone asks:** *But the failure to encounter a contradictory statement doesn't call the certainty into question. So where's the risk?*

No! It doesn't call the certainty into question, but it throws it into increasing undecidability. And so it weakens the subject of this certainty.

**The same person:** *Right! But since you can only formulate this negative proposition by anticipated certainty, nothing can be changed.*

Right.

**He goes on:** *So, strictly speaking, there's no risk . . . but how should I put this? Undecidability sets in . . . What I'm disputing is not the conclusion* that undecidability will set in but the risk involved in making it do so. If undecidability sets in, it's against the will of the person who's reasoning by the absurd, since he's convinced of his certainty. You can't both have and not have certainty. It's precisely because you have certainty that you allow yourself to assume not-A.

Yes, but be careful! If it's a strategy, it's because the person reasoning by the absurd doesn't simultaneously consider his certainty a *truth*. Let's not confuse things! If that were the case, he wouldn't attempt to prove it. He thus admits that only what is proven, even if by the absurd, is really established in the element of truth. He assumes—and that's the subjective-strategic element—he, too, assumes the difference between certainty and truth. He has certainty, but not to the point of thinking that certainty is the standard of truth. He, too, thinks that the standard of truth is ultimately provability. The tactic adopted therefore openly exposes him to the risk of endless errancy, in the course of which, moreover, the only initial subjective point of support—certainty—seems to be gradually crumbling away.

There's a striking illustration of this point: that of the Jesuit Father Saccheri, who, at the beginning of the eighteenth century, was the first to attempt to prove Euclid's fifth postulate on parallel lines by *reductio ad absurdum*. Previously, this postulate had been considered as a truth to be proved. For a long time, it was seen not as a genuine axiom but as a theorem whose proof had not yet been found. Many attempts, right from the time of the Greeks, began with a direct proof of the concept of equidistance—which was incidentally a vicious circle: there was no way out of it. It was not until Saccheri that a method of *reductio ad absurdum* was explicitly proposed: he would assume that the axiom of parallel lines was untrue and derive contradictory consequences from it. But, in so doing, he actually invented part of Lobachevskian geometry by taking a very skewed and peculiar position, which, except in rare, fleeting moments, seems not to have diminished his certainty that it was a provable axiom, whose historical destiny turned out to be an absolute risk: quite simply, that of proving the relativity—the plurality—of geometries.

**The same person as before:** *But when he begins, is it a risk for him or, on the contrary, something that will ultimately guarantee his certainty? His failure to obtain the guarantee of that certainty by placing it in the element of truth won't necessarily affect his certainty. I think that, at the beginning, the risk is more like a reverse risk, so to speak, it's sort of the way in which you have a chance to guarantee your certainty, which is always somewhat in the element of precariousness, after all. And someone who's in this element of precariousness doesn't take a risk but rather assumes a kind of self-protection. He's more geared toward that, insofar as he'll protect his precarious certainty through the guarantee of truth, not in the element of a risk that would jeopardize his original certainty. He does it to protect himself . . .*

I think you have to make a distinction between two things. When I said "risk," I didn't mean to suggest that the subject who's certain is trembling with fear when he uses *reductio ad absurdum* reasoning. Right? . . .

**Someone comments almost inaudibly:** *When I think about risk, it's in the sense that certainty has more to do with desire than with truth . . .*

**The previous commenter, interrupting:** *Risk means being in the element of desire, where precisely nothing is guaranteed. So there's a precariousness, in my view, which then, since you're entering the realm of proof—and therefore the transmissible—may well move into a register in which it's guaranteed.*

You're forgetting something: the distinctive feature of *reductio ad absurdum* is that if you're wrong, you won't know it. That's the inherent element of risk: the price you pay for being wrong will be endless errancy. It's more dangerous, I think, to risk undecidability than failure. Because failure—the proof of the falsity of the hypothesis—is, on the contrary, very reassuring. For someone whose standard of truth is provability, if they prove the contrary, they were wrong. But they were wrong in the element of certainty, actually. In other words, their mistake itself is in an element that equates certainty and truth, whereas a mistake made in *reductio ad absurdum* reasoning is deferred *ad infinitum*, with ever-increasing undecidability, and which fails to establish any security of decision. What happens then is that the only point of support—certainty—may crumble away or be confronted with permanent errancy. And you won't even have that distinct advantage of the explainable punishment for failure, for the mistake, for the false hypothesis. That's what I meant when I was talking about "risk."

**The commenter continues:** *I didn't make myself clear then. Let's leave aside whether it's a risk or not . . . What I think the motivating factor is, is precisely a certain precariousness about what you call certainty. Someone reasoning constructively has certainty, while someone reasoning by the absurd has a vulnerability in their certainty.*

Absolutely.

**The person goes on:** *And it's because of this vulnerability, I wouldn't exactly say that they take the risk but rather that they want to have access to a regime of homogeneous and transparent certainty, which someone who uses constructive reasoning has.*

I'd agree wholeheartedly with that. But only to say that, as a result, the risk factor concerns the person reasoning by the absurd, not the one reasoning constructively. And this risk comes into play in this particular instance of the possibility of errancy. Reasoning . . .

**The commenter interrupts:** *What I mean, if you don't mind, is . . . well, I want to make you say that there's something sort of pathological about certainty. Isn't there?*

In the case of *reductio ad absurdum* reasoning?

**The commenter confirms:** *Yes, in the case of* reductio ad absurdum *reasoning. It's the point of departure, as it were.*

I think there's only a pathological aspect to certainty because it's anticipatory. What you're calling pathology is only the fact that the certainty depends on anticipation.

**The commenter agrees:** *Yes, yes . . . anticipation is the symptom of pathology. Someone who has that absolute certainty of self-homogeneity will reason by what you call the absurd. And when something anticipatory appears, it's the symptom of vulnerability in the certainty, the symptom of pathology. The certainty isn't pathological because it's anticipatory: anticipation is the sign of a pathology of the certainty.*

You mean a symptom?

**Someone else comments:** *There's something extremely important about* reductio ad absurdum *reasoning: it's that this truth is no longer to the credit of whoever proves it. This truth is achieved by whoever thinks . . . It's the height of errancy: he thinks he possesses certainty about it thanks to his imagination, but nothing happens. I think that's actually what errancy is.*

**The previous commenter:** *This is a useful digression, since it's at the heart of the problem you raised in your book . . .*

Which one?

**The commenter:** *. . . or in the demonstration of the presentation of truth in Ornicar?*[1]*. That's why I'm harping a bit on this. I agree with what she said, but if I used the term "pathology," it was intentional, because we're touching on a point of the real here. We don't agree on this point because, in my opinion, considering anticipation as something that reflects a prime symptom might, if you like, give you food for thought, and . . . you might even give me special credit!*

Special discredit is more like it! But I'm a bit uncomfortable with "pathological" in this instance. With the term "pathological." That's all.

**The commenter goes on:** *It's the original discourse that came out of psychoanalysis. There's always something here that brings us back to our initial reference point. That was simply the perspective I adopted . . .*

In a certain way, I'd see the word "pathological" coming into play precisely when certainty is proposed as a standard of truth.

*I understand. I'm talking here about pathology . . .*

If there *is* pathology, the cause is suggested right away.

*When I was talking about pathology—in connection with the beginning of psychoanalysis—I was playing devil's advocate here by adopting the traditional clinician's perspective. When you're in a regime that you're actually making a system out of, that's always how it happens or when you abandon ontology.*

If we're getting into ontology now, or rather if we're coming back to it, let's go on! The first feature of *reductio ad absurdum*, which we've just been debating, was, at any rate, its strategic nature. Consequently, an element of risk results from the anticipation of certainty: it may be fulfilled and end up as truth, but if not, it just wanders. So there you have it! That was the first feature.

The second feature is that the fiction declares itself as such in assuming not-A: the reasoning will be, in a certain sense, split; it will be in two parts, since the regime of consequences will be applied to a statement that I assume is false. There's a fictitious mediation of the hypothesis. I pretend that the fiction is true, and specifically I apply that regime of constructive truth—the examination of the consequences—to it. My pretending that it's true has a real payoff: that of applying the regime of the explicitation of the consequences to it. With this type of reasoning, I move, or I hope to move, from certainty to truth via a fictitious mediation, identified as such, with the remarkable feature that I'll identify it as such only retroactively. I indicate it as such, I indicate it subjectively as fictitious, but I'll only call it fictitious retroactively—when I reject it, when I say: my hypothesis has to be rejected. *Reductio ad absurdum* reasoning is really a retroactive naming of the fiction.

Finally, the third feature, which is very germane to our discussion about Parmenides: the conclusion of the proof, which is specifically and explicitly detached from any belief—obviously, since it operates within the assumption of the false. If there's one thing that's not required, it's believing in the hypothesis.

**Someone comments:** *That's what you said about Pascal's formulation of the wager as retroactive belief.*

Yes, but Pascal's formulation of the wager isn't a *reductio ad absurdum* argument. It's an examination of the consequences of two choices in order to show that one of the wagers is better than the other. I didn't say that every wager is a *reductio ad absurdum* argument. I said that *reductio ad absurdum* is explicitly detached from the effect of belief, precisely because it indicates the fiction. I pretend the statement is true, and I don't expect anyone to believe it, of course. I simply expect them to apply the neutral regime of consequence to it. But you can see that at the heart of *reductio ad absurdum* reasoning there's an uncoupling of belief and consequences. I will rid the notion of examining the consequences of any assumption of belief, since I am drawing the consequences of a fiction about the true. Thus, in all the steps that follow my hypothesis, the constructions and the objects involved are fictitious and therefore require attention to be focused exclusively on the rule of consequence, but detached from any effect of belief. In that sense, *reductio ad absurdum* is diametrically opposed to narrative. And it is so because it announces itself as a narrative; it declares: "Assuming this is true, then such and such a thing would happen." But the assumption that it's true is part of a strategic regime that fictionalizes it. The narrative of the consequences is thus identified as a pure narrative, as a transitory fiction that is expected to be retroactively invalidated. It's as though you had a fairytale that began, like all fairytales, with "Once upon a time" but would end with "Well, actually no, *not* once upon a time." Just imagine a twisted fairytale like that! Naturally, the fairytale is a narrative with an effect of belief for children: the "Once upon a time" is kept ambiguous as to whether it's real or not. Whereas, in this case, the tale would abolish its own conditions as a tale. A tale that un-tells itself, a narrative whose ultimate figure is the elimination of the assumption it's based on. That's the third feature!

The fourth, which is just as important, is *reductio ad absurdum*'s organic presupposition. I presuppose the overall coherence of the method. Because if, when I come across a contradiction, I reject the hypothesis, I obviously do so under the presupposition that there are no contradictions, that there can't be any, as opposed to narrative, in which, if there are any, they'll either be related to reality, given that we're in a regime of reality, or they'll become clear from a different perspective. But with the retroactive fictionalization of all the consequences I've derived from my hypothesis, the bottom line is that there are no contradictions in the system in which I'm operating. Why? Because there's a law, an abstract and irrevocable law, which will be encountered as such at a given moment, as such at the point of the real, at the point of the impossible, hence in a contradiction. Which is precisely what is impossible, but this impossibility acts here as the encountering of the law. Note that the law is encountered here in its overall effect, in its overall existence, in the "It is impossible for there to be any contradiction," which applies to the whole field of possible proofs. Whereas in constructive reasoning there's also a law, of course, but it acts locally: it regulates the movement from one truth to another and is never encountered as such. It is moreover because it is not encountered as such that constructive reasoning can have the appearance of a coherent narrative. So, with *reductio ad absurdum* reasoning, if it's successful, if it doesn't end up in errancy, there is an ultimate emergence of an impossibility, which is the equivalent of the encountering of the law in its overall effect, and it's on this basis, it should be noted, that I conclude, because it's on this basis that I reject the not-A hypothesis.

The fifth feature: the statement I ultimately prove, after the emergence of an impossibility equivalent to the encountering of the law in its overall effect, is actually proved not in terms of its meaning value but purely in terms of its position vis-à-vis the law. The thing is, it's impossible for this statement not to be true. But the fact that it's *impossible* for the statement *not to be true*—you can see the negative overload of that sentence—minimally elucidates the meaning of the statement itself. That the statement is ultimately grasped in its pure logical necessity—what I call its relationship with the law and the impossible, its conjoined and eclipsed relationship with the law and the impossible—has a very obvious symptom: it's not *the statement* that I prove this way, not the *statement* itself, simply because it's its double negation. It's not A that I prove but not-not-A. That's clear, isn't it? Given that not-A has to be rejected—it has to be rejected because, if I don't reject it, it's the law itself, which I encountered at the point of impossibility, that I must reject—it naturally follows that not-not-A has to be immediately accepted. So, if I conclude that A is true, *I obviously do so under the assumption that not-not-A is the same thing*. But that they are the same—something the intuitionists categorically reject—is only defensible at the furthest remove from the meaning of A. Because if you start getting into the dialectic of the meaning of A and the dialectical explicitation of that meaning, this equivalence between A and not-not-A is anything but obvious. This is well known. It is moreover what the Hegelian dialectic rejects.

The whole point, where *reductio ad absurdum* reasoning is concerned, will be that it is a procedure of positioning, not of meaning. I would say that it's because it has to do with being (to return indirectly to Parmenides) that there's a conclusive value. In the final analysis, *reductio ad absurdum* consists in the fact that it's impossible for the statement not to exist. Then, indeed, the negation of what doesn't exist is to exist. If not-A doesn't exist, then not-not-A must exist, thus reviving A's existence. This is one of the fundamental reasons why Parmenides used *reductio ad absurdum* reasoning, which came naturally to him, so to speak. What is involved is being qua being, which possesses no dialectical proliferation of meaning.

---

Focusing now on the transmission values of this type of reasoning—since the issue turns on the question "What does this kind of transmission transmit about transmission?"—I will isolate the main facts, which are as follows:

First of all, the fiction is explicit and, at the same time, distanced, in that it's identified as such: "I assume that. . . ." This is what I'd call an "effect of unbelief." *Reductio ad absurdum* conveys an effect of unbelief, an effect of unbelief intimately linked to the truth/fiction dialectic. It has always been criticized for this effect of unbelief. People have often said: "This type of reasoning doesn't really convince, it's indirect; I accept it, but I don't get it, you know?" It's true that the effect of unbelief is inescapable because the distancing of the fiction requires unbelief; it arouses a fundamental unbelief. That's what the effect of unbelief is. You can see how it's at the breaking point with the figure of narrative.

Second of all, the subordination to the law, which is characteristic of all demonstrative discourse, occurs in an encounter—the encounter with contradiction, with the impossible. The law is called upon, in its power, at a point of impossibility. This is what solicits and requires it in its overall power. It's what I'd term "the effect of the real" of *reductio ad absurdum*, connoting at once encounter, impossibility, and law—the effect of the real that is the way the law is called upon by the encountering of a point of impossibility. It is therefore to this triptych of the encounter, the impossible, and the law that I'll link *reductio ad absurdum* reasoning owing to its effect of the real, whereas constructive reasoning has the outward appearance of reality: it moves through, or it is in the realm of the possible.

Third of all, the validation of the statement does not lie in the clarification, the explicitation of, or the connection with, its meaning. In this sense, *reductio ad absurdum* is not an effect of persuasion but an effect of constraint. This is what I'd call its "effect of force." It is an effect of force in the sense that the ultimate belief is forced. And it is forced without our having been led to it by the explicitation of the meaning. This is a feature it has often been criticized for:

being brutal. There is, in fact, an element of brutality—it's a forcing-through—connected to the element of the real and the element of unbelief. Belief and reality are gentler than unbelief and the real.

Finally, the statement is validated through the adventure of a strategy at risk of errancy. This is its "risk effect" or "anticipation effect."

The transmission values of *reductio ad absurdum* lie in these four terms—risk, the real, force, and unbelief. Or, more precisely, in the capacity they all have to designate a value of rupture with narrative.

Now let's read a passage from Fragment 8 of Parmenides's poem [once again in Graham's translation]. It has to do with being:

> Never was it, nor shall it be, since it now *is*, all together, one, continuous. For what birth
> would you seek of it?
> Where [or: how], whence did it grow? Not from what-is-not will
>    I allow
> you to say or to think; for it is not sayable or thinkable
> that it is not. And what need would have stirred it
> later or earlier, starting from nothing, to grow?
> Thus it must be completely or not at all.
> Nor ever from what-is-not will the strength of faith allow
> anything to come to be beside it. Wherefore neither to come to be
> nor to perish did Justice permit it by loosening its shackles,
> but she holds it fast. And the decision concerning these things
>    comes to this:
> it is or it is not. Thus the decision is made, as is necessary,
> to leave the one way unthought, unnamed—for it is not a true
> way—the other to be and to be true.
> And how would what-is be hereafter? How would it have come to be?
> For if it has come to be, it is not, and similarly if it is ever about to
>    be.
> Thus coming to be is quenched, and perishing unheard of. (217)

In this passage, as is always the case with a very terse Parmenides, we probably have the earliest instance of *reductio ad absurdum* in the intellectual history of humanity, and, as such, an event, an event of thought, closely related to the ontological proposition itself but which in fact concerns the question of its coding. He attempts to answer the question typically associated with that of myth: whether being was created, or came to be, and whether it can perish. He poses the question of the origin of being itself: the question that is usually the central issue of origin myths, even if in the form of how the world and its offshoots were created. But to address it, he actually has only one axiom: being is and nonbeing is not, which is the relation of exclusion. It's clear that, from this statement, no specific predicative proposition can be drawn about being. The degree of elaboration of the meaning of being itself is not sufficient to prove constructively, or through the explicitation of this meaning, a statement such as: being does not come to be, in terms of its uncreated nature. So Parmenides will reason indirectly in the form of examining the opposite hypothesis. That is why the passage is chock-full of interrogative sentences, beneath which the false assumption is purely and simply concealed. And the demonstrative structure is as follows: Assuming that being is created, it can only be so from what-is-not or from what-is. *Reductio ad absurdum* reasoning, as often happens, will split into two branches. If being is created, it is created from what-is-not (the first hypothesis) or from what-is (the second hypothesis). "Impossible in both cases!" Parmenides will say, because if it was created from what-is-not, it couldn't be being. Why? Because if there were a relation of creation between what-is-not and what-is, there would be a relation of creation between being and nonbeing. We'd have this nameable relation that would be the relation of creation. Therefore, a contradiction would occur with the one axiom we've got, namely, there is no relation between being and nonbeing. So being cannot be created from nonbeing without immediately contradicting the basic law of the coding, which is that there is a radical disconnection, a complete exclusion, an irreducible difference, between being and nonbeing. Now, can it be created from what-is? No! Because then it would be self-antecedent, which contradicts the fact that it knows no difference. The fact that being knows no difference is also a consequence of the initial axiom: the radical exclusion between being and not-being prohibits being from containing difference. It's a constructible consequence. Here, on the other hand, we can't assume that being can be created from what-is, because there would have to be self-antecedence, hence difference—which being precludes. That is the argumentative structure of this passage dealing with the question of the coming to be of being, which concludes that it does not come to be: there is no coming to be.

As you can see, this conclusion is not drawn directly from the nature of uncreated being but from the impossibility of denying it, hence from the impossibility of denying that there is no coming to be. It is drawn from the assumption that there *is* one. But if there *is* a coming to be, then it's an impasse: we're at a point of impossibility with regard to the foundational axiom of the whole setup. Which is a radical rejection of experience: no sense experience is involved here. The conclusion is reached solely on the basis of impossibility. The axiomatic framework of the ontology requires rejecting the hypothesis of a coming-to-be as a fiction.

What's remarkable is that the elements of *reductio ad absurdum* are virtually identified as such in Parmenides's text itself: the interrogative form refers to the hypotheses, and the word "impossible" refers to the encounter. Isn't it amazing that at the very heart of this text Parmenides should say: "Thus the decision is made, as is necessary, to leave the one way unthought, unnamed"? What is decided is that the hypothetical way must be ignored and that the other way—"Being and Truth"—is situated at the point of impossibility of the first way. And when he concludes "Thus coming to be is quenched and perishing unheard of," he does so right after some negative phrases: "For if it has come to be, it is not, and similarly [it is not] if it is ever about to be." The very essence of *reductio ad absurdum* reasoning is involved here in the negative conclusion.

———∞∞∞———

This leads me to believe that it is suited to two types of questions to which it is connected in its essence: negative properties and questions of existence. I'm not saying that, in some cases, it can't be proved constructively that a given thing doesn't have a given property, but negative properties call for *reductio ad absurdum* reasoning because they call for a positive hypothesis: let's assume that they *do* have that property. I already pointed out to you that all the properties of being, according to Parmenides, are actually negative properties—which already anticipates or makes certain of Hegel's arguments possible. And it's really in this case, to prove the existence of a negative property, that *reductio ad absurdum* is called for: there is no coming to be of being. As for existence, describing it seems to call for the indication, the evidence, or the showing, of the thing that exists. Yet, in the order of the proposition of transmission, whose origin is in Parmenides's text and in pure mathematics, too, existence is very often proved by the absurd, that is to say, by the negation of the assumption of non-existence. In a way, the Parmenidean discourse combines the two. Since its distinctive feature is ontological radicality (proving that being is in an absolute sense), it seeks, if I can put it this way, the very essence of existence. But its aim is also to prove the parallel series of negative properties of being. In this text, there is an emergence of thought because the detachment of faith in the narrative of beliefs suggests that it's possible to conclude solely on the basis of impossibility, to conclude not because it's credible, or possible, or plausible, or narrated, or can be experienced, or because it can be shown, but to conclude on the basis of the point of impossibility, because the other way is forbidden. This requires, in a certain way, that the fiction be shown, that a voice be hypothetically given to someone who thinks the opposite, even if means telling him, as Parmenides sternly does: "I will not allow you to say [this]." But note that when Parmenides says: "Not from what-is-not will I allow you to say or to think," it's because he has just permitted it. He won't allow it, because, on a deeper level, he has just given himself permission, not to think it but to *say* it. This prohibition actually means: "Say it and we'll see; we'll draw all the consequences from that assumption!" This is a radically new mode of transmission because the fiction shows the necessary other side, as it were, of the element in which truth takes root, namely, the combination of impossibility, law, force, and the real. Philosophy springs from that, with its own, invariant knot—being, nonbeing, and thinking—but it comes to be because it is under the condition of the matheme in that precise sense. And the condition of this condition is that the conclusive nature of the absurd has become known. For the matheme to be transmitted as the horizon of discourse, I claim that, for all the reasons I've explained, and for which constructive reasoning wouldn't suffice, the conclusive nature of the absurd has to have become known.

It is in this respect that mathematics is a *condition* of philosophy. This should not be understood as meaning a temporal succession, a chronological condition, i.e., that mathematics has to come before philosophy. We will see how Szabó claims that it's the other way around, that mathematics was made possible by Parmenides. If we think in terms of historico-empirical conditions, we can probably agree with him, although the dating is very complex. It was the Eleatic School that brought about the possibility of the matheme by its commitment to apagogic reasoning. It's not in terms of "Who influenced whom?" that the question should be asked. In order for a thinking to be possible, for the possible discourse of this thinking to emerge, it must, as a *condition*, be freed from both objects and narrative. There must be the establishment without belief of a being that is free from the sensible.

---

Mathematics would epitomize that figure. Mathematics is therefore on the horizon of Parmenides's proposition; it is a condition for it— apart from the question of its historical status in Parmenides's day, an extremely thorny problem. Hence the need, actually, for a joint inception. It is impossible, in the destinal form of the kind I'm prescribing here, for philosophy so conceived to emerge unless mathematics *also* emerges. It is possible that it can therefore be said that philosophy is also a condition of mathematics. There is a dual conditioning, a dialectic of conditions. There is a birth in each of the components, a split birth, the birth of two systems of thought, whose common basis is, in terms of discourse, the break with narrative. And, in thought, a subtractive position of being. Next time I will conclude regarding Parmenides with a more detailed and in-depth analysis of this foundational doublet.

# Session 10

## January 28, 1986

I'll be fairly brief today. Let me begin by reminding you that Parmenides's founding gesture was a double gesture. He proposed a Borromean knotting of the three components, "being," "nonbeing," and "thinking." And he also proposed a type of discourse that was on the horizon of the matheme in that *reductio ad absurdum* (or indirect or apagogic) reasoning played a key role in it.

I'm not claiming a causal connection here. I'm not arguing that philosophy grew out of the invention of mathematics, or, conversely, that mathematics was only possible thanks to the existence of philosophy. No! The relationship assumed here is not that of a dependence in the sense of a causal externality. It is that of an intrinsic condition: for there to be philosophy, there must be the horizon of the matheme, which is a figure of thought, an indivisibly mathematico-philosophical figure. So there's no need to ask which it was originally, mathematical or philosophical. I would say instead that, historically, philosophy *and* mathematics were involved simultaneously in the emergence of this figure of thought. They created it through a dense dialectic, but the horizon of the matheme is what the relationship itself was based on. And this is what was involved in Parmenides's double foundation. It could be claimed that the proposition concerning the Borromean nature of the knot of thinking, being, and nonbeing was the philosophical element and that *reductio ad absurdum* was the logico-mathematical one, but that would be a trivial analysis. Rather, what should be asserted is that the speculative proposition, on the one hand, and the proposition about the transmission of the proposition, on the other hand, ushered in philosophy under condition of the matheme—and *that* was an *event* of thought. Yes, it was an *event* of thought. And, over the course of history, this event would be divided into mathematics and philosophy in what I'd call separate regimes of fidelity. Mathematics as pure ontology is a mode of fidelity to the event of thought I'm talking about. Philosophy, because of its originary intertwining with mathematics, has historically constituted another regime of fidelity. However, the event that introduced the horizon of the matheme as a figure of transmission is unique. It is no more specifiable to mathematics than it could be to philosophy. And chronology won't provide us with any criterion for deciding.

If Parmenides was the founder, if he can be construed as the founder, it's because he was a witness to the event rather than the initiator of a well-defined regime of fidelity. He is still, he can still be seen as, a witness to the event, as an actor in the event, or as an event participant. It is not possible then (and this will be my main point of disagreement with Heidegger) to conceive of or think this event as a period in the history of being through the metaphor of proximity. Parmenides's discourse doesn't imply a greater or a forgotten proximity to the Openness of being, because what's involved is a knot and a coding, i.e., a regime of connection in the double mode of the philosophical connection *stricto sensu*, of the Borromean knot, and a proposition about transmission. It is therefore not a figure of presence but truly an event of thought, that is to say, a proposition about relationship. Nor, if we consider the question of language, does it have to do with a dimension of reception, as Heidegger will say. Language is not originary here because it is supposedly involved in the concealment of being, open to the Open, or has poetic resonance. If there's anything to be said about language, and therefore about the richness of transmission of what goes on in it, it is much rather the capacity of language to endure the impossible. And that's not poetry's capacity but the matheme's. It is already (I say "already" because I'm using one of Lacan's terms) "the impasse of formalization" that is directly involved in *reductio ad absurdum* reasoning. So, here again, it is in the formalization of language, i.e., in its law, that the capacity to endure the point of impossibility and to move beyond it, that is to say, to conclude, develops.

That is why philosophy, in my opinion, doesn't originate in a question: the question of being, followed by the questioning of the question, the infinitely open nature of such questioning . . . Philosophy originates in the ability to conclude, with the invention of a new regime of the time for concluding.[1] This is a novel proposition. It can be argued that to conclude, there must be a question, but thinking that the essence of what is originally given is the question is not the same as thinking that that essence has to do with the time for concluding. What can be heard in Parmenides's tone, in the loftiness of his tone, is the audacity of concluding, and of doing so without recourse to narrative. Narrative is also a regime of conclusion. It closes off the question and covers it over. It covers it over with its twists and turns, its saturation, its rambling complexity, and its wide variety of figures. It is well known that a narrative, an origin narrative, a mythological narrative, or even a fictional narrative provides relief from anxiety about the question, but only because it diverts it. It diverts it in the sense that it answers it on a path that gradually becomes unrecognizable. That is why, if narrative is a means for concluding, it is so because of its diversion of the question, whereas the Parmenidean time for concluding is its audacity: it is the audacity of concluding by directly enduring the point of impossibility. So, even with all due caution, I cannot help but see in

Heidegger's interpretation something deliberately diversionary, in the sense I just mentioned, which does not really lead us back to the audacity in question.

**Someone interrupts**: *But aren't there some diversions that do in fact lead back? I was thinking of free association. I know this is a digression, but...*

Free association isn't a narrative to which the metaphor of diversion can be applied. It only makes sense if it's thought simultaneously with interpretation and the cut, because, in itself, it is elusive; in itself, the freedom of free association is something unassignable. Make no mistake about it: free association—when rigorously conceived—is not at all about the desire to close off the question. Why? Because in reality, what is called "freedom" here is essentially necessity. What is expected of free association is that a regime of necessity should appear in it that is no longer evident in the coding of what's non-free because it's been overwhelmed by another one. Anyone who'd conceive of interpretation as the narrativizing of free association would most certainly be a terrible analyst!

---

To return to what I was saying, there's something deliberately diversionary about Heidegger insofar as he doesn't restore the original audacity to us because he doesn't point out the innovation with respect to the time for concluding. He automatically assumes there is an originary proximity: lurking within him, then, is what I'd call the assumption of a "proto-narrative," a narrative that would be the absolutely primal narrative, a narrative that would be the matrix of narrative in general and the narrative of being, the way in which being articulates its own narrative. And no doubt, for him, it's an epic, no doubt there's ultimately an epic of being. There's something about Heidegger that inevitably reminds us, as a basic matrix, of

Homer's *Odyssey*, i.e., of a displacement, of the story of a wayward hero in search of his birthplace, who, over the course of his return, goes through a variety of interpretable figures, interpretable, in fact, in the sense that everything is only a return. In a certain way, the *Odyssey* is Heidegger's proto-narrative, the odyssey of being. By contrast, it's clear that what's involved in the Parmenidean matrix is not a proto-narrative; what's involved is a decision, and this decision has to do with the event of a figure of thought. That's why Heidegger can completely ignore mathematics in his interpretation of the Greek foundation of philosophy. And yet, empirically, that's a huge symptom that I've always been astonished doesn't immediately attract attention. Because, after all, how was it possible to think the "originarily Greek" essence of philosophy, to insist on this point with the utmost rigor, to think it in the element of an event of thought—of what Heidegger calls the "historial destiny" of being—and to think all this in totally oblivious disconnection from the emergence, the constitution, and the invention of logico-mathematical discourse, despite the fact that that reference was widespread among the Greek philosophers?

Even though I'm not dwelling on this, it's a crucial point. I think that, once all the historico-socio-political explanations have been taken into account, Heidegger's potential for being susceptible to the Nazi narrative—Nazism is really a pure narrative or criminal fable structure whose murderously ancient kernel can be isolated—comes down to the fact that the whole framework of thought is reduced to the proto-narrative mode and therefore to a sort of conceptual myth. But the fact is, Heidegger had a certain kind of receptivity to this. Even leaving aside the "documentary evidence," the receptivity and lack of self-criticism are undeniable: on the one hand, a rapturous discourse about the deep and originary connection between the Führer and the German people; and, on the other hand, not a word, to the day he died, about the extermination of the European Jews.[2]

**Someone comments:** *After he died, it was rumored that he'd been in Berlin during the Nazi rallies and that he'd stood at the window and told his students "Here are myths come to life!"*

He may well have done so. The fact is that, for perfectly accountable reasons, German philosophy is obliged to think Germany. This is a unique situation since French philosophy, for example, does not have to think France. But it's an imperative for German philosophy to think Germany, to have a philosophical concept of Germany, or to turn Germany into a philosophical concept. Yet, it so happens that in this demand, in this temptation, the question of Greece is a mediation. So it would be fascinating to ask why, to ask: Is Germany the new Greece? Just about every German thinker has had to ask: Is it or isn't it? And every philosopher has strong reason to think it is, after all, because Germany is indeed the foremost country for philosophy in the modern world, just as Greece was in the ancient world.

**Someone in the back of the room asks:** *Couldn't the history of thought in Germany provide some insights?*

Of course!

*After all, there's an origin. Don't you think we could go much further back? This identification with Greece is a theme that dates back to Goethe, if I'm not mistaken.*

What do the experts from Germany have to say about it? The history of German thought explains its genealogy, I'm convinced. From the late eighteenth century, when German philosophical supremacy emerged, up to Heidegger, there's been the Germany = Greece equation. It's really striking to see how in a progressive writer from East

Germany, Heiner Müller, the Greek mediation is still so prevalent. The identification with Greek figures is still crucially important among German novelists and poets. This issue is by no means over.

**Someone else comments:** *I could suggest an explanation. It's associated with the great classical movements, like in poetry, with Hölderlin, at the very time in history when German nationalism arose. At the time when the Germans began to think of themselves as such, this idealization of Greece predominated . . .*

It's quite true that German nationalism developed in the climate, in the figurative articulation, of a civilization dominated by neoclassicism and Greek art as a frame of reference. What's really remarkable is the extraordinary tenacity of that conjunction—or its intellectual continuity, if you like: the fact that it survived the period of German state-building, two hundred years of German history, and that it has lasted as such a tenacious intellectual and speculative figure. In any case, the question "What is Greece?" is not a historical, ancient, or cultural question. It's a basic question of identity because it mediates the question "What is Germany?," the latter being an obligatory question of German thought. So, determining whether or not the invention of mathematics is included in the basic definition of Greece involves defining what Germany is. I'm not saying this is the only diagnostic criterion. It's also essential to know, for example, whether Athenian political democracy is included, or which concept of Greek art is involved. I would say that these are the three issues: science, the Polis, and the Temple, or sculpture. But to return to Heidegger, his susceptibility to the Nazi protonarrative can be seen even in his vision of Greece, and maybe even primarily in his vision of Greece, because in his interpretation of Greek philosophical originarity he completely separated the philosophical proposition properly speaking from the proposition concerning transmission, i.e., from the horizon of the matheme. This is the exact opposite of the French vision of Brunschvicg, according to whom Greece represented the philosophical activation of mathematical idealities. Heidegger de-mathematized Greek originarity. This wasn't simply an irrationalist project. The issue involved cannot easily be thought in terms of rationalism or irrationalism. The heart of the matter is "What transmits?" and therefore "What did Greece transmit to us in terms of originarity?" Was it just the miracle of a presence, or was it a decision about the impossible?

We should give thinkers the best chance possible. I'm only making a case about Parmenides here for my own purposes. There is something truly great about Heidegger's project as regards the origin of Parmenides's proposition itself. Heidegger provided new guidelines for thinking about this issue. Our debt to him should be acknowledged. But that won't stop us from thinking that his Greece is a "bad" Greece and that that's also why his Germany is a "bad" Germany, ultimately sutured to a German nightmare. And it's for this reason that Heidegger couldn't submit to any self-criticism. When he distanced himself from the Nazi regime, his philosophy, his orientation of thought, fell back, at precisely that time, in fact, upon Greece: it was from that time on that he began, as though it were an innocent project, his profound and penetrating analyses of the original great Greek thinkers. But if the self-criticism called for was to be conducted philosophically, only a thorough, philosophically conducted self-criticism could be required of a philosopher like him—even though we would have preferred that it be as an ordinary citizen. Yet if a self-criticism were to be conducted philosophically it certainly couldn't be done in the form of this withdrawal, because this Greece was really also that of the "bad" Germany, even though it was empirically innocent. Of course, analyzing Anaximander's only surviving fragment of writing isn't the same thing as encouraging your students to enthusiastically perform their duty as Nazi soldiers. But in terms of continuity, of philosophical depth, Heidegger would have had to completely revise his own account, his account of the history of being. Not because it was irrational but because it sidestepped the founding decision. It couldn't accommodate the completeness of the decision. Mathematicity would have had to be reintroduced in one way or another. To that end, Greece needed to be revisited. It needed to be revisited, whereas Heidegger had instead taken refuge in it. But he had taken refuge in the Greece that was the Greece of the Germany that he was fleeing, that he was fleeing in place. So he didn't leave his country; he simply retreated into the Greek patriotic interior of that Germany. There was something that he couldn't approach—the facts bear this out—that he couldn't revisit, that he couldn't re-think, for the deep reason that Greece had been the illusion of a refuge for him. All of which is to say that the question of the originary mathematicity of Greece has a progressive, German function and thus a progressive universal function as well. Because we, too, must assume that the question of Greece is part of the question of Germany. The question of the originary Greek mathematicity is part of the assessment of Germany and therefore of the philosophical assessment of Nazism.

This is actually a very complex question. Let me list the reasons why.

The first has to do with the wide-ranging debate about continuity and discontinuity: is mathematics really originarily Greek? Is there really a Greek beginning, an absolute beginning, a break?

The second great debate—assuming the first was decided in favor of a Greek origin—concerns the "When?" When did it begin? This is the issue of dating and its symbolic effects, because the determining factor is the signifying act. To say that it happened at one date rather than another imposes a regime of meaning. It's not just a question of empirical truth.

The third great debate is the one about connections: the relationship between mathematics and philosophy.

We'll see all this next time when we read Árpád Szabó's book *The Beginnings of Greek Mathematics*. Its value lies in proposing a coherent way of deciding on these three questions and in showing the inner relationship among them. So that's it! We'll conclude with this next Tuesday.

# Session 11

## February 4, 1986

Precisely because it bears witness to an event of thought, Parmenides's text can only be understood, as regards its originary function, in terms of the intricate relationship between the emergence of the philosophical proposition and the advent of mathematical discourse. This is what I think I showed right here in this seminar. I'm not going to go back over the steps of the proof. The question of Greece, Greece as a concept, was involved in that proof in the form of "What is Greece?" That question, "What is Greece?," which is not exhausted by the multitude of answers about its sites, history, events or developments, requires a decision. Something must be decided. This is exactly what the German tradition resolved to do: to decide about Greece in order to decide, ultimately, about Germany. And the essential feature running from Goethe to Heidegger was precisely to exclude the matheme from the identification of Greece, or to decide about Greece by excluding the matheme—what I called a "de-mathematizing" of Greek originarity—and therefore, I said, to refound Greece in the context of narrative. The inevitable consequence of the exclusion of the matheme was to return or reattach Greece to the figure of narrative.

Indeed, the German Greece was a Greece whose key figures were those of myth. The decision about Greece would thus be immersed in the obscurity of the question "Matheme or myth?" Why "the obscurity of the question"? Because it's not that simple, not least because of the many attempts to make myth itself the vehicle for a matheme. Take the classic example of Freud's Oedipus theory, in which the myth is proposed as the vehicle for a matheme. The story has a formal structure consistent with the ideal of science. By contrast, in Greek philosophy itself the mythic constitution of the matheme can be discerned. Consider Plato's *Timaeus*. The elements of its cosmology are mathemes: the theory of regular polyhedrons, and so on. But the overall structure is a mythical proposition. Twists and turns combine in spaces that are by no means completely and clearly separate, in which a decision has to be made about two immanent and disconnected alternatives. So there's an obscurity about the question, and Plato's work bears exemplary witness to this. It is suspended between myth and matheme, proposing both, one as a vehicle for the other and vice versa. In this respect, it is Greek in exemplary fashion. But of an already totalized Greece, so to speak. The decision about Greece is, at any rate, suspended between two questions: are the great myths the vehicles for the Greek proposition about thinking? Are they the ultimate and incontestable vehicles for it, or does the originarity lie instead with the matheme? These are at any rate the elements of the decision.

There is, as I said, especially where Heidegger's interpretation of Parmenides is concerned, a decision system with respect to Greece that excludes the matheme, which is to say, that truly decides the issue. To decide otherwise about Greece, and therefore about Parmenides, means saying: the matheme is included in the origin. Mathematics and philosophy emerge together, with "together" really becoming the locus of the origin. So there is the Two in this origin, which, in Parmenides's proposition, as you'll recall, is that the One of the Two is its coding, or that the One is the proposition of transmission. But there is the Two, and this Two subsequently led to a widening gap that, probably very early on, historically, gradually autonomized mathematical discourse as such, separating it little by little, though never completely, from philosophical discourse.

In my opinion, the originary Two is documented in Árpád Szabó's book *The Beginnings of Greek Mathematics*. It sheds light on the importance of a wide range of debates that historians often engage in over their theories. These disputes over doctrine, interpretations, and revisions are part of a great tradition of the historiography and history of antiquity. In Szabó's book, the debates specifically concern, either directly or indirectly, the question of the inclusion or non-inclusion of the matheme in the figure of the origin, which also focuses the debate on the meaning of the vague notion of "the West." The theory of the West could be discussed at great length. But the question that concerns us is whether the matheme is included in the Western paradigm and with what status. Of course, Heidegger included science in the Western paradigm—science and technology—but with the very special status of the forgetting of the origin. In his view, science is not included in the Western paradigm with an originary status but with the status of forgetting, thus fomenting the nihilistic figure of the West, its figure as self-divestiture. So this is an intellectually crucial question.

This is because it's not just exclusion or not that would jibe with the origin. The historians' controversies that Szabó discusses— doubtless highly technical but actually fundamental—are about the origin of rationality, the figure of Western intellectuality, whether it exists or not, the significance of the originarity of Greece, and so on. The book sets out three major debates. The first is the one that concerns discontinuity: With respect to the matheme, to mathematics, did Greece really start something? The second debate is the one about chronology: Assuming something did have its start in Greece, when would this have been? Finally, the third one— the debate about connection—concerns the precise nature of the philosophico-mathematical entanglement. What answers to these three questions help the case of those who exclude mathematics from the Greek foundation? And therefore help Heidegger's case?

As for the first issue, what helps the supporters of narrative is that, as far as the matheme is concerned, Greece didn't start anything, obviously. Hence the immediate disqualification of the matheme's inclusion in Greek originarity: if it didn't begin there, there's no point in being concerned with it. The theory of the matheme's exclusion is thus consistent, clearly consistent, with what I'd call the Babylonian-Egyptian theory, which essentially holds that mathematical discourse already existed to a large extent before Greece, in Egyptian and Babylonian texts, which themselves referred to preexisting documents.

As for the second question, "When?," it's the opposite, so to speak. The theory that the originarity has nothing to do with the matheme is consistent with the fact that mathematics only developed later, much later, than the Greek origin: Greek mathematics would instead be contemporary with the time of the *forgetting* of the origin rather than with that of the origin itself. So the exclusion theory is perfectly consistent with the idea that the actual Greek invention of mathematics is Platonic, contemporary with Plato and not with Parmenides or Heraclitus. Hence the considerable advantage of being able then to see in Plato, in his reliance on mathematics, in the effective use he makes of the mathematical paradigm, something that, in Heidegger's sense, has already forgotten the originary presence, is already on the way to the oblivious reign of science. So the later the better! Consequently, the matheme exclusion theory requires that mathematics be a non-Greek and very ancient invention and that, in Greek history, its full development be contemporary with what Heidegger called the time of the turn, i.e., the time when the question of being is itself forgotten in the question of the supreme being or the Idea. It's like killing two birds with one stone, in a way: not only is mathematics not originary but it can be blamed for the forgetting! You can see the importance of dating where our hypotheses are concerned, even when the supporters of the exclusion theory aren't involved and it's the scholars who are dealing with it.

As for the third question—that of the connections between philosophy and mathematics—which encapsulates the other two, the matheme exclusion theory will include two propositions: (1) There is no originary connection between philosophy and mathematics; and (2) There is a belated connection, with the emergence of Platonism, but it's a connection that, far from being a step forward or a breakthrough in speculative thought, is actually a step backwards or a loss.

So, clearly, the theory of the matheme's inclusion in the origin—the theory that holds, as I do, that the invention of mathematics is consubstantial with the originarity of the philosophical proposition—will feel more closely related, in all respects, to the diametrically opposed historical theories. It will more easily accept—since the invention of mathematics is part of philosophical originarity—a historical discontinuity and will for that very reason diverge from the Babylonian-Egyptian theory. As regards the debate about chronology, it will push Greek mathematics as far back in time as possible. It will be based on the historical theory that establishes a quasi-contemporaneity with the great pre-Socratic philosophers of the development of mathematics on the horizon of the matheme. The third and final point is that it will defend a theory of connection.

―⁂―

How are these three controversies specified to specific disputes?

Regarding the first issue, choosing between the Greek theory and the Babylonian-Egyptian theory about the origin of mathematics requires making a decision about the essence of mathematics itself. In particular, does mathematics exist as soon as mathematical objects—geometric shapes and numbers, on which intellectual operations are performed—appear? Does the definition of mathematics in fact ultimately involve the emergence of a certain kind of objects? If so, then the Babylonian-Egyptian theory would have to be supported, because, without a doubt, numerical operations were already being used in those civilizations, along with the earliest recognition of geometric shapes, and there were already calculations, spatial idealities, and concepts such as the circle or the triangle. Or does mathematics only exist when there is reasoning *stricto sensu*, when there is a proof, or even, as I claim with Szabó, when there is the explicit form of *reductio ad absurdum* reasoning? If mathematics exists only when the indisputable and explicit proof-form exists, then the Babylonian-Egyptian theory can no longer be supported, even by the admission of its supporters. There were triangles, circles, and numbers before the Greeks. So the dispute is not about "Did this exist or not?" No! The crux of the matter is the matheme form of transmission—the demonstrative and universal form—or, in other words, the ideal of an integral transmission, without remainder, by strictly demonstrative means. The question then becomes: "In the current state of the literature, is the idea and use of a proof whose conclusion must be accepted by every thinking subject a Greek invention or not?"

---

As regards the second issue, the dating, the focus is whether certain of the key mathematical ideas of Greek thought were contemporary with Platonism or clearly prior to it. And whether certain generalizations, crucial on account of the way they paved for proofs, dated from the time of Platonism or were pre-Platonic. Regarding all this, Szabó undertakes a fascinating textual analysis of Plato: in particular, the discussion with the slave about the doubling of the square in the *Meno* and, even more so, the mathematical passages about the question of irrationals in the *Theaetetus*. For a very long time, a whole interpretation—innocently German, so to speak—by late nineteenth-early twentieth-century German academic scholarship had expounded the theory, based on these texts, that a decisive development of Greek mathematics had occurred in Plato's time. Much of Szabó's book consists in rereading these texts closely and showing, conclusively, in my opinion, that not only do they not suggest that the discoveries Plato talked about were contemporary with him but that these texts are only fully intelligible if it is assumed that these discoveries were made earlier. You can see how subtle this is: what Szabó attempts to show—and this is the strength of his innovative interpretation of the text (although its intricacies can unfortunately not be reproduced here)—is not just the anteriority of the discoveries but that it was on this anteriority that Plato based himself to transmit what he wanted to transmit. The mathematical references could only work in Plato's presentation if they were references familiar to an educated, informed, knowledgeable audience, hence established references and not scientific theories that were supposedly being grasped at their inception. Szabó shows how Plato's references in the dialogues were intended for the public, the "general public," not reserved for esoteric use, for the teaching that took place in Plato's school through the master-disciple relationship. The fact that the mathematical references were dealt with allusively, that they were presented allusively in the manner of someone trying to transmit philosophy publicly, whereas the matrix of philosophical transmission in Antiquity was a master-disciple relationship, a direct relationship, makes it highly unlikely that these were mathematical innovations at the time of their emergence, their gestation, their creation.

**Someone comments:** *But that's Szabó's theory . . .*

Yes, it's Szabó's theory.

**The person continues:** *So what about the German scholars then?*

You mean the German scholars' theory as opposed to Szabó's? Well, here's what it was: the texts concerned, in Plato, were actually the first announcement, the first mention, of recent discoveries. As for the allusiveness, it was due to the cautiousness of the discoverers: they didn't want to say too much about them. The second dispute focused on the issue of dating and anteriority, which was clearly crucial, because if Plato or Platonism were originary in terms of mathematics, then mathematics was only linked to the development stage of philosophy, not to its original proposition. It's really interesting to see how the German scholars gave Plato credit, quite innocently, in my opinion, for this theory. Out of their tremendous respect for him, they wanted to give him credit for everything, including mathematics: it was something like the reconstruction of a foundational Platonism, on a vast scale. Ultimately, though, their theory was still the same as the exclusion of the origin. So there was a convergence, a convergence of thought, between them and Heidegger, who was not interested in the issue in its historicist form.

---

As for the third issue, the connection between philosophy and mathematics, it's more complicated, because the heart of the debate concerns the origin of both mathematical idealities and the proof. It's all intertwined: the question of the connection in terms of demonstrativity, the connection between philosophy and mathematics with regard to transmission, the question of number and that of shapes. Those are the elements of the debate.

As regards demonstrativity, I'm not going to go over it again because I've already dealt with it extensively. The whole question has to do with the value of apagogic reasoning, of *reductio ad absurdum* reasoning, because the assessment of it will differ depending on which theory is supported. The supporters of the theory of the non-originarity of mathematics regard *reductio ad absurdum* as an inferior type of reasoning precisely because it doesn't presentify. So it has no intrinsic value, let alone originary value—in any case, it certainly does not provide a connection between mathematics and philosophy. In Szabó's theory and the one I proposed, the opposite is true: not only is *reductio ad absurdum* the key to the question, to integral transmission, precisely because it is subtractive, and because it acknowledges the fiction, but, in addition, as regards this question of demonstrativity, it's really *reductio ad absurdum* that sutures philosophy and mathematics, in exemplary fashion in Parmenides's work—and immediately thereafter in Zeno's. As for the question of objects, and in particular the fundamental question of the general concept of number, which is the key to the origin of arithmetic in its universal sense and in its specifically mathematical sense, the debate takes the form of a theory about the relationship between the Pythagoreans and the Eleatics. Let me explain why.

Pythagoreanism, about which not much is known, was supposed to have been a philosophico-mathematical doctrine that considered number as being itself, or something like that, projecting nascent mathematicity onto a cosmological doctrine. The school of Pythagoras is said to be slightly later than Parmenides, which therefore suggests that the arguments of Zeno, i.e., of the second generation of Parmenideans, were explicitly directed against the Pythagoreans. You see the pattern: Parmenides claiming the absolute unity of being; the Pythagoreans, on the contrary, claiming its constitutive multiplicity—therefore, the Parmenideans proponents of the One, the Pythagoreans proponents of the multiple, and Zeno defending his master against the Pythagoreans, the proponents of the multiple, via *reductio ad absurdum* arguments such as: if you support the multiple, here's what happens, it doesn't work, and so on. This is the common historical pattern, in which nascent mathematicity is uncoupled from Parmenides; it's attributed to the Pythagoreans and is incorporated into a doctrine of the multiple in reaction and opposition to the doctrine of the Parmenidean One. As for Zeno, he turns the Pythagoreans' own weapons against them by using *reductio ad absurdum* proofs directed against the multiple. Thus, once again, the originarity of philosophy is separated from the originarity of mathematics and is even partly competitive with or opposed to it. According to the Pythagorean theory, there has to be a break with Parmenides, with the absoluteness of the One, in order for mathematics to be possible.

In this theory that attributes the originarity of mathematics to the Pythagoreans, there is once again an uncoupling from the originarity of philosophy and even a polemical uncoupling. Indeed, it is in the context of the anti-Parmenidean polemic that the abstract concept of number emerges, in the context of a doctrine of the multiple. Concerning this issue, Szabó's theory is that the Parmenides-Pythagoras opposition is wrong. In reality, the ultimate foundation of the Pythagorean notion of number is actually Parmenides's ontology, i.e., the One, the concept of the indivisible unity of being in Parmenides. How does Szabó prove this? By means of a very precise and detailed history of the Greek mathematical texts dealing with the relationship between number and the One. His point of departure is to note that, in all of Greek mathematics, including in its absolutely systematic forms, as in Euclid, number is defined as that which is composed of units, thus implying that the One is not a number. It's a process that goes to the point where, when the Greeks had to do an arithmetic proof, they were forced conceptually—not technically but conceptually—to reason first in the case where the number was not One and then in the case where the number *was* One, while for us moderns there is always only one proof. And Szabó asks why, even among the mathematicians of the Classical Age, there was this peculiarity of the absolute need to distinguish first the general case of numbers and then the case of the One. His interpretation is as follows: the Parmenidean One subsists at the heart of the concept of number as its split-off foundation. The One is not a number strictly speaking because this One is actually the Parmenidean One, that is, incapable of being multiple, incapable of being divided, impenetrable, and so on. The Greeks' arithmetical One has all the attributes of Parmenidean being. Parmenides's ontology, Szabó adds, made the concept of number possible, in the form of the concept of the unit: number is that which is made up of units. Szabó's theory is that the Pythagoreans, if indeed there were Pythagoreans, didn't divide the Parmenidean One; theirs wasn't a doctrine of the multiple or of division opposed to a doctrine of the One. On the contrary, they *multiplied* the One—which is something very different. Szabó disputes the idea that the concept of number is the result of the One being divided, since it is instead the result of it being multiplied. And therefore, Pythagoreanism was a proliferating Parmenideanism, not a shattered Parmenideanism. There was no anti-Parmenidean creation of Pythagorean arithmetic. There was an arithmetization, it's true, an emergence of number, and therefore an excess over Parmenides, but an arithmetization whose ultimate guarantor is what I call the proliferation of the Parmenidean One. And so, even in the late arithmetic proofs, there's the proof of the Pythagorean case, a number, and then the separate proof of the Parmenidean case: if it's One, then it is necessary to think in a different way, to prove in a different way.

That's the evidence in the case. What Szabó deals with in his book could be summarized as follows: there is a triple originarity of mathematics, a triple foundational mathematico-philosophical connection, and a triple instance of the originary nature of mathematicity, which is, first, the question of *reductio ad absurdum* reasoning; second, the pre-Platonic, necessarily pre-Platonic, nature of already developed Greek mathematics; and third, the Parmenidean genesis of the concept of number despite the appearance of an absolute antagonism between the concept of number and Parmenideanism.

---

Let's wind up this Parmenides seminar now. In a simultaneously political and personal debate with Heidegger, we need to shed new light on the question of Parmenides's originarity by saying: *There is a distinctive Parmenidean originarity of philosophy*—the part of the statement I share with Heidegger—*but under the condition of the matheme, in the sense that this condition is at the same time based on that origin.* The latter point, however, is one of deep, very deep, disagreement. That's why it's a mistake—with potentially adverse consequences—to conceive of science as being part of a figure of forgetting. Whatever the destinal meaning of this metaphor may be, to conceive of science as a figure of forgetting is a decision, in this case a decision about Greece, but it is also, in a way, a decision about Germany, and a decision about philosophy. A decision that remains unjustifiable. Therefore, we must think that, in its mathematical figure, science is originarily linked to the philosophical proposition, through a linkage that is in no way the historically traced identity between them. I assume you've understood that the theory I'm defending here is not a positivist one: still less could it be concluded that *science can replace philosophy*. There is an originary linkage. Then comes the history of this linkage, including the figures of de-linkage that such a history introduces.

**Someone interrupts:** *Would you say that we need to reintroduce the fact that science is originarily linked to the rejection of narrative?*

I would say that philosophy is originarily linked to the possibility of disrupting narrative. I would put it like this: narrative must be able to be disrupted in the very transmission. Which doesn't mean that philosophy has no relationship at all with narrative. That would be a maximalist thesis, and what's more, a positivist one, in the long run. Nor am I saying that the matheme *is* philosophical transmission. No! I said that the existence of discursivity, of philosophical transmission, was originarily under condition of the matheme. Even if philosophy is only narrative, even if it can be proved that, to a great extent, it is only narrative, the narrative that it is remains under the condition of the matheme. More precisely, philosophy requires that it be possible to disrupt the narrative—the Parmenidean foundation tells us so. To be sure, there is poetic narrative in Parmenides, but there is narrative only under the condition that it can be disrupted. Maybe it is only disrupted in order to found a different narrative regime, but it is disrupted. Even if the entire history of philosophy only offers us narratives, it also offers us—because they are under the condition of the matheme—the recurrent possibility of assessing the narrative as a narrative. And this is true to such an extent that Heidegger will say that we're no longer capable of doing so, because what he means by "being capable" is remembering what that narrative meant. As a result, there is, in his view, the loss of a memory and a language. The language of the originary narrative has become obscure to us. So language, speech must be restored to it. But doesn't philosophy's greatness lie not in restoring this supposed language but rather in disrupting it, in disrupting the narrative, even if only to replace it with a different one? It is the condition of the matheme that makes it possible for the narrative to be shown as a narrative, and thus displaced, transvalued.

That's how I wanted to conclude.

Next Fall we'll be talking about the Reverend Father Malebranche[1] . . . What a fantastic narrative that one is!

# Notes

### Parmenides's Subtractive Ontology: Introduction to Alain Badiou's *Parmenides: Ontological Figure, Being 1*

1. The seminars of 1983–84, *The One: Descartes, Plato, Kant* and 1984–85, *Malebranche: Being 2—Theological Figure* have been published by Columbia University Press. The seminars *Infinity: Aristotle, Spinoza, Hegel* and *Heidegger: Being 3—Figure of Withdrawal* are forthcoming with Columbia University Press.
2. Plato, *Complete Works*, ed. John M. Cooper, trans. Nicholas P. White (Indianapolis, IN: Hackett, 1997), 262. See also Georg Wilhelm Friedrich Hegel, *Lectures on the History of Philosophy, Volume I: Greek Philosophy to Plato*, trans. E. S. Haldane (Lincoln, NE: University of Nebraska Press, 1995), 254.
3. I am grateful to Joseph Spencer, who pointed out to me that philosophers in the analytic tradition have often emphasized this aspect of Parmenides's thought. See for example, Richard D. McKirahan, who writes: "Whereas his philosophical predecessors had employed rational criteria in criticizing earlier views and developing their own, Parmenides was the first to make systematic use of another form of rational thought: the systematic use of argument, deductive argument in particular, to prove his points." *Philosophy Before Socrates: An Introduction with Texts and Commentary*, 2nd ed. (Indianapolis, IN: Hackett, 2010), 150.
4. Aristotle, Diogenes Laertius, and other ancient authors report that Parmenides believed in two "elements," fire and earth; but if so, they seem to function on a cosmological level, not that of being. In the extant fragments of Parmenides's text, the only reference to either fire or earth comes in the section on "opinion"—not the section on "truth." As Daniel Graham points

out, "It is questionable whether Parmenides has these two physical elements in mind . . . But his theory does seem to use something like a conception of elements, that is, realities of fixed nature which continue in existence but interact to produce different products. . . . Parmenides seems to be the first thinker to explain the multiplicity of phenomena by deriving things from elements." *The Texts of Early Greek Philosophy: The Complete Fragments and Selected Testimonies of the Major Presocratics: Part 1*, ed. and trans. Daniel W. Graham (Cambridge: Cambridge University Press, 2010), 240. All further references to Graham's edition of Parmenides's text will be cited by fragment number and page in the body of the text.

5. Hegel, *The Science of Logic*, ed. and trans. George di Giovanni (Cambridge: Cambridge University Press, 2010), 60.

6. This is of course a version of what Heidegger calls the "ontological difference," or the difference between ontology (Being) and ontics (beings). Martin Heidegger, *The Beginning of Western Philosophy: Interpretation of Anaximander and Parmenides*, trans. Richard Rojcewicz (Bloomington: Indiana University Press, 2015), 90.

7. In the introduction to his translation of Parmenides, Daniel Graham points out that the path of "Opinion" cannot be dismissed as simply false knowledge, since "this was apparently the longest and most detailed part of the poem, setting forth for the first time some of the most important astronomical discoveries made by early Greeks." We can compare this with what Plato calls "ortho-doxa"—right opinion—in the *Republic*. In both cases, at stake is a type of knowledge without reason that is to be distinguished from true knowledge. See Graham, *Texts of Early Greek Philosophy*, 1:204.

8. Heidegger, *Beginning*, 96.

9. It is not clear that Gorgias believed his own argument; it is perhaps, like his "Encomium on Helen," meant as a dazzling display of his own rhetorical skills. The treatise is divided into three parts: "the first one that nothing exists, the second that even if it exists, it is incomprehensible to man, the third that even if it is comprehensible, it surely cannot be expressed or communicated to another." Graham, *Texts of Early Greek Philosophy* II:741

10. A similar statement is found elsewhere in the Poem: "The same thing is for thinking and is wherefore there is thought" (8:217)

11. Badiou would no doubt agree with Irad Kimhi's argument that fragment 3 cannot be understood, as some critics have suggested, as implying a "correspondence" between thinking and being or that "the truth of thinking depends on something which is external to thinking." See Kimhi, *Thinking and Being* (Cambridge, MA: Harvard University Press, 2018), 6–7.

12. Martin Heidegger, *Introduction to Metaphysics*, 2nd ed., trans. Gregory Fried and Richard Polt (New Haven, CT: Yale University Press, 2014), 153. The translation for this edition is revised and expanded.
13. "Vernehmung ist Durchgang durch die Kreuzimg des Dreiweges. Das kann sie nur werden, wenn sie von Grund aus *Ent-scheidung* ist *für* das Sein *gegen* das Nichts und somit Auseinandersetzung *mit* dem Schein" (Martin Heidegger, *Der Anfang der abendländischen Philosophie* [*Gesamtausgabe* 35], (Frankfurt: Verlag Vittorio Klostermann, 2012), 177.
14. All references to Plato are from the aforecited *Complete Works* translated by Nicholas P. White. In quotations from the *Sophist*, I am using "Stranger" rather than White's "Visitor" as the translation of Plato's term ξένος [xénos] to refer to the speaker from Elea, in keeping with Badiou's usage of "l'Étranger" in his seminar.
15. In his 2007–2010 seminar, In the end, the parricide foretold is a relatively modest one. It's not even certain that Dad's been killed outright.
16. Badiou is alluding to the title of Lacan's 1971 seminar. See Jacques Lacan, *Le Séminaire. Livre XVIII. D'un discours qui ne serait pas du semblant*, ed. Jacques-Alain Miller (Paris: Seuil, 2006).
17. Badiou already discussed these questions in relation to Plato's *Parmenides* and *Sophist* in his seminar *The One: Descartes, Plato, Kant*, trans. Jacques Lezra with Susan Spitzer (New York: Columbia University Press, 2023).
18. The first use of *reductio ad absurdum* is sometimes attributed to Xenophanes of Colophon (who may have been Parmenides's teacher), but this is by no means certain.
19. In topology, a ring is the simplest kind of knot, referred to as an "unknot."
20. We can understand Lacan's specimen utterance as suggesting that although the analysand believes that they enter into analysis so that the analyst can relieve them of their symptoms and make them happy, insofar as those goals are different from (and contradictory to) their unconscious desires, their request conceals the *demand* that the analyst *not accept* the explanations or symptoms that the analysand *presents* them with, because they know that they are at least in part red herrings, meant to misdirect the analyst from the real of the analysand's desire. Each moment is linked to one of the others only via the mediation of the third; there is no stable or coherent dyad among them, so its structure is intrinsically triadic. Lacan argues that the center of this knot-like structure of language is the *objet a*, the absent cause of desire that structures the analysand's unconscious fantasy. When he returns to the Borromean rings in next year's seminar, *Encore*, Lacan comments, "Object *a* is no being. Object *a* is the void presupposed by a demand" (126). As in the Borromean knot involving being,

thinking, and nonbeing that Badiou will locate in Parmenides, nonbeing (the *objet a* as "the void") is the element that allows for the articulation of meaning and being. Jacques Lacan, . . . *or Worse: The Seminar of Jacques Lacan, Book XIX*, ed. Jacques-Alain Miller, trans. A. R. Price (Cambridge: Polity, 2018), 65–77. Jacques Lacan, *On Feminine Sexuality: The Limits of Love and Knowledge, Book XX: Encore 1972–1973*, trans. Bruce Fink (New York: Norton, 1998), 126.

21. Badiou writes, "The One of the Borromean knot is that of a consistency that affects the whole, it is a One of adherence, the collective property of the terms, whereas the One of the chain prescribes the places of the connection, which have a separating function." Alain Badiou, *Theory of the Subject*, trans. Bruno Bosteels (London: Continuum, 2009), 227.
22. Badiou, *Theory of the Subject*, 229.
23. Badiou, *Theory of the Subject*, 231.
24. "Ce lien entre la question du deux et la question du néant a donné lieu à tout le déploiement de la dialectique jusqu'à Hegel. . . . Platon appelle ce deux 'l'autre,' qui est le signifiant du négatif, c'est un signifiant sans signifié (cf. le Phallus pour Lacan). L'autre c'est ne pas être par rapport à être. Cet autre-là (le néant) est requis pour que les autres signifiants soient rapportables les uns aux autres. S'il n'y a pas de deux, il n'y a pas de chaîne signifiante, pas de chaîne de l'intelligible." ["This link between the question of the two and the question of nothingness gave rise to all deployments of the dialectic up to Hegel. . . . Plato calls this two 'the other,' which is the signifier of the negative, a signifier without signified (cf. Lacan's "Phallus"). The other is not being in relation to being. This other (nothingness) is required so that the other signifiers can relate to each other. If there is no two, there is no signifying chain, no chain of the intelligible." Badiou, *Le séminaire. Vérité et sujet: 1987–1988* (Paris: Fayard, 2017), 275.
25. Badiou bases his argument about Parmenides's innovative use of *reductio ad absurdum* reasoning on the work of the Hungarian classicist and historian of mathematics, Árpád Szabó. See Szabó, *The Beginnings of Greek Mathematics*, trans. A. M. Ungar (Dordrecht, Holland: D. Reidel, 1978). In *Being and Event* Badiou returns to Szabó's account of Parmenides: "Szabo remarks that a typical form of reasoning by the absurd can be found in Parmenides with regard to being and non-being, and he uses this as an argument for placing deducible mathematics within an Eleatic filiation. Whatever the historical connection may be, the conceptual connection is convincing. For it is definitely due to it treating being-qua-being that authorization is drawn in mathematics for the use of this audacious form of fidelity that is apagogic

deduction." Badiou, *Being and Event*, trans. Oliver Feltham (London: Continuum, 2005), 250.
26. It is worth noting that Badiou uses the expression "constructive reasoning" to refer to what is often called "direct" reasoning; but since constructive reasoning is sometimes used to describe intuitionistic logic, as opposed to classical logic, I am not using that term here.
27. As part of classical logic (which should not be confused with logic of the "classical" historical period), both direct and indirect reasoning assume certain principles, including the laws of non-contradiction, the excluded middle, and double negation elimination.
28. In *Being and Event* Badiou clarifies that the equation of A and not-not-A functions on the level of ontology: "The entire question concerning the double negation -- A thus comes down to knowing what it could mean to deny that a multiple—in the ontological sense—does not exist. We will agree that it is reasonable to think that this means that it exists, if it is admitted that *ontology attributes no other property to multiples than existence*, because any 'property' is itself a multiple. We will therefore not be able to determine, 'between' non-existence and existence, any specific intermediary property, which would provide a foundation for the gap between the negation of non-existence and existence. For this supposed property would have to be presented, in turn, as an existent multiple, save if it were non-existent. It is thus on the basis of the ontological vocation of mathematics that one can infer, in my view, the legitimacy of the equivalence between affirmation and double negation, between A and --A, and by consequence, the conclusiveness of reasoning via the absurd" (250).
29. Szabó, *Beginnings*, 218.
30. In Meditation 11, "Nature: Poem or Matheme?" Badiou writes, "The Greeks did not invent the poem. Rather, they *interrupted* the poem with the matheme. In doing so, in the exercise of deduction, which is fidelity to being such as named by the void . . . the Greeks opened up the infinite possibility of an ontological text. Nor did the Greeks, and especially Parmenides and Plato, think being as φύσις [phusis] or nature, whatever decisive importance this word may have possessed for them. Rather, they originally *untied* the thought of being from its poetic enchainment to natural appearing" (*BE* 126).
31. Badiou, *The Immanence of Truths*, trans. Susan Spitzer and Kenneth Reinhard (London: Bloomsbury Academic, 2022), 40.
32. See Kenneth Kunen, "Elementary Embeddings and Infinitary Combinatorics," *Journal of Symbolic Logic* 36, no. 3 (1971): 407–13.

## About the 1985–1986 Seminar on Parmenides

1. Alain Badiou, *Le Séminaire: Malebranche: L'être 2, figure théologique* (Paris: Fayard, 2013). Published in English translation as *Malebranche: Theological Figure, Being 2*, trans. Jason E. Smith with Susan Spitzer (New York: Columbia University Press, 2019).
2. Alain Badiou, *Le Séminaire: Parménide: L'être 1, figure ontologique* (Paris: Fayard, 2014).
3. Alain Badiou, *Le Séminaire: Heidegger: L'être 3, figure du retrait* (Paris: Fayard, 2015). English translation forthcoming from Columbia University Press.
4. See in particular Barbara Cassin, *Parménide: Sur la nature ou sur l'étant. La langue de l'être?* (Paris: Seuil, 1998).
5. Parmenides, "On Nature," fragment 8, in Daniel Graham, ed. and trans., *The Texts of Early Greek Philosophy: The Complete Fragments and Selected Testimonies of the Major Presocratics*, Part I (Cambridge: Cambridge University Press, 2010), 217.

### Session 1: October 22, 1985

1. At this relatively early stage of the seminar, there were some administrative problems of organization at the University of Paris 8 that were ultimately resolved very quickly.
2. Badiou's phrase "interpretation by the cut" alludes to the Lacanian practice of cutting short an analytic session when something real emerges in the analysand's utterance (as opposed to its apparent meaning). Lacan also refers to this as "scansion" or "punctuation," suggesting that the imposition of a full stop repunctuates the act of saying in order to bring out an unexpected signification.

### Session 2: October 29, 1985

1. Martin Heidegger, *Introduction to Metaphysics*, 2nd ed., trans. Gregory Fried and Richard Polt (New Haven, CT: Yale University Press, 2014), 106. Subsequent page references to this edition will appear in parentheses in the text.
2. G. W. F. Hegel, *Science of Logic*, ed. and trans. George di Giovanni (Cambridge: Cambridge University Press, 2010), 60.
3. Unless otherwise noted, in this and other citations throughout the seminar the words in italics in square brackets are Badiou's interpolated comments.
4. Parmenides, *Poem* in *The Texts of Early Greek Philosophy: The Complete Fragments and Selected Testimonies of The Major Presocratics, Part I*, ed. and trans. Daniel W. Graham (Cambridge: Cambridge University Press, 2010), 211.

5. The Bremner-Rhind Papyrus, cited in *Egyptian Cosmology: The Animated Universe*, Moustafa Gadalla (Greensboro, NC: Tehuti Research Foundation, 2017), 16.
6. *The Rig-Veda*, vol. 1, trans. Stephanie Jamison and Joel P. Brereton (Oxford, England: Oxford University Press, 2014), 1609.
7. *Chandogya Upanishad* 6, 2:1–2, in Geoffrey Parrinder, *The Routledge Dictionary of Religious and Spiritual Quotations* (New York: Routledge, 2001), 76.
8. Guy Lardreau and Christian Jambet were philosophers trained at the École Normale Supérieure and militants in the post-1968 Maoist organization, the Gauche Prolétarienne, though they renounced their Maoist positions in their jointly published book *L'Ange: pour une cynégétique du semblant* (Paris: B. Grasset, 1976). See also Christian Jambet, *Logique des Orientaux: Henry Corbin et la science des formes* (Paris: Seuil, 1983); Guy Lardreau, *Discours philosophique et discours spirituel: autour de la philosophie spirituelle de Philoxène de Mabboug* (Paris: Seuil, 1985).

**Session 3: November 5, 1985**

1. Badiou relies throughout the seminar on Jean Beaufret's *Le Poème de Parménide* (Paris: Presses Universitaires de France, 1955). Since he comments below on this translation, heartily approving of Beaufret's rendering of Parmenides's line here, *to gar auto noiein esti te kai einai*, it seemed necessary to retain the French in this case.
2. This line (*tauton d'esti noein te kai houneken esti noema*), discussed by Hegel in his *Lectures on the History of Philosophy*, has been translated more idiomatically as "Thinking, and that for the sake of which there is thought, are the same" in Heidegger's essay "Moira (Parmenides VIII, 34–41)" in *Early Greek Thinking*, trans. David Farrell Krell and Frank A. Capuzzi (New York: Harper & Row, 1975), 82–83.
3. Cf. Mao's 1930 speech "Oppose Book Worship": "You can't solve a problem? Well, get down and investigate the present facts and its past history!" See https://www.marxists.org/reference/archive/mao/selected-works/volume-6/mswv6_11.htm. Accessed October 21, 2024.
4. This odd phrase is usually translated as "essence" in English. The shorter phrase *to ti esti* ("the what it is") is sometimes used by Aristotle to convey approximately the same idea. See Marc S. Cohen, "Aristotle's Metaphysics," trans. W. D. Ross, in *The Stanford Encyclopedia of Philosophy* (Summer 2016 Edition), ed. Edward N. Zalta, http://plato.stanford.edu/archives/sum2016/entries/aristotle-metaphysics/.

5. Aristotle, *Metaphysics*, trans. W.D. Ross, in *The Complete Works of Aristotle*, vol. 2., revised Oxford Translation, ed. Jonathan Barnes (Princeton, NJ: Princeton University Press, 1995), 1555; translation slightly modified to conform to the French. Subsequent references to this edition will be given in parentheses in the text.
6. Although Xenophanes was traditionally considered part of the Eleatic "school," this is now in doubt. We thank Daniel Graham for pointing this out to us.
7. There is a play on words here between *un rigoriste*, "a rigorist," and *un rigolo*, meaning "a joker, a clown," or, more pejoratively, "a fraud, a phony," as is the case here.
8. Aristotle, *Physics*, trans. R. P. Hardie and R. K. Gaye, in *The Complete Works of Aristotle*, vol. 1, ed. Jonathan Barnes (Princeton, NJ: Princeton University Press, 1984), 316. Subsequent page references to this edition will be given in parentheses in the text.

## Session 4: November 12, 1985

1. Daniel W. Graham, *The Texts of Early Greek Philosophy* (Cambridge: Cambridge University Press, 2010), 217.
2. Cf. "Nature is . . . not objectivity nor the given but the gift, the gesture of opening which unfolds its own limit as that in which it resides without limitation." Alain Badiou, *Being and Event*, trans. Oliver Feltham (New York: Continuum), 123.
3. Graham renders this as "incomplete," but in keeping with Badiou's discussion of the French phrase *sans terme*, it seemed more appropriate to translate the Greek *ateleuteton* as "without end" here.
4. Aristotle, *Physics*, trans. R. P. Hardie and R. K. Gaye, in *The Complete Works of Aristotle*, vol. 1, ed. Jonathan Barnes (Princeton, NJ: Princeton University Press, 1984), 316. Subsequent references to this edition will be given in parentheses in the text.
5. Badiou's point here depends on the Lacanian distinction between "reality" (understood as the realm of symbolic and imaginary representation) and "the real" as the "impossible," or what is constitutively left out of reality. Hence Aristotle extracts Parmenides's concept of being from its "real" and tries to "realize" it—that is, reduce it to the realm of reality.
6. Badiou elaborates on this point involving the gap in the seminar transcription online at http://www.entretemps.asso.fr/Badiou/85-86.htm. Accessed October 21, 2024.

## Session 5: November 19, 1985

1. It is not Pythodorus who comes to see Cephalus but rather Antiphon whom Cephalus goes to see because Antiphon has learned by heart Pythodorus's account of the meeting between Parmenides, Socrates, and Zeno. See the additional description later in the chapter.
2. Plato, *Parmenides*, in *The Dialogues of Plato*, vol. 4: *Plato's Parmenides*, rev. ed., trans. R. E. Allan (New Haven, CT: Yale University Press, 1998), 15; trans. modified.
3. Jean-Claude Milner, *Détections fictives* (Paris: Seuil, 1985).
4. The literal meaning of the famous French proverb Badiou cites here, *Rien ne sert de courir; il faut partir à point*, is "Nothing is gained by running; you must start at the right time."
5. The dialogue is actually set at least thirty years after Socrates's death, as Badiou explains in the transcription of the seminar online. See http://www.entretemps.asso.fr/Badiou/85-86.htm.
6. Plato, *Plato's Theaetetus, Part I of the Being of the Beautiful*, trans. Seth Benardete (Chicago: University of Chicago Press, 1986), I.84.
7. Plato, *Sophist*, trans. Benjamin Jowett, http://classics.mit.edu/Plato/sophist.html.

## Session 6: December 3, 1985

1. Plato, *The Sophist*, in *Theaetetus and Sophist*, ed. and trans. Christopher Rowe (Cambridge: Cambridge University Press, 2015), 129; trans. slightly modified. Subsequent page references to this edition will be given in parentheses in the text. We have kept the more traditional appellation "The Stranger" in preference to "The Visitor," as he is referred to in Rowe's translation.
2. Badiou discussed this topic in Session 8 of his seminar *The One: Descartes, Plato, Kant*, trans. Jacques Lezra with Susan Spitzer (New York: Columbia University Press, 2023).

## Session 7: December 10, 1985

1. The Graham translation being used here omits "namely" (*à savoir*, in Beaufret's translation). Other translators interpolate it. Katherine Freeman, for example, renders the line: "There is only one other description of the way remaining, (*namely*), that (*What Is*) Is." See Hermann Diels, *Ancilla to the Pre-Socratic Philosophers: A Complete Translation of the Fragments in Diels, Fragmente Der Vorsokratiker*, trans. Katherine Freeman (Cambridge, MA: Harvard University Press, 1983), 43.

2. Badiou cites the same lines here in Beaufret's translation. He does the same with the next citation, giving his own version, followed by Beaufret's. See Jean Beaufret, *Le Poème de Parménide* (Paris: Presses Universitaires de France, 1955).
3. We have omitted Badiou's interpolated comment here, in his own translation of these lines, because it focuses on a point of French grammar (the expletive *ne*) that is not immediately relevant to the English translation. The gist of his remark is that there should be no subject ("it") preceding "is or is not" in the first line, which the expletive *ne*, on the contrary, would imply. Beaufret, whose translation of the same lines Badiou then cites, adds the "it," as do Graham (see below) and other translators.
4. In keeping with his remark above concerning the expletive *ne* in French, Badiou translates this as "*est pas*," rather than "*n'est pas*."
5. "L'Action restreinte" ("Restricted Action") is the title of an essay in Mallarmé's *Divagations* that Badiou often cites, including in his play *The Incident at Antioch: A Tragedy in Three Acts*, trans. Susan Spitzer, introd. Kenneth Reinhard (New York: Columbia University Press, 2013), and in his seminar *Images of the Present Time*, trans. Susan Spitzer, introd. Kenneth Reinhard (New York: Columbia University Press, 2023).

## Session 8: January 14, 1986

1. See chap. 1, p. 82 of Hegel's *Science of Logic*, trans. A. V. Miller (New York: Humanities Press, 1969).
2. Cf. ". . . it is precisely because desire is articulated that it *is not articulable*." Jacques Lacan, *Écrits: The First Complete Edition in English Paperback*, trans. Bruce Fink, with Héloïse Fink and Russell Grigg (New York: Norton, 2007), 681.

## Session 9: January 21, 1986

1. The reference here is to Alain Badiou, "Six propriétés de la vérité" [Six properties of truth], *Ornicar?* 32 (January 1985): 39–67; continued in *Ornicar?* 33 (April 1985): 120–149.

## Session 10: January 28, 1986

1. Badiou's concept of "the time for concluding" derives from Lacan's version of the "Prisoners' Dilemma" thought experiment in his essay "Logical Time and

the Assertion of Anticipated Certainty" from 1945. For Lacan, the prisoners' dilemma is an allegory of the logical moments involved in the emergence of a subject, and "the time for concluding" is the moment when an act of subjectification breaks through the purely reciprocal or specular relationship to the other and produces the "I." Jacques Lacan, *Ecrits: The First Complete Edition in English*, trans. Bruce Fink, with Héloïse Fink and Russell Grigg (New York: Norton, 2006), 161–175. In *Theory of the Subject*, Badiou discusses Lacan's concept in terms of the distinction between the punctual moment of "subjectification" and the extended "subjective process." *Theory of the Subject*, trans. Bruno Bosteels (New York: Continuum, 2009), 248–253.

2. See Alain Badiou and Barbara Cassin, *Heidegger: His Life and His Philosophy*, trans. Susan Spitzer, introd. Kenneth Reinhard (New York: Columbia University Press, 2016).

### Session 11: February 4, 1986

1. Alain Badiou's Malebranche seminar has been published as *Malebranche: Theological Figure, Being 2*, trans. Jason E. Smith with Susan Spitzer (New York: Columbia University Press, 2019).

# Index

Adeimantus, 79
Aesop, 85
Althusser, Louis, 122
Anaxagoras, 48
Anaximander, xxi, 18, 20, 182
anti-philosophy, viii, xvi
Antiphon, 79, 207n1
apagogic reasoning. *See reductio ad absurdum* reasoning
*Apology* (Plato), 86
Aristophanes, 86
Aristotle, xxii, xxxvii, xlviii, 77–78, 117, 128, 130, 135–136, 199n4, 206n5; being and nonbeing, 132; critique of Parmenides, 113–114; *Physics*, 56–59, 61, 63, 206n8; and the risk of nonbeing, xxvii–xxxi
Athenian political democracy, 181

Babylonian-Egyptian theory, 188–190
Beaufret, Jean, 17, 42–44, 205n1, 208n2, 208n3
becoming, xxii, xxxvi
*Beginnings of Greek Mathematics, The* (Szabó), 184, 187

being, xxi–xxii, xxxii, 110; historial destiny of, 179; naming regime of, 127; of nonbeing, xxxi, xxxi, 22, 35, 111, 114; *vs.* nonbeing, 131–132; relationship with nonbeing, 137–140; and Socrates, 96; and thinking, 77, 120, 124–126, 129–130, 135–138
*Being and Event* (Badiou), vii, xviii, xxi, xxxi, xxxiv, xl, xlii–xliii
being is being, 71, 117
being is One, xxii, 57, 61–64, 69–70, 72, 117–118
Borromean knot/knotting, xxxii, xxxvii, xlii, 91, 113–115, 127–129, 132, 136, 144, 175–176, 201–202n20, 202n21; of being, xxxii–xxxviii; of nonbeing, xxxii–xxxviii; between real, symbolic, and imaginary, 128; of thinking, xxxii–xxxviii
Borromean nature of the thinking/being/nonbeing relationship, 114
Borromean rings, xxxii–xxxiii

Canto, Monique, xvii
Cantor, Georg, xliii

Cartesian "meditations," vii
Cassin, Barbara, li
*Century, The*, xx
Cephalus, 78–79, 207n1
Char, René, 18
Châtelet, François, xiv
Christian spirituality, 37–38
Classical Age of Greek philosophy, 19, 21–22, 195
classical logic, xxxix, 151, 202n27, 203n27
coding, l, 128–133, 135–138, 140–146, 169–170, 176, 178, 186; differential, 140; history of, 136; minimal, 137–138, 141; Parmenidean, 140–141, 145–146; Plato's, 135–136
Cohen, Paul, vii
Colophon, 20, 201n18
communism, xlvii
consciousness, 10
constructive reasoning, xxxii, 152–156, 160, 165, 167, 172, 202n26

Deleuze, Gilles, xiv, xx
democracy, xlvii, 98, 181
Democritean philosophy, 16
Democritus, xliii, 16–17
Derrida, Jacques, xiv, xviii
Descartes, René, xiv, xxxvii, xxxvii, xlviii, 12, 14, 16
*Détections fictives* (Milner), 84
direct reasoning, xxxix, xl, xli, 151, 203n26
*Discours philosophique et discours spirituel* (Lardreau), 36

"effect of the real," xli, 167
"effect of unbelief," xl, 167
Eleatic exception, 52
Eleaticism, xliii, xliii, xliii, 16, 95

Eleatic philosophers, xxvii, 53, 79, 83–84, 193
Eleatic philosophy, 20
Eleatic School, xl, 20, 51, 172, 206n7
Eleatic Stranger, xxviii, xxix, 90, 94–100, 103–106, 108, 110
epistemological break, 122
equivalence of truth, 154
Euclid, xxiii, xxxix, 88, 158, 194
Existent, 31–34, 203n28
experiential language, 130

fiction, xlii, 153–155, 163–164, 167, 170, 172, 193
fidelity, 176, 202n25, 203n30
Foucault, Michel, xiv
Freeman, Kathleen, xxvi, 207n1

German nationalism, 181
German philosophy, 180
Germany, 180–183, 185, 196
Gorgias of Leontini, xxv, 200n9
Graham, Daniel, xxvi, xxvi, 122–123, 168, 199–200n4, 199n4, 200n7, 206n3, 206n6, 207n1, 208n3
Greece, 181–183, 185–191
Greek philosophy: Classical Age of, 19, 21–22, 195; pre-Socratic age of, 20–21

Hegel, Georg Wilhelm Friedrich, xxi–xxii, xxxvi, xlviii, 12, 15, 18, 23, 46, 118, 133, 202n24, 205n2
Hegelian dialectic, xiii, 166
Heidegger, Martin, viii, xxi–xxiii, xxiv, 1–3, 132, 136, 145, 176, 178, 182–183, 192, 196, 200n6; on "Anaximander's Saying," 18; on *auto*, xxvi; on being, 8, 18; co-belonging, 43; on essence of philosophy, 6, 30;

historial destiny of being, 179; on metaphysics, 8; on Parmenides, l, 23–25, 28–29; on *Vernehmen*, xxvi. See also *Introduction to Metaphysics* (Heidegger)
Heraclitus, xxii, 78, 88, 188; dynamic vitality, 24; notion of becoming, xxii
historial destiny of being, 179
Homer, li, 84–85, 179; *Iliad*, 85; *Odyssey*, 179

*Images of the Present Time* (Badiou), viii, 208n5
*Immanence of Truths, The* (Badiou), vii, xv, xvi, xxi, xlii–xlv, xliii
"Inconsistency Theorem," xliv
indirect reasoning, xli. See *reductio ad absurdum* reasoning
Infinite, the, xxi, xlviii, 8, 14–15, 63–64, 203n30
*Introduction to Metaphysics* (Heidegger), 17–18, 23, 27, 41, 47
Islam, 36–38

Jambet, Christian, 36–38, 205n8

Kant, Immanuel, xlviii, 2–3, 12, 14
Kimhi, Irad, 200n11
knots/knotting, l, 129, 133; of being, nonbeing, and thinking, xxxv, 119–120, 135, 175; Borromean (See Borromean knots); formalism of, l
Kunen, Kenneth, xliv

Lacan, Jacques, xi, xv, xxxii, 98, 124, 128, 153, 177, 201n20, 208n1; antiphilosophy, viii; Borromean rings, xxxiii; psychosis, 67; the real, xli
lack-of-being (*manque-à-être*), 8–9, 11, 13

Lacoue-Labarthe, Philippe, xv
L'Action restreinte, 208n5
Laertius, Diogenes, 199n4
Lardreau, Guy, 36–38, 205n8
"La technique littéraire des paradoxes de Zénon (Milner)," 84
Lautréamont, Comte de, xiii
*Leaves of Hypnos* (Char), 18
*Lectures on the History of Philosophy* (Hegel), xxi, xxi, 199n2, 205n2
Lenin, Vladimir, xxxiv
logico-mathematical discourse, 176, 179
*Logics of Worlds* (Badiou), vii, xviii
*Logique des Orientaux* (Jambet), 36
logos, 102; *patrikos*, xxix, 102–103, 111–112
Lyotard, Jean-François, xiv

Malebranche, Nicolas, viii, xxi, 16; *Treatise on Nature and Grace*, 17–18
Malis, Marie-José, xv
Mao, xxxiv, 46
Marx, Karl, xxxiv
mastery, 81–83, 86–87, 94, 96–97, 104
*Matérialistes de l'Antiquité, Les* (Nizan), 17
mathematics, xxxix, 3–6, 173, 176, 188–195; Borromean knot, 129; contemporary, xliii; demonstrative, l; and ontology, xl; and philosophy, xxiii, xxxii, xxxvii, 175–176, 186; pure, 129, 141, 171
matheme, xxxii, xxxvii–xxxix, xl–xliii, xlix, li, 113, 146–148, 172, 175–177, 182, 185–190, 196–197, 203n30
McKirahan, Richard D., 199n3
meaning, 144, 165–167, 172; and mathematics, 143; metaphorical, 35; plurality of, 45–46; for word cause, 47–51, 56

memory, xxxiv, 111–112, 197
meta-ontology, xxiii
Milner, Jean-Claude, xvii, 84–87; *Détections fictives*, 84
mythic thinking, xliii

narrative, xli, 146–148, 152–154, 177–178, 197; of beliefs, 171; coherent, xxxix, 165; mythological, xxxviii; Nazi, 179; poetic, xxiii, xxxviii; proto-narrative, 178–179; pure, 164, 179
Nazism, 179, 183
Nietzsche, Friedrich, viii, 24–25, 118
Nizan, Paul, 17
*noein*, 124
nonbeing, xxxii, 110, 113, 120–121; Aristotle and risk of, xxvii–xxxi; *vs.* being, 131–132; being of, xxxi, 22, 35, 111, 114; being relationship with, 137–140; Borromean knot of, xxxii–xxxviii; and Plato, 131; Plato and risk of, xxvii–xxxi; as pure name, 121, 123–127; renaming, 130–131; and thinking, 135–136
non-relationship, 137–138, 141, 143, 145
*nous*, 124

*Odyssey* (Homer), 179
*Off the Beaten Track* (Heidegger), 18
"One, The," xxi, xliv, xlviii, l, 8, 13–14, 16, 18, 50–51, 53, 55, 57, 61–62, 64, 68–69, 72, 83–84, 120, 128–130, 135, 137–139, 141, 186, 193–195, 202n21
One-being, xliii, 16, 62–64, 66
One of being, 72, 132; as pure name, 129–130
ontological difference, 200n6
"On What-Is-Not" (Gorgias of Leontini), xxv

Openness of being, 176
"Other, the," xxxvi, xlii, 111–112, 131, 140

Paris Commune of 1871, xxxiv
Parmenideanism, 64, 195–196; proliferating, 195; radical, 64; shattered, 195
Parmenideans, 53–55, 57, 61, 63, 103, 193
Parmenides, viii, xxvii, 77, 98–102, 108–114; 1985-86 seminar on, xlvii–lii, xlvii–lii; "being is being," 117; coded relationships, 137; coding, 132–133, 138, 140–141, 145–146; discussion with Socrates in the *Parmenides*, 78–87; experiential language, 130; *The Immanence of Truths*, vii–viii, xxi, xlii–xlv; as master of Plato, 96–97; *reductio ad absurdum*, xxxviii–xlii; relationship between thinking and being, 130; signs, 117–119; Subtractive Ontology, xxi–xlv; threefold ways, xxiii–xxvii
*Parmenides* (Plato), 78–87, 93
*Parmenides: Ontological Figure, Being 1,* xxi–xlv
*patrikos logos*, xxix, 102–103, 111–112
*Philosopher* (Plato), 94–95
philosophy, 177; anti-philosophy, viii, xvi; classical, 15; Democritean, 16; Eleatic, 20; German, 180; Greek, 19, 21–22, 195; and mathematics, xxiii, xxxii, xxxvii, 175–176, 186; pre-Socratic age of Greek, 20–21; Western, 36–38
*Physics* (Aristotle), 56–59, 61, 63, 206n8

Plato, xiii, xvi, xvii, xix, xxi, xxxvii, xlviii, 77–78, 99–100, 103–114, 117, 128, 130, 131, 136, 140, 191–192, 200n7; *Apology*, 86; and nonbeing, 131; *Parmenides*, 78–87, 93; *Philosopher*, 94–95; position on mastery, 97–98; prohibition for, 131–133; and the risk of nonbeing, xxvii–xxxi; on sophist, 98; *Sophist*, 78, 87–91, 93–98; *Statesman*, 94–96; *Theaetetus*, 78, 88–90

Platonism, 80, 91, 93–94, 97–98, 103, 109, 189–190, 192

poetic: discourse, xxxii; language, 27; metaphor, 65; narrative, xxiii, 197; prophesying, l; resonance, 177; speech, 59; thinking, xliii, 35

*Poème de Parménide, Le* (Beaufret), 17, 205n1, 208n2

precariousness of the transmission, 79–80, 93

pre-Socratic age of Greek philosophy, 20–21

pure being, xxxvi, 23, 139

pure nothingness, xxxvi

Pythagoreans, 193–195

radical Parmenideanism, 64

Ranciere, Jacques, xiv

real, the: effect of, 167, 168; fullness of, 137

reasoning: *ad infinitum*, 160; constructive, xxxii, 152–156, 160, 165, 167, 172, 202n26; direct, xxxix, xl, xli, 151, 203n26; *reductio ad absurdum* (See *reductio ad absurdum* reasoning)

*reductio ad absurdum* reasoning, 115, 148–149, 151, 154, 155–160, 161,
163–171, 176–177, 193–194, 202n25; development of, xxxix–xl; matheme in, xxxii; negative logic of, xlii; voluntaristic aspect of, 156

Regnault, François, xvii

*Republic* (Plato), xvi, 200n7

Rimbaud, Arthur, xiii

risk effect, 168

risk of nonbeing, xxvii–xxxi

*Saint Paul: The Foundation of Universalism* (Badiou), xx

Sartre, Jean-Paul, 9

*Science of Logic* (Hegel), xxii, xxxvi, xxxvi, 18, 69

self-criticism, 179, 182

Serres, Michel, xiv

Shanghai Commune, xxxiv

Shiite Islam, 36, 38

signs, 117–120, 139

*Sinthome, Le* (Lacan), xxxiii

Socrates, xviii, xxviii, 22, 78–84, 86–91, 93–97, 105, 109, 148, 207n, 207n1, 207n5; discussion with Parmenides in the *Parmenides*, 78–87; as master of Plato, 96–97; respectful relationship with Parmenides, 93–94

*Sophist* (Plato), xxi, 78, 87–91, 93–98; Platonism, 93

Spencer, Joseph, 199n3

Spinoza, Baruch, xlviii, 15

"spiritual discourse," 37–38

*Statesman* (Plato), 94–96

"subject-process," 8–9, 13–14

*Symposium* (Plato), xix, 108

Szabó, Árpád, 184, 187, 190–195, 202n25

*Theaetetus* (Plato), 78, 88–90, 93–95
Théâtre de la Commune in Aubervilliers, xvi, xvii
*Theory of the Subject* (Badiou), vii, xiii, xxxiii
Thiault, Aimé, li
thinking, xxxii; and being, 77, 120, 124–126, 129–130, 135–138; Borromean knot of, xxxii–xxxviii; and nonbeing, 135–136; poetic, xliii, 35
"time for concluding, the," 177–178, 208n1
transgression, 75, 100, 102–103; of Parmenides's prohibition, 77, 98
*Treatise on Nature and Grace* (Malebranche), 17–18

unknot, 201n19
*Upanishads*, 34–35

*Vérité et sujet* (Badiou seminar), xxxvi
Vodoz, Isabelle, viii
von Neumann, John, xxxi, xliii

Wahl, François, xiii
Western-centrism, 36, 39
Western philosophy, 36–38
Wittgenstein, Ludwig, viii, 124
*Wittgenstein's Antiphilosophy* (Badiou), xx

Xenophanes, xxvii, xxvii, 20, 25, 55, 201n18, 206n6

Zeno of Elea, xxvii, xxviii, 55, 79–90, 193–194, 207n1
Žižek, Slavoj, xvii
Zusammengehörigkeit, xxvi

List of the seminars
(*in chronological order*)

| 1983–1984 | L'Un. Descartes, Platon, Kant. |
| 1984–1985 | L'Infini. Aristote, Spinoza, Hegel. |
| 1985, 4e trim. | L'être 1. Figure ontologique: Parménide. |
| 1986, 1er trim. | L'être 2. Figure théologique: Malebranche. |
| 1986–1987 | L'être 3. Figure du retrait: Heidegger. |
| 1987–1988 | Vérité et Sujet. |
| 1988–1989 | Beckett et Mallarmé. |
| 1989–1990 | Platon: La République. |
| 1990–1991 | Théorie du Mal, théorie de l'amour. |
| 1991–1992 | L'essence de la politique. |
| 1992–1993 | L'antiphilosophie 1. Nietzsche. |
| 1993–1994 | L'antiphilosophie 2. Wittgenstein. |
| 1994–1995 | L'antiphilosophie 3. Lacan. |
| 1995–1996 | L'antiphilosophie 4. Saint Paul. |
| 1996–1998 | Théorie axiomatique du Sujet. |
| 1998–2001 | Le xxe siècle. |
| 2001–2004 | Images du temps présent. |
| 2004–2007 | S'orienter dans la pensée, s'orienter dans l'existence. |
| 2007–2010 | Pour aujourd'hui: Platon! |
| 2010–2012 | Que signifie «changer le monde»? |